Speaking Truth
to Power

ANCHOR BOOKS
DOUBLEDAY
NEW YORK
LONDON
TORONTO
SYDNEY
AUCKLAND

ANITA HILL

SPEAKING TRUTH TO POWER

AN ANCHOR BOOK
PUBLISHED BY DOUBLEDAY
a division of Bantam Doubleday Dell Publishing Group, Inc.
1540 Broadway, New York, New York 10036

ANCHOR BOOKS, DOUBLEDAY, and the portrayal of an anchor are
trademarks of Doubleday, a division of Bantam Doubleday
Dell Publishing Group, Inc.

Speaking Truth to Power was originally published in hardcover
by Doubleday in 1997. The Anchor Books edition is
published by arrangement with Doubleday.

BOOK DESIGN BY CLAIRE NAYLON VACCARO

The Library of Congress has cataloged the hardcover edition
of this book as follows:

Hill, Anita.
Speaking truth to power / Anita F. Hill.
p.   cm.
Includes index.
1. Hill, Anita. 2. Women lawyers—United States—Biography.
3. Sexual harassment of women—Law and legislation—
United States.
I. Title.
KF373.H46A3   1997
340′.092—dc21
[B]   97-1316
CIP

ISBN 0-385-47627-2

1   3   5   7   9   10   8   6   4   2

THIS BOOK IS DEDICATED
WITH LOVE AND GRATITUDE
TO MY PARENTS
ERMA AND ALBERT HILL

INTRODUCTION

Midway through the morning of my testimony at the Thomas confirmation hearing, Senator Howell Heflin, Democrat of Alabama, summed up the Republican attack on my credibility. A former state supreme court judge and trial attorney, Senator Heflin appeared to be deliberating aloud as he explained his approach.

"I, and I suppose every member of this committee, have to come down to the ultimate question of who is telling the truth. My experience as a lawyer and a judge is that you listen to all the testimony and then you try to determine the motivation for the one that is not telling the truth.

"Now, in trying to determine whether you are telling falsehoods or not, I have got to determine what your motivation might be. Are you a scorned woman?" he asked.

"No," I said, a bit surprised by the line of questioning but certain of my answer.

"Do you have a martyr complex?" With his heavy accent and deliberate pacing, "martyr" came out sounding like "mah'duh."

"No, I don't."

"Maybe she is a martyr and doesn't know it," someone behind me snickered.

"Do you have a militant attitude relative to the area of civil rights?"

"No, I don't." I was not certain what he meant, but I knew I was not a militant in the way the term was defined in the 1960s.

"The reality of where you are today is rather dramatic," Senator Heflin said. "Did you take, as Senator Biden asked you, all steps that you knew how to take to prevent being in the witness chair today?"

"Yes, I did. Everything that I knew to do, I did." I felt like a child who was being chastised for wandering into traffic.

Senator Heflin's questions revealed a truth about the hearing. Generally, questions about motive are raised in the context of a criminal trial. They are designed to elicit the impetus for a criminal act. The prosecution presents the theory that the accused committed the crime out of greed, rage, or passion. The defense attorney attempts to show that none of these factors existed in the case. Heflin's questions revealed that I was being treated as a defendant. The Republicans had accused me of lying about Clarence Thomas' sexual harassment of me when I worked for him ten years earlier. They effectively shifted the hearing on whether Thomas was suitable to serve on the Court to a hearing on whether I could rebut their presumption that I was lying. Primed by all the rhetoric before the hearing, the American public was predisposed to be suspicious of my statements and my behavior. Before anyone would even listen to my charges, I had to prove that my character was such that I was not guilty of inventing them. Throughout the country, people were poised to register their verdict through the polls taken during the hearing.

Years have passed since October 1991. My world has been forever changed by the events that culminated in the "Hill-Thomas hearing." I am no longer an anonymous, private individual—my name having become synonymous with sexual harassment. To my supporters I represent the courage to come forward and disclose a painful truth—a courage which thousands of others have found since the hearing. To my detractors I represent the debasement of a public forum, at best, a pawn, at worst, a perjurer. Living with these conflicting perceptions is difficult, sometimes overwhelming.

The transformation of my life began before the hearing with the news reports of my claims. Overnight my world expanded and the number of persons to whom I was accountable grew exponentially as I was questioned about my experience. After the hearing the number of people who felt accountable to me grew just as surprisingly as people sought to explain the event.

I knew on October 11, 1991, that the experience would remain with me forever. I did not know that it would live with me. Gradually, the events that took place in the days and weeks following the hearing revealed that the public would not quickly or easily forget the episode. The continued media interest, like the initial intrusion of the press on my privacy, was unanticipated and uninvited on my part. To them the event was a news story. To me it was my life.

In my first dealings with the press on October 2, I was cautious though naive. By October 13 I was thoroughly skeptical and doubted that the press would discuss sexual harassment with any insight or sensitivity. Nor did I believe that all the journalistic prying was motivated by service to the public's right to know. Some of my suspicions were confirmed when I received a telephone call from an Oklahoma City attorney who represented the owner of a bar popular with lesbians. Apparently, a tabloid reporter had called the owner to find out if I frequented her establishment.

Tuesday, October 15, 1991, the day of the vote on the nomination, became my focal point. Like the first day of a long-awaited vacation, that date stood out in my mind. I saw the vote as an end to the media attention, not a referendum on my testimony, and I convinced myself that once the nomination was debated and voted on by the entire Senate, the corps of reporters would leave Norman, Oklahoma, throw away my telephone number, and move on to the next story. This mental compartmentalization allowed me to go on about my work. But I could find no way to contain the public interest. The telephones in my office rang off the hook with calls from around the country. Each day I would go home to an answering machine filled with messages and out of tape. Daily, I received an average of thirty faxes offering sympathy, extending invitations, or expressing anger over the hearing. Even before I arrived home from Washington, D.C., local florists had begun delivering plants and flowers to my office at the University of Oklahoma College of Law. The pinks, yellows, and reds of the arrangements added a curious kind of festivity to the chaos. The fragrance filled the administrative offices and conference room until they smelled like a perfumery. Still, lovely colors and smells seemed out of place amid frazzled nerves and constantly bleating phones. One of the secretaries in the main office, Rose Martinez-Elugardo, made sure that I saw all the arrangements, collecting the card from each, and students volunteered to take them to local hospitals and nursing homes. Selfishly, I regretted that I could not preserve them all.

The enormous amount of mail was testament to the extraordinary level of public interest in the hearing. Beginning on Tuesday, October 15, the Postal Service started delivering trays of letters addressed to me. Some of them must have been written and mailed on the day of my testimony. And as the days passed, the volume of letters increased. By October 19 I was receiving two trays of cards and letters, each tray containing about seven hundred pieces of mail. I told myself that this probably represented a backlog of mail and would stop. I was wrong. The following day brought five trays, and the deliveries continued at this pace for three weeks. The mail came from around the country and then from around the world.

Teaching a full load at the law school and working as a faculty representative in the office of the provost on the main campus left me little time to read, let alone respond to, the incoming mail. The telephone calls, as well, went mostly unreturned. A group of women in the university community organized to help me with the mail after work hours. Fifteen or so cheerful, enthusiastic volunteers gathered in the law school lounge, eager to be helpful in any way that they could. After a few hours of opening and sorting, we had finished only a fraction of the letters. The mood shifted when it dawned upon us that the time and cost of responding to them all was prohibitive. We could not even afford to acknowledge receipt of most of the correspondence.

People of all ages, races, and backgrounds wrote. Just about every category of person imaginable who had seen, heard, or read about the hearing took time to put their reactions into words. Some letters were from old friends who wanted to reconnect after years of no communication, but most were from strangers expressing their concern about what they had witnessed. "This is the first time I have ever written a public figure," many began. The letters spelled out a huge range of emotion, from sympathy to anger to joy. Many writers were outraged at what they considered insensitivity on the part of certain senators, or frustrated by the unsatisfactory resolution of the issue. Many had experienced sexual harassment firsthand. Many more related to sexual harassment as a violation of basic human dignity. Some decried the way that politics had pervaded the judicial appointment process. Others were deeply concerned about the quality of political representation evidenced by the behavior of the senators on the Judiciary Committee. Each letter in its own way established a link between the writer and me. We had a common experience so potent as to create a bond between total strangers. "I feel like I know you," many wrote.

In the quiet of my office, after classes were over and most of the staff had left, I tried to read at least forty letters a day. Many, especially those from harassment victims, were heart-wrenching. Because of their intensity and my fatigue, reading my assigned number of the letters at the end of a workday often proved impossible. I would become despondent and unable to continue, or angered by my own helplessness to change things. I changed my routine, setting aside time to read the mail first thing in the morning. But this was a mistake because after reading of all the embarrassment, anger, grief, I could not focus on my work. This letter speaking of abuse or that letter describing disillusionment stayed with me all day.

Not all of the letters caused me dismay. I laughed at humorous characterizations of my senatorial detractors. A letter from proud parents of an infant brought a smile to my face, and still does. "If this photo brings you half the joy she brings us, we will be pleased," they wrote.

Though there were the threatening, vulgar, and just plain cruel messages, they were few, and I thank God for that. So as not to delude myself into believing that everyone saw my testimony in a positive light, I read those as well. The outrage I felt over the abusive experiences described in some of the letters numbed me to any cruelty my detractors could dish out. In the face of so much pain, their hostility seemed trivial.

The people who took time to write, even those who expressed anger at me, seemed to want to make sense out of the hearing. They wanted to understand for themselves and in some cases for me. I cannot overstate the importance of these letters, notes, and other messages. They were crucial to my endurance and ultimately to my recovery. I had been deeply wounded by the allegations about me during and after the hearing, but I had had no place to heal. The scrutiny of critics and curious onlookers, from the tabloid press to people on the street, seemed constant. Certainly, talking about the experience with my family and friends was a great relief. And prayer sustained me daily. Yet it was knowing that people I had never met shared my concerns that lifted me spiritually when I was alone in my office with their letters. If the hearing had left me feeling isolated and out of touch with the world, the correspondence afterward helped me to reconnect with it.

The event known as the Hill-Thomas hearing has been described variously as a watershed in American politics, a turning point in the awareness of sexual harassment, and a wake-up call for women. For me it was a bane which I have worked hard to transform into a blessing for myself and for others. And because it brought to bear for the average public issues of sexual harassment, issues of race, gender, and politics, the hearing and all of the events that surrounded it deserve honest assessment.

But I am no longer content to leave the assessment to others, for they cannot know what I experienced—what I felt, saw, heard, and thought. Whatever others may say, I must address these questions for myself. I have not lived one day since the hearing without feeling its significance or the immeasurable weight of responsibility it has left with me. During her testimony before the Judiciary Committee, Judge Susan Hoerchner commented that I did not choose the issue of sexual harassment; rather, it chose me. Having been chosen, I have come to believe that it is up to me to try to give meaning to it all.

During his inquiry Senator Heflin suggested "other motivations" for my testimony. "Are you interested in writing a book?"

"No, I'm not interested in writing a book," I replied.

The transcript of the confirmation hearing recorded the chuckles and snickers that went through the room as "laughter." The suggestion that all of this might have been motivated by aspirations to write a book must have seemed preposterous to anyone. In any case, the exchange provided one of the few moments of comic relief during the hearing.

This book is not intended as a detached or dispassionate chronicle. I am objective enough only to realize that I cannot write such a book. Instead, I write to offer my own perspective. I do this not simply to survive the tragedy but to transcend it. I do not undertake this endeavor lightly. I have never had much interest in writing anything beyond legal articles and essays. The very idea of writing a book of personal reflection is counter to my nature. I do not eagerly share with strangers the personal aspects of my life. Sometimes I fear that my writing will not communicate the power of my experience effectively. Sometimes I fear that it might, thus provoking further attacks on me. But it is as important today as it was in 1991 that I feel free to speak. If I let my fears silence me now, I will have betrayed all of those who supported me in 1991 and those who have come forward since. More than anything else, the Hill-Thomas hearing of October 1991 was about finding our voices and breaking the silence forever.

And so, despite my reply to Senator Heflin, I begin.

PART ONE

CHAPTER ONE

Senator Joseph Biden, Democrat of Delaware, is a man who chooses his words carefully and speaks them clearly in a mildly nasal voice. He has thinning brown hair, a pleasant face, and a rather remarkable smile—a grin that spreads from ear to ear in an instant, disclosing perfectly straight teeth.

In September 1991, as he chaired the first round of the Senate Judiciary Committee hearing on Clarence Thomas' nomination, Biden's smile flashed frequently, but by October 11 it was appearing less and less often. As I gave my statement that morning, his face looked sober.

About 8:00 the previous evening, Senator Biden's staff had informed my lawyers that Judge Thomas would be the first witness to address the committee. I had expected to give my statement first. On October 8, when Senator Biden called me to say that the committee would hold a second round of hearings on my allegations, he told me that I had the "option to testify whenever I wished, . . . first and last," as I chose. What I did not know was that between that phone call and the eve of the hearings, he had given the same assurances to Judge Thomas. Nor had anyone informed me how long Judge Thomas might testify or when I could expect to be called.

Because of this eleventh-hour change in procedure, I was in my room at the Capitol Hill Hotel when the hearing opened shortly after ten o'clock and Thomas gave his statement. From my window I could see

the Library of Congress, a building I had frequented as a young government lawyer, while across the street the bells of St. George's rang from its
Gothic spires throughout my stay. Just outside was a huge oak tree, its
leaves a brilliant red-orange. And while no amount of autumn sunshine
could have made it cheerful under the circumstances, I tried to look
upon the tree as a reminder that seasons change and this, too, would pass.

There were two televisions in my room, each perched precariously on
stands shaky from use. Both of them were on as I watched Thomas'
testimony intently. It never occurred to me not to watch it. In my heart I
was sure that he would acknowledge the immorality of his behavior,
however obliquely, and offer an explanation, if not an apology. And
though I was shocked by his "categorical denial," it did not change what
I had to do. After listening to Thomas, I left the hotel with my attorney
Charles Ogletree and my friend-turned-legal-adviser Sonia Jarvis, and
we made our way to the Russell Building in the northeast quadrant of
Capitol Hill, where the hearing was being held.

Rushed from the car into the Rules Committee room, I had no time
to prepare for what I learned would be a full day of testimony. Someone
informed the Judiciary Committee of my arrival. By then Thomas had
left the hearing room, and the committee had assembled in a room
adjacent to the caucus room. Chairman Biden insisted that my testimony
begin immediately. The Capitol policemen escorted me out of the Rules
Committee room, instructing me to stand immediately behind them as
they led me and my advisers down the corridor to the caucus room for
my testimony.

We walked swiftly through a gauntlet of reporters and camera operators filling the hallways. Every one of our steps echoed down the long
corridor of the Russell Building, with its fifteen-foot ceiling. Senate
staffers stepped out of their offices to watch the parade. As I walked
down that corridor, I was certain that every journalist in the country was
there. I was wrong. There were far more in the caucus room—reporters,
photographers, camera operators, crew members—all waiting to capture
the story.

The scene inside the hearing room startled me momentarily. The focal point of the large room was a long table draped in a bright green cloth. At the center of the table sat a single microphone, a glass of water, and a name card: "Professor Anita Hill." I sat down in the lone chair at the table. Immediately to my right and left were throngs of photographers; behind me were my advisers, more journalists, staffers, and other nameless observers. In front of me, facing me and the bank of journalists, was the Senate Judiciary Committee—fourteen white men dressed in dark gray suits. I questioned my decision to wear bright blue linen, though it hadn't really been a decision; that suit was the only appropriate and clean suit in my closet when I hastily packed for Washington two days before. In any case, it offered a fitting contrast.

Senator Biden called the hearing to order, explained the procedure the committee would follow, and swore me in. After I finished reading my statement, he gave me that smile and said, "Professor, before I begin my questioning, I notice that there are a number of people sitting behind you. Are any of them your family members you would like to introduce?"

"Well, actually my family members have not arrived yet," I said with regret and anxiety. Sue Ross, one of my attorneys, whispered that my family was waiting in the hallway. "Yes, they have," I corrected myself. "They are outside the door. They were not here for my statement."

"We will make room for your family to be able to sit," said the chairman.

"It is a very large family, Senator."

A short time later, my relatives began filing into the hearing room. Each took a turn greeting me. My mother, who would be eighty in five days, embraced me as cameras flash-froze the moment for posterity. Chairs were shifted around and brought in from adjacent rooms.

"We will try to get a few more chairs, if possible, but we should get this under way." Senator Biden was beginning to sound a bit impatient.

By now, the entire first row had been cleared, but we needed more room still. The press corps made up the next layer of spectators. Most journalists were not about to give up their seats, and Senator Biden did not request them to.

"Fine, we can put them in the back as well," Biden said.

But my family did not travel across the country to sit in the back of the hearing room. And they paid little heed to Biden's suggestion.

"Now, there are two chairs on the end here, folks. We must get this hearing moving. There are two chairs on the end here. We will find everyone a seat but we must begin." The instant smile had completely vanished.

"Now, Professor Hill, at the risk of everyone behind you standing up, would you be kind enough to introduce your primary family members to us."

"I would like to introduce, first of all, my father, Albert Hill."

"Mr. Hill, welcome," the chairman said.

"My mother, Erma Hill."

"Mrs. Hill."

Four of my sisters were there—the eldest, Elreatha, and JoAnn, Carlene, and Joyce. I introduced them too.

"I welcome you all. I am sorry?"

"My brother, Ray Hill," I interrupted, limiting my introductions to my "primary" family members, as the senator had requested. I forgot my sister Doris and deliberately omitted my nieces and nephew, Anita LaShelle, Lila, and Eric.

I had simply said that I needed their support. Some I had expected; others I was surprised to see. With less than forty-eight hours notice, twelve of them had come to Washington, D.C., to be present on Friday morning at the opening of the hearing. My parents had arrived from Tulsa with my sisters Elreatha and JoAnn. My sisters Doris, Joyce, and Carlene and my niece Anita LaShelle had flown in from California. My niece Lila had come from New York. When I first told my family of the hearings, I did not know who would be able to make the trip to Washington on such short notice. They all had jobs and would have to take vacation time to attend.

My family was as relieved as I had been when they were allowed into the hearing room. Like me, my family had watched Thomas' opening statement from a hotel room. And like me, they had little information about when I would appear. As soon as they were notified, they had hailed three taxis for the trip to the Russell Building. As I greeted each of them, I felt despair and humiliation that we should be brought together under such painful and public circumstances. Even at the age of thirty-five I wanted my family to be proud of me. At the same time, I wanted to protect them—especially my parents, who were both approaching eighty at the time of the hearing. This event placed them squarely in harm's way, and I could neither help feeling responsible nor shield them from what was happening.

At that moment when I hugged my mother, I felt the gravity of the situation most intensely. For the first time during the ordeal I wanted to cry, but my desire to show her my strength moved me beyond the tears. As difficult as it was for me to have my family there in the midst of the turmoil, their presence gave me courage. I could read the determination on their faces.

What I know of my family story goes back two generations on my father's side and one on my mother's. They came from Arkansas, North Carolina, and Texas, traveling to Indian Territory and Oklahoma to escape the racial hostility of those states. But what they and even their descendants found was merely a different, sometimes less violent, brand of inequality.

Like my parents, my grandparents and great-grandparents were farmers. The latter group all began as slaves on farms in the South. My mother's father, Henery Elliott, was born a slave in Arkansas in 1864. His parents, Sam and Mollie Elliott, were separated by sale, before he was born. Henery's mother and a stepfather, Charley Taylor, were brought together by the circumstances of their status. At the end of slavery, they married and raised my grandfather. Sam Elliott remarried as well, to a woman named Alice. Alice Elliott was known to her step-grandchildren and the generation that followed as "Granny."

My maternal grandmother, Ida Crook Elliott, was born in Texas in 1872. Over a span of twenty-five years, she and my maternal grandfather had fourteen children—a large family even by farm standards. Amazingly, given the times and the family's economic conditions, all but three of their children survived. I have the impression from them that my grandparents were much like my mother, their youngest daughter, quiet and determined. From the one photograph of my grandparents that exists, and a few stories my mother and her brother, my Uncle George, tell, I learned almost all I know about them. Ida Elliott was one of two children, born and raised in Texas. Her only brother, Danny, was killed when he resisted whites who were trying to drive him from his farm. My mother and her brother, my Uncle George, tell the story in a way reminiscent of the stories of loved ones killed at war.

The story that stands out the most is the one about how my mother's family came to Oklahoma. It begins in the fall of 1913. Henery and Ida Elliott were living and raising their children on a farm in eastern Arkansas. About that time, as a small boy "in shirttails," my mother's brother George recalls being "visited" by a white neighbor on horseback. Consistent with the times, the call was work-related, social interaction between the races at that time being virtually unheard-of. Approaching the Elliott home, the neighbor cut a trail through my grandparents' field, leaving to waste all of the cotton in his newly carved path. "My wife needs some help with her cleaning and cooking," the neighbor said. He "asked" my grandfather if my grandmother was available to work for him. "She's pretty busy just taking care of these children," my grandfather responded on her behalf. But whatever care Henery Elliott took not to offend, his explanation that my grandmother was far too busy to work outside her home fell on deaf ears. "Have you forgotten who you're talking to?" the rider demanded. Even at the turn of the century, his status as a "freeborn white man" left neither my grandfather, a former slave, nor my grandmother, a descendant of slaves, the option to say no. "I'll be around to see you tonight," he threatened as he rode away, cutting another path of wasted cotton through my grandfather's field.

During the early twentieth century in much of the United States, even a polite, reasoned rejection by a black person of a white person's request could be viewed as "uppitiness." My grandfather knew through tales passed along from his father and through his own experience in Arkansas that the lessons for "uppitiness" were harsh and arbitrary, ranging from threats to burned crops to lynching. And those lessons were often doled out at the hands of night riders.

Between 1882 and 1968, Arkansas was the site of 284 reported lynchings. The incidents of lynching in North Carolina, South Carolina, and Tennessee, states with higher black populations, were fewer than in Arkansas. Higher incidents of lynching occurred only in the states of Mississippi, Georgia, Louisiana, Alabama, and Texas. The grimly illustrative statistics on lynching do not begin to take into account the night rides and other tactics employed by organizations and individuals. A black family's attempts at self-preservation and protection included the telling and retelling of these stories as warnings to young blacks that the informal "system of justice" born of racism was neither just nor systematic. Racial violence and the threat of such were ever present in the collective black psyche of that time.

Though the night visit the neighbor promised my grandfather never occurred, Henery and Ida Elliott decided that for the sake of their children they would no longer live under such threats. That night my grandfather began preparations to move his family. After the season's crops were harvested and the Elliotts had collected their pay, they would leave. Throughout the black communities in Arkansas, Louisiana, and Tennessee rumors spread that Oklahoma provided escape from the racial tension prevalent in these more southern states. "Mama and Papa were told that things were so much better in Oklahoma," my mother recalls with a chuckle. Like thousands of other southern rural blacks, my maternal grandparents packed their wagons and moved to farmland in Oklahoma where a number of all-black or predominantly black communities were developing.

Farming was all my grandfather and grandmother knew. Immediately following slavery, 60 percent of the blacks in the country were employed in some type of farm labor. But between 1915 and 1940 many blacks had been encouraged by economic and social opportunities to migrate to northern urban areas, trading in the farm and farm labor for more modern living conditions and factory jobs. And for those who stayed, farmwork rarely led to farm ownership. As late as 1930, 80 percent of black farmers were working land owned by someone else. My grandparents never owned any of the land that they worked in Arkansas or in Oklahoma. But unlike many southern blacks, my grandfather with his large family chose to remain a farmer.

In January of 1914 Ida and Henery Elliott and ten of their eleven children moved to Wewoka, Oklahoma. Their departure was tearful as they left behind family members including my Aunt Zodia and my great-grandparents, Sam and Alice, as well as Charley and Mollie Taylor. Uncle George remembers the day they left for Oklahoma as "the first time I ever saw my papa cry." They all cried as they said good-bye to Zodia, my mother's oldest sister. Though my grandparents wanted the promise of Oklahoma for all of their children, Zodia was a new bride whose husband wanted to remain in Arkansas. She stayed with him as much of the rest of the family made their way to Wewoka, a town with a relatively large black population, many of whom were members of the Seminole Nation or their descendants. When Henery Elliott's father, Sam, died a few years later, he brought his stepmother, Alice Elliott, the woman my mother knew as Granny, to live with him and his family. Later, when my mother was thirteen, the family moved to a small rural community called Lone Tree in Okmulgee County.

The only photograph of my mother's parents, a snapshot, pictures them in an open, flat landscape that looks like it could be almost anywhere in Oklahoma. The only thing that separates Henery and Ida Elliott from this austerity created by the background and the black-and-white photography is a patch of flowers and a young boy who seems to be running to escape the camera. They are dressed in simple clothing— the clothing of farmers. Yet the clothing gives some hint that it is Sunday or some other special occasion—my grandfather wears a jacket, and my grandmother a long full dress and cotton stockings but no apron. I try to place the picture among all of the stories. To me my grandfather looks like a man who would have been a deacon in the church. A serious man who would have been approached by neighbors in the Lone Tree community about rebuilding the membership in the Lone Tree Baptist Church. A man who would have succeeded in such a challenge. The season appears to be fall, and though my grandparents appear to be in the winter of their short lives, they stand tall and straight, looking soberly into the camera. Unsmiling, they both appear to be gazing beyond the camera. I like to think that they are looking into the future—into the faces of grandchildren they would never know.

My grandmother's posture is stiff-backed, almost to the point of appearing uncomfortable. Her very demeanor, her serious expression, and her deliberately erect carriage remind me of my mother. In their shared demeanor, my grandmother and mother are alike in a way that my mother and I will never be. Ida Elliott did the impossible, giving birth to thirteen children and raising fourteen with none of the benefits of the modern conveniences we take for granted today. Amazingly, she lived until 1937 to the age of sixty-four, surviving my grandfather by one year, if not the Great Depression.

Alice Elliott lived with her stepson and his wife, Henery and Ida, until the three could no longer care for each other. By that time, my mother and her siblings were adults with homes of their own. In 1932 Henery, Ida, and Alice Elliott moved to my Uncle Tutulus and Aunt Fanny Elliott's home. There were no pension programs for aging farmers and the family chose home care rather than nursing home care partly because of cost, partly because of tradition, and partly because of love. Their step-granddaughter- and daughter-in-law, my Aunt Fanny, cooked and cared for them. My mother and her siblings helped to look after her parents and step-grandmother as first Henery, then Ida, and finally in 1939 Alice Elliott died. She was the last member of the generation that had experienced slavery firsthand. Sadly her thoughts on it and life after it are unrecorded.

My paternal grandparents were Allen and Ollie Hill. Allen Hill was the youngest of four children. According to my father, his grandparents had come to Oklahoma "as hoboes" before the turn of the century, before Oklahoma became a state. Along with two other families of freed slaves and their children, my paternal great-grandparents, Ed and Sally Hill, hopped freight trains from North Carolina to Oklahoma when my grandfather was just a small boy. This, too, was a blended family. My great-grandfather had two children by a previous "slave" marriage. My great-grandmother had one under similar circumstances. Together they then had two children including my grandfather. In Oklahoma Ed Hill farmed and ran a junk business, scrapping spare parts from the junked equipment of the many oil fields that sprang up throughout Oklahoma Territory.

Ollie Nelson Hill, my paternal grandmother, was born in Texas and lived there until, when she was twelve, her mother, Nellie Nelson, died. Gus Nelson was her father. He was born Gus Simms but he'd been given the name Nelson as a slave when purchased by a man with that name and retained it throughout his life. Upon his wife's death, Gus Nelson, a minister, brought my grandmother, Ollie, a brother, and two sisters, along with a younger sister of Nellie's, to Oklahoma, where he raised them alone. Late in his life, after his children were adults, he remarried.

Allen Hill and Ollie Nelson were married when they were in their late teens and served as proof to the theory that opposites attract. Though married for over thirty years, they appear to have lived separate lives. Mama Ollie, a religious woman, was a member of the fundamentalist Church of God in Christ. Musically gifted, she was quiet and reserved. She happily shared her talent with her children but allowed them to play only the music of the church. Daddy Allen, on the other hand, loved to go to dance halls and baseball games. Always outgoing and gregarious, he joined church only late in life. According to my mother, Allen Hill's confession of his sins came when he was well past committing most of them—as he stood at death's door.

For a time, Allen Hill ran a taxi service with a surrey between Muskogee and Okmulgee, Oklahoma. It was the first of its kind in the area. But mostly, Allen and Ollie Hill were farmers. Unlike my maternal grandfather, Allen Hill did not work the land he leased. He had sharecroppers, his two sons, and hired help do his farming. Late in life, at my father's suggestion, he bought land, the first in his family to do so. That, along with an adjacent parcel that my father purchased at the same time, was the beginning of the family holdings.

The professionally taken photographs of Allen and Ollie Hill tell a different story from the snapshot of my maternal grandparents. The professional studio settings of the one show prosperity, whereas the bleak farm background of the other shows only austerity. Allen and Ollie Hill are photographed separately, speaking to me of their very different personalities. The one photograph of my grandmother shows her serious nature. In her time her square-jawed, well-defined features might have been described as handsome. The lines and wrinkles on her face show the stresses of her middle-aged years, but her eyes indicate a sense of peace. Photographs of my grandfather are more numerous than of any other grandparent. In each his dress is complete with jacket, tie, and overcoat and hat tilted to the side. The photograph of Allen Hill as a young man shows not only his style but his soft good looks. As he aged, he retained the style but his looks became hardened—perhaps by years of "good living," perhaps by illness. That he enjoyed his life is not apparent from his expression.

I never knew any of my grandparents' generation. I do not even have familiar names to refer to them. I study their photographs searching for some clue of the stories that time, personality, and the circumstances of birth have robbed me of. These photographs, along with a few vignettes that my Uncle George and parents tell, are for me the only tangible pieces of evidence of my past. They make up an incomplete portrait of my American heritage. Though Ida and Henery Elliott and Allen and Ollie Hill never knew me, I often wonder what they, having lived so close to slavery and through racial hostility, might have thought of their granddaughter's life—a life with so few barriers as to be incomparable.

Both sets of my grandparents were like thousands of blacks, some former slaves and some barely a generation from slavery, who arrived in Oklahoma with hopes of greater opportunity. The history of the area, a place of aspirations often unrealized, is a complex one. Much of it had formerly been Indian Territory, and served as the home of the Cherokee,

Choctaw, Seminole, Chickasaw, and Creek tribes after the Louisiana Purchase and their relocation to the land in the 1830s. Blacks came with each of these tribes, either as slaves or as freedmen. For example, blacks made up 37 percent of the tribal roll of the Creek Nation. They had also been prominent in the tribal leadership of the Seminole tribe and constituted two separate bands of the Seminoles. Prior to 1889, the five tribes, and later approximately seventy additional relocated tribes, existed together on the land despite differences in language, culture, and tradition. But in 1889 the government opened the "unassigned" land to settlement by whites and divided the area into Indian Territory and Oklahoma Territory. And it was the settlement of whites within the boundaries which opened the door for statehood in 1907.

In addition to the blacks who came to Oklahoma Territory with the relocated Indians following the Civil War, a number of black freedmen had relocated to Oklahoma from the South to escape the harsh treatment they'd received there. In the late 1800s the antilynching advocate Ida B. Wells encouraged groups of black settlers to leave Tennessee and relocate in southeast Oklahoma, then part of Oklahoma Territory. Several viable black townships sprang up with the help of the railroad. The best known is Boley, Oklahoma, which, in its prime, boasted a post office, two banks, and its own city government. Prior to statehood in 1907, rumors that the federal government might set aside all or part of Oklahoma Territory as a freedmen state encouraged even more blacks to come. These talks reportedly went all the way to the secretary of state in Washington.

By this time, however, what had been Indian Territory had been opened to settlement by non-Indians, first with the opening of the Cherokee strip and subsequently with the land run of 1892. And many of the whites settling into Oklahoma Territory politics were southern expatriates. When these individuals negotiated statehood for Oklahoma with the federal government, they promised the federal government the protection of rights of Indians and blacks in lieu of establishing a freedmen state. According to the terms of the Enabling Act, under which Oklahoma was admitted into the Union, territory officials agreed not to pass any laws which would violate the Thirteenth, Fourteenth, and Fifteenth Amendments to the Constitution. But in 1907 when the nation granted Oklahoma statehood, neither the letter nor the spirit of those protections was honored.

Legislators passed countless provisions at the state level to institute the same kinds of Jim Crow laws in Oklahoma that existed in the southern states. For example, the state legislature amended the Oklahoma constitution to include a "grandfather clause." Such a clause granted the right to vote to those whose grandfathers had been eligible to vote prior to the granting of the right to vote to black men under the Fifteenth Amendment to the United States Constitution. Such clauses effectively disenfranchised blacks because their black grandfathers had never been eligible to vote prior to the amendment's passage and their white grandfathers were not legally recognized as part of their lineage. This type of provision stood in the way of black political participation in Oklahoma until challenged in the U.S. Supreme Court by *Guinn v. United States* in 1915 and *Lane v. Wilson* in 1932, in both of which cases it was ruled unconstitutional.

My mother's family traveled the segregated trains from Arkansas to Wewoka, Oklahoma, to arrive there in 1914. My mother remembers her excitement "at being lifted onto the train by Brother John" (her sister Zodia's husband), but of the segregated conditions only allows that "that's just the way things were. If we wanted to travel, we had to travel in the 'colored' car." But by 1914, in *McCabe v. Atchison, Topeka, & Santa Fe Railway Co.,* black residents in Oklahoma challenged the kind of segregated facilities *Plessy v. Ferguson* had legalized. Black attorneys in Oklahoma also successfully challenged the systemic exclusion of blacks from juries in *Hollings v. Oklahoma,* in 1935. Nevertheless, segregation and racial violence and threats were a part of the life my grandparents found in Oklahoma.

Just as the all-black townships emerged in the state, "sundown" towns, white towns with ordinances or de facto rules prohibiting blacks from their boundaries after dark, developed as well. Norman, Oklahoma, the site of the University of Oklahoma, was one such town. Henryetta,

Oklahoma, very near the all-black town of Wildcat, was another sundown town notorious in reputation for its harsh treatment of blacks who dared to violate the curfew. My Uncle George once recalled to me his misfortune late one afternoon of having his car break down at the outskirts of Henryetta. Reluctant to seek assistance, he eventually knocked on the door of a local residence. To his surprise, the people in the house were "quite friendly." The men of the house helped him to repair his car but he was relieved to be out of town before dark. My uncle's fear was warranted by the reputation of the town, if not by the attitudes of all of its residents.

Oklahoma certainly had its share of lynchings. From 1882 to 1968, 122 blacks are reported to have been lynched in Oklahoma. At least two of these lynchings were of women. In 1911 a black woman named Laura Nelson was lynched along with her fifteen-year-old son in Okemah, Oklahoma, a town some ten miles from Henryetta. She'd been accused of murdering a deputy sheriff who allegedly discovered stolen goods in her home. Members of the mob raped Miss Nelson before hanging her. And in 1914 a mob of white men lynched Marie Scott, a seventeen-year-old girl, alleging that her brother killed one of two white men who had previously assaulted her.

In 1921 Tulsa, Oklahoma, was the site of one of the country's bloodiest race riots. Seventy-five people, mostly black, were killed as a prosperous section of town known as the Greenwood District was bombarded from the air. Accounts of these violent events vary. Some sources suggest that it all started when a mob gathered to lynch a black youth who had been accused of attempting to rape a white woman. Others suggest that this was only an excuse to destroy the source of affluence for blacks in Tulsa. Prior to the riots the Greenwood District had been dubbed the Black Wall Street. Over the three days of unrest blacks were rounded up and held in a camp at the fairgrounds, only to be released in the custody of a white person for the purpose of reporting to work. Few contemporaneous accounts of the riot exist, but modern accounts indicate that in addition to the seventy-five people who were killed, hundreds more were injured and thousands were left homeless. By 1923, two years after the Tulsa race riot, the population of Oklahoma was approximately 2 million, of which 103,000 were reportedly members of the Ku Klux Klan. Little of the story of the race riot in Tulsa is documented. The course material in the required Oklahoma history class I took in junior high school never mentioned it or the black townships as part of the state history.

This was not the Oklahoma that the Hills or Elliotts had heard about when they decided to leave North Carolina and Arkansas for better opportunities for their children. But it was the Oklahoma they got. They stayed on and, as blacks throughout the country did, learned to deal with the hardships.

M y parents' early lives were remarkably similar to my grandparents'. My mother, like hers, gave birth to thirteen children. And the rural and racially segregated conditions under which each raised her children were much the same. Yet there were differences as well. Erma Hill was born in 1911 in Arkansas, moving to Oklahoma at age three. She was thirteen years old when her parents left Wewoka and moved to Lone Tree, where she lives today. The timing of my mother's life places her on the bridge between the slavery into which her father was born and the civil rights era during which many of her children came of age.

When my parents met in the 1920s at an interschool spelling bee, they were children. And they married only two years later. "I thought marrying was the thing to do," my mother remarks with some regret. "I often say I was getting married when I should have been getting an education."

At a time when children were defined by who their family or "people" were, my mother was the daughter of a deacon/farmer who had helped to bring life back into the floundering Lone Tree Baptist Church. My father, on the other hand, was the son of a farmer with a reputation for philandering who leased rather than owned large acreage worked by sharecroppers.

Just before my mother's seventeenth birthday they gave birth to their first child, a daughter, Elreatha. Following soon after was their first son, Albert, Jr., "June." "I only wanted to have two children," my mother once confided in me. But in 1931 there was little available reliable birth control. My mother became pregnant with her third child, my brother Alfred, or "Bubba" as we called him. At the time, my parents were living with my father's family along with my father's brother and his wife, my Aunt Sadie. "I refused to have another baby in my in-laws' home." My father found a small house and moved them to a plot of land within a few miles of his parents. The children came like clockwork, every two years. Two boys, Winston and Billy, were the fourth and fifth children. Then came my sister Doris, my mother's second daughter. When the next child, Allen, was born, my parents' small household was full with five boys and two girls. With the births of Joyce and Carlene, in the next four years, there was no space left. My father bought a four-room frame house and moved it onto a patch of land directly facing Lone Tree Mountain. The family remained in the frame house, perched on a small rising about a hundred yards from a creek and a wooded area. And as the family grew, so did the house.

When my parents moved there, Lone Tree was just a collection of small farms separated by anywhere from one-half to six miles of farmland, woods, and unpaved roads. Farms housing blacks or whites were interspersed throughout Lone Tree—a physical integration which belied the region's social racial segregation. Blacks and whites paid few social visits to each other. Blacks only visited the "white" churches for funerals, and whites visited our "black" churches for the same occasions even less. No blacks or whites complained.

Except for the fact that my father owned the land on which it stood—a first in his family—the house was typical for most blacks in 1946 rural Oklahoma. It had no electricity or running water and its unpainted exterior was covered with tar paper for insulation. To make it home, my mother planted small plots of yellow jonquils and orange and black marigolds in the front yard and a half-acre garden immediately to the north of the house.

Along with the children who were big enough to do so, my mother and father worked for seventy-five cents a day and dinner (a luncheon meal generally consisting of beans or peas and a baked potato) chopping cotton in the Oklahoma summers, with temperatures often reaching one hundred degrees. In the fall, sometimes in near-freezing weather, they worked picking cotton for one cent a pound. In sacks nine to twelve feet long, the adults and teenagers of my family could count on picking 150 pounds a day. When my father purchased a car, he hired himself out to haul pickers to various cotton fields in the area. He earned five cents for every hundred pounds pulled by those he hauled. Soon the members of my family were not only hiring themselves out for others but were busy working our own land, land on the creek bottom just south of our house. And when my brothers John and then Ray were born, my parents just built on another room.

For years my parents slept in a closetless bedroom with whoever was the baby at the time. The older girls shared a second room and the older boys shared the third. This sleeping arrangement accommodated our family as at first it expanded and then contracted, the children leaving home one by one. The births of John and Ray came at about the same time that Elreatha left home for college and Albert, Jr., for the army. Two years later, Alfred enlisted in the army.

In 1948 an unfulfilled need for cheap labor in oil pipeline construction opened up opportunities for blacks who until this time had been farm laborers. With Winston, Billy, and Allen old enough to handle the family farming, my father started helping to build oil pipelines at various locations in the Tulsa and Sand Springs areas. "I was used to earning no more than a dollar a day in the fields and that was seasonal. The construction companies offered forty dollars a week for a ten-hour day," my father recalled. "To us that was big money."

My parents added an expanded kitchen onto the house just in time for the birth of my sister JoAnn in 1950. In the meantime Elreatha had married and given birth to my parents' first grandchild, Lila. But then for the longest stretch since she started childbearing, my mother went without conceiving. It was only just before JoAnn turned four that I was born. As they struggled to name me, my sisters Joyce and Carlene prayed that I would be the last. As teens my sisters were a bit embarrassed by the fact that our mother, now in her mid-forties, had continued to bear children.

Outside the farm, with the introduction of a union, my father's wages increased to seventy-eight dollars per week. But the boys were starting to leave home—Allen had just left to join the air force to become a para-trooper—and John and Ray, the only two now left, were too young at fourteen and twelve to handle the planting by themselves. By 1962, in order to keep the farm, my father had to leave the construction work and return full-time to farming.

About the same time that my father returned to full-time farming, the market price of cotton declined. In the late 1950s and 1960s there was less and less field work outside of the family plots. By the time I was nine, and big enough to be expected to pull cotton, relatively little was planted. By that time we only worked our own fields and thus I never hired out to chop or pull cotton. Our family crop went from cotton to peanuts. But peanuts, too, had to be chopped and harvested. And harvesting peanuts can be just as backbreaking. But above all, because the peanuts grow underground, it is dirty work—done in the often muddy fields of late autumn.

In Lone Tree during the 1950s and 1960s many of the families farmed small farms for a living, and others used their own farming to supplement jobs they held in town or hired their labor out to larger farmers. Unfor-tunately, even then the depression that was to hit the farm industry was being forecast, anticipated, and, in some cases, experienced. The family farm was slowly disappearing. The level of security and comfort a farm offered seemed each year to diminish. Even as late as 1960, 11 percent of the farm operators in this country were black, equal to blacks' represen-tation in the general population, but black farm ownership had declined even from 1920 figures. Though farm declines for whites seemed to plateau in the early 1980s, the trend in decline for black farm ownership continued. Farm displacement rates for blacks during that period were two and a half times that for whites. The dual hardships of unfavorable economic forces and racial bias in lending eventually took their toll. In

1990, 62,000 (or 1.5 percent) of the 4.5 million farmers in this country were black. By the year 2000 the U.S. Civil Rights Commission predicts that black farm ownership will be altogether extinct. Our family farm was a part of this trend. We were a typical midwestern/southern farm family with one added dimension—we were a black farm family. Even today my parents, having lived through both the heyday and the demise of the black-owned, working family farm, are still farmers at heart.

My family's home was the center of my world. As a child, once I stepped off the orange bus that brought me home each day and headed west for the half-mile walk to the house with tar paper siding, there was little else of consequence. The only thing one could see from the house was the yard, the field, the abandoned cars, the tractor, combine, and other equipment, and the occasional cow that crossed too near the house to graze on my mother's roses. There were no neighbors to visit with over the backyard fence; no cars to pass along the street in front of our house. There was no street, only an unpaved, rocky dirt road. And it wasn't until 1972 that the telephone intruded on our isolation.

At home, I came into the world surrounded by family—people of all ages—and as only a child can conceive, they all belonged to me, and I to them. And this marvelously rich world of human interaction more than made up for what we lacked in cultural experience. We did not travel, we did not take vacations or go to the movies. We were farm people. Our family outings consisted of going to church and prayer meeting, visiting nearby relatives, the yearly all-black rodeo, and the segregated, until I was six, county fair.

My parents' adult lives have been so consumed by family that it still takes effort to see them as independent personalities. Erma Hill, my mother, is a mixture of stern restraint and lavish generosity. Years into my adulthood I began to understand her. Underneath the crop of fine hair that has been gray or graying as long as I have known her lies a complex mind. She is never unnerved or flustered. She can appear almost haughty, and one glance can freeze its target. But upon closer examination, I have come to recognize that much of her moderation and even her severity can be attributed to shyness and modesty. Despite the fact that she is a farmworker and the mother of thirteen children, she is never less than dignified. Her erect posture suggests the propriety of an Edwardian lady. Those were the days in which she and her friends came of age. Those are the ways her behavior reflects. And she taught her children to carry themselves in that same way despite the differences in the times of our upbringing.

My mother was at her best during our Sunday morning routine preparing for church. "Finish eating your breakfast and wash the dishes, so that we can get to Sunday school on time." A few minutes later she would call again to her children from her bedroom, "Are you all ready for church?"

"Yes," we'd groan in response, anticipating the next command.

"Well, sit on the couch and don't move until I tell you," the command always came back. "And don't get your socks dirty."

My mother often expected from us what we considered to be the impossible, especially on Sunday mornings. But we dutifully complied. Even in the summer, when we walked the three miles along the dusty road between our home and the church, we arrived with our white anklet socks spotless and only a hint of dust on our patent-leather shoes. My mother's church friend often served as her reinforcement. A woman nearly six feet tall and over 190 pounds in her prime, Mattie Hutton was her closest friend. We called her Miss Mattie. One Sunday morning when I was about twelve years old, she presented me with a purse. "Never let me see you at church without one again," she warned to remind me that I had come of age. As my Sunday school teacher, Miss Mattie watched my progress in this respect. She hovered over us like her own. From the time she and my mother taught us the children's "Jesus Loves Me" until we learned the more complex spiritual "Will the Circle Be Unbroken" (a song mourning a mother's death), they reminded us that we were first the children of God and only after that theirs.

Miss Mattie no doubt reasoned that if I were carrying a purse, I wouldn't be able to play tag with the boys between Sunday school and church as I liked to. Well, I carried the purse, but I certainly continued to play chase. Years later, in deciding on a gift for me, she would choose a handmade apron. I treasure the gift but I do not wear it, preferring to wear the evidence of my cooking on my clothes.

Another of my mother's friends, Bertha "Red" Reagor, Miss Red, tried to make a similar impression on my role identification. Miss Red gave me a sewing basket for my birthday one year, and a miniature butter churn the year after. "I just thought this was the cutest thing for Faye" (everyone referred to me by my middle name). She laughed nearly each word, as was her customary way of talking. When I went away to college, my mother confiscated the sewing basket rather than let it go to waste. The butter churn I keep as a memento, knowing that butter will never be formed in it. Most of the gifts my mother's friends gave to help ground me in what they considered my proper role and carriage, I still have. They serve as tangible reminders of the intangible gifts—the poise, the self-respect, the discipline—that were of far greater value.

But if she was the person who kept us in line, my mother was also an unselfish nurturer. My most distinct early memory of her is of her feet as they moved up and down with the treadle of the sewing machine that she had inherited from her mother. My mother sewed all of her daughters' clothes until one by one they learned to sew for themselves. I would have my turn sewing soon enough, but then I was no more than four or five years old and too young for most household duties. During her sewing we would play a game for as long as her patience lasted. Having been taught the alphabet by my older sister Joyce, I would make up letter combinations, most of them nonsensical.

"What does 'd-g-t' spell?" I would ask. Though I had learned the letters, I had not learned the difference in vowels and consonants and the significance of vowels in correct spelling. "Nothing," my mother would respond. "Nothing," I would repeat incredulously. I had somehow gotten the impression that every letter combination spelled a word. Occasionally, I would hit upon a combination of letters that actually did spell a word. This only spurred me on. I am sure I would have played the game for hours if allowed. Though I never tired of it, eventually my mother did. "That's enough spelling for now," she would announce when her ability to endure my admittedly poor efforts waned.

Usually those words were enough. But certain signals alerted me that it was a bad idea to press any point. We all took my mother seriously. I knew that the appropriate response was to stop, at least for the moment. She often guided me to the next activity: "Let's go outside and get the eggs." Or the always welcomed "Are you ready for some lunch?" She would indulge me enough to try to distract me with food—a baked sweet potato or sardines and crackers. Though I remember enjoying these foods with my mother, I don't think I ever really enjoyed the taste of them. We enjoyed mostly the communion of that time, so much so that I would never complain about the flavors.

I enjoyed a luxury shared by none of my other siblings. That was time alone with my mother. For the four years between the time when my youngest sibling, JoAnn, started school and the time I entered the first grade, my mother and I were nearly constant companions. Similarly, when JoAnn went away to college and I was in high school, my mother and I spent the summers together. And outside of her farm responsibility, I had her constant attention. By that time Mama had been raising children for thirty years, and knowing that I was the last child she would raise to adulthood, she seemed to take extra care with me. I never believed that she favored me, though my siblings might disagree. Certainly, she may have hung on to me a little longer. But she never excused me from discipline or the work that had to be done on the farm.

My favorite meals were the ones that my mother cooked for the family when I was a child. Food and physical warmth were two things that Mama lavished upon her family. She always assumed that her children were as hungry or as easily chilled as she. A sudden unexpected drop in the temperature (common in Oklahoma) during a spring day never caught us off guard. We were prepared with sweaters just in case. Each winter morning she rose before the rest of us to build a blazing fire in our wood-burning stove. And my mother did nearly all of the cooking. Meals of biscuits or corn bread, rice or fried potatoes, stew, pork chops or fried chicken, and greens were her specialties.

Summer and winter, my mother was invariably the first to rise in the household. In summer with no fire to attend to, she began the day by starting the preparation for breakfast. The sound of rattling pots was our alarm clock, followed shortly by the sound of my father sharpening the hoes for the day's work in the fields. "You all get up, now. It's almost seven," she cried out at 6:35. Following breakfast my mother gathered us and we trekked to whatever field we were working, often on foot. (My father worked with the tractor and looked after the cattle.) Midday, we broke. My mother prepared the noon meal. We returned to often oppressive heat of the cotton or peanut patch for an afternoon of work. We ate a light meal at about sunset, washed up, and shortly thereafter fell into bed exhausted. My mother and her children kept this routine every summer until only I and my mother were left to do the "chopping."

My mother regularly coordinated meals, field work, and home chores. In any given year, the household included as many as eight of the thirteen children. When my parents learned that an elderly man once married to my father's aunt had again been widowed, they brought him into the household. At the age of four, I could not understand how Charley Arvier, who spoke a kind of Cajun French and broken English with a Louisiana accent, was related to me. Yet we called him Uncle Charley, and he lived with us as part of the family until he died eight years later. She did this without any fanfare or self-consciousness. This was simply a part of her routine. As an adult I marvel at it.

My father's personality is just as strong as my mother's. Despite their differences in interests and background, as a young man my father, with his broad smile, smooth brown skin, and curly black hair, must have been quite appealing to her. He was handsome (though "Handsome" was the nickname that went to his older brother, Ralph), energetic, and athletic. And he probably served as an antidote to the sobriety of the Elliott family. Where my mother was shy and reserved, my father was always outgoing and charming. Still, they were never an odd couple so much as a matched set.

My father loved to tease, to make us laugh, and to laugh at his own jokes even when others did not. I recall once having incurred my father's wrath. Late at night, when my mother was away, I was whining about having to share my bed with two visiting nieces and nephews, having been used to sleeping only with my sister. My father took objection to being kept up past his bedtime to listen to my protest. I learned then that my father had his limits too. His one demand of us as small children was that we be quiet. "You all cut out that noise," he would bellow in the evenings. Daddy still has great charm about him and the ability to relax and feel at home in almost anyone's company. Yet he can also be detached and reserved. Like my mother, he is a product of his time—a time when fathers were not necessarily expected to be emotionally available twenty-four hours a day.

My earliest clear memory of him is watching him getting ready to go to the Sunday night musicals where he would sing tenor with his quartet, the Oklahoma Spirituals. Though as a farmer he was in the home much of the day, he did not work alongside us in the fields. He drove the tractors and tended the cows. On Sunday, however, we were all together. He would shave his face of all but his thick mustache and slick back his hair with Murray's pomade. The orange tin of hairdressing was for his exclusive use. In the background, Negro spirituals played on the radio broadcast from a station in Muskogee. "Be quiet so I can hear the announcements," my father commanded. The "memory lane" segment was a "must hear" for him. The announcer told who had died that week and which of the black mortuaries "has the body." All the children were dressed, heeding our mother's admonition to sit quietly. My mother, having concluded her responsibility to us, was also finished with her routine. But my father was a different story. He regularly finished his routine as the rest of the family waited, fully dressed. No one dared urge him to quicken his pace. We'd just wait patiently for him to enter the living room and ask of those gathered, "Are you all waiting for me?" My mother never learned to drive a car. Had she mastered this skill, I suspect that we would have waited at church for my father's arrival.

My father's most memorable church activity was his singing. I often anticipated hearing him sing "Pass Me Not O Gentle Savior" in his untrained falsetto voice. This voice was inviting and pleasant yet so unlike his speaking voice, it seemed completely unreal. As a child, I could not understand how my father's gravelly speaking voice could turn to a high-pitched singing voice. By the same token, my achievements at school were a source of pride and delight for my father. Though he expected me to do well in school, he never understood my attachment to learning. And I am certain that he never saw the significance of it for my future. I was, after all, always his "baby girl."

Every Sunday the family went to Sunday school at Lone Tree Missionary Baptist Church, the church my paternal grandfather had helped to establish. And on every first and third Sunday we went there to church. The alternating Sunday church service was a part of the rural tradition of the "circuit" minister who pastored two or more churches and visited them on a rotating basis. Our pastor's visit fell on these two Sundays. Presumably, he spent other Sundays at another church. This was typical of small rural communities and continues even today. The whitewashed wood-frame building now sits quietly during the week attracting little attention from passersby, as it awaits Sunday services.

In earlier days when my parents' family was young, the building rattled with activity daily. Prior to 1960 it was the home of the grammar school for the "colored" children in the rural neighborhood. At one point two teachers taught as many as sixty schoolchildren at a time within its walls. Before my memory, on occasion on Saturday nights when musicals were not held in the church, there was a different kind of bustle in the building. That week's farmwork completed, the members of the community dressed in close to their Sunday best and gathered at the "church house" for family movies. A man who traveled about with projector, film, and screen collected nickels from families and created a makeshift theater, thus compensating for the lack of entertainment available to rural blacks. My sisters Joyce and Doris recall watching the films *The Wolf Man* and *Dracula* in the church building and being afraid to walk the three miles home afterward. This was the 1950s. The family never went to the movie theater together, so it was not part of our experience. I saw my first movie in an actual theater in 1967 when my brother Ray took JoAnn and me to see *Bonnie and Clyde*.

On Wednesday night the school and social center became a place of worship as church deacons led parishioners in prayer meeting. Prayer

meeting was my favorite church activity. I particularly enjoyed the traditional hymns as they were performed in the church. "I love the Lord, he
heard my cry and pitied every moan," Deacon Jesse Barnett (my friend
Pocahontas' father) would call out to the worshipers. "I love the Lord, he
heard my cry," they would sing in response, almost moaning the words.
"Long as I live, when troubles rise, I'll hasten to his throne," again
Deacon Barnett called. As the song went on, the imagery was so strong,
coupled with the words and singing, that I would see Jesus "bowing his
head and chasing my griefs away." Perhaps childhood griefs were so
limited that they vanished with ease.

On Friday night Lone Tree conducted business meetings. From appearances, the men mostly ran the church's business, but the women of
Lone Tree firmly yet diplomatically let their opinions be known. On
Saturday night Lone Tree might offer a musical, bringing in choirs, solo-
ists, and duos from Okmulgee and surrounding counties. My parents'
friends S. L. and Red Reagor were among the most interesting with
their a cappella selection of jubilees—a lively syncopated form of gospel
song that evoked images of happy times or deliverance. Due to their years
together, the Reagors as a duo had mastered the form of singing like no
other couple had and were known throughout the rural churches because
of it. During service it was the tradition that the women sat on the right
side of the church and the men sat on the left. Couples who came in
together separated at the door and walked separately down the church's
two aisles to sit on one of the wooden pews. Young children sat with
their mothers. When it came time for the Reagors to sing, they approached the front of the congregation from separate corners and returned separately when they concluded. It was our tradition and we
never questioned or commented on it.

Lone Tree Missionary Baptist Church was the center of the family
spiritual and social life. The women of Lone Tree were my role models.
Most were farmers and homemakers who came out of the fields to clean
their homes and the church building. The lessons they taught, both
religious and social, are the most valuable to me. They were not "femi-

nists," in the modern sense of the word. They worshiped in a service which prohibited women from preaching or leading. When women and men sat separately in church, it was most likely out of this denigration of women's roles. Yet they were essential to the operation of the church and voiced their opinions. Importantly, they expected just as much from the girls in the church as from the boys. Even more importantly, by example, they taught me about concern for the collective—the community. Some Sundays family members and friends assembled at our home around 2:00 P.M. for Sunday dinner. It was as though they just materialized. We had no telephones to communicate an invitation or to announce an event. Miraculously, or so I always felt, whether there were ten or thirty extra mouths to feed, my mother always seemed to have enough food. Each of those days seemed like a mini-reunion that gave me a sense of being in touch with people outside of the farmwork and my everyday school life.

Neither my parents nor the other people in rural Oklahoma were naive about discrimination and its impact on their lives. No doubt that is why Erma and Albert Hill insisted that their children finish high school and provided for their education beyond high school. In the fall of 1945 my parents had eight children and one due shortly. Elreatha, my oldest sister, then seventeen, graduated from high school in the spring. My parents were both thirty-four and neither of them had finished high school. My farmer parents' vision extended well beyond their circumstances. They sent "Reat" to college at a time when only 5 percent of the black women in the country had white-collar jobs and 60 percent were working as domestics. On the average in Okmulgee County, females completed 8.9 years and males 8.6 years of formal education. Yet Elreatha was one of the few hundred black women who that year would begin her college education. The fact that Oklahoma made it a criminal offense to educate blacks and whites of any age together was not a deterrence. All of the children in the family attended segregated schools.

Before Oklahoma became a state, parents of two black children in a town named Guthrie challenged unsuccessfully the dual education system in Oklahoma Territory. Again, in 1946, a woman named Ada Lois

Sipuel began to challenge educational segregation in a case argued in the U.S. Supreme Court two years later by Thurgood Marshall, *Sipuel v. Board of Regents of the University of Oklahoma*. Though, in 1949, she ultimately won her right to attend the School of Law at the University of Oklahoma, the victory in the case only affected professional and graduate schools in the state. The practice of segregated education for elementary, secondary, and undergraduate education continued until well after the 1954 decision in *Brown v. Board of Education*. Elreatha attended Langston University, the historically black college set up in the state to avoid integration of such institutions as the University of Oklahoma and Oklahoma State University. She never graduated, choosing instead to marry and raise children—eleven, in fact.

Eleven of my brothers and sisters attended segregated schools. In 1958 JoAnn was the first to begin her education at the integrated Eram School. Neither she nor I, who followed her in 1962, ever attended segregated schools. Interestingly, Eram School was integrated because of fiscal necessity rather than because of the mandates of the law. Eram was a rural school district whose size in a dwindling farm community would have required its closing without the numbers of black children who still resided in the area. Rather than close, the board made the choice to integrate in 1958, and Carlene, John, JoAnn, and Ray began attending there. Prior to attending Eram, Ray had been in classes at Lone Tree.

All of my brothers, except for one, chose to go into the military following high school. My parents waited patiently at home as each went off to duty. Amazingly, only one, Albert, Jr., was involved in combat. The promises of the military to give young men the opportunity to see the world was fulfilled in my brothers. The promise to promote their educational development was not as readily fulfilled. Yet each enlisted in a branch of the service one after the other, until my youngest brother, Ray, broke the chain. Ray chose to go directly into college.

My school life and activities were typical of girls in rural Oklahoma in the 1960s and 1970s. When I began my formal education, there were five children at home. Carlene, John, Ray, JoAnn, and I each day began with the near-half-mile walk to the bus stop. Ray, JoAnn, and I traveled north to the two-room elementary school at Eram. Carlene and John, though they earlier had attended Eram Grade School, were bused south to the segregated high school in Grayson. At Eram grades one through four studied together in one room with a single teacher and grades five through eight with another. In each classroom four rows of aqua-blue seats with attached desktops faced a single blackboard. Each row was designated for a single grade, which averaged about eight students. Next to the blackboard was a huge gas heater that heated the entire room. Due to my nearsightedness, I often sat near the front and close to the heater. Accordingly, I was often scalding hot while my classmates in the rear shivered.

My first-grade teacher was Mrs. Johnson, whose husband taught in the other classroom, where my brother was. Later Mrs. Broadhead, then Mrs. Morton and Miss Pope—all women, all white—taught each of the four classes in her charge each of the required subjects. Mrs. Harris and her husband, Lee Wade Harris, rounded out the school staff as cook and bus driver/janitor, respectively. Under Mrs. Broadhead and her successors, I excelled, often doing the next grade's work in order to be challenged. But the highlight of my promotion from grade to grade was that it brought me away from the inner wall and the cloakroom and closer to the outer wall of the schoolroom and the area I loved most. I knew from grade one that, once in the fourth grade, I would be allowed to sit next to the wall. I could hardly wait—for underneath the large windows was the room's library. There, lining the shelves were the encyclopedias, geography books, and the Nancy Drew mystery series just waiting for me to finish my work.

In grades one through three, when I finished an assignment early, I would ask permission to cross the room to the library. But by the fourth grade I could simply reach out and pull whatever I wanted from the shelf without leaving my seat or drawing attention to my idleness. I liked my schoolwork and did well in it, but I loved reading the library books even more. Perhaps they were a greater incentive to complete my assignments quickly and correctly. By the end of fourth grade, having read all of the books in the first library, I was anxious for the promotion to the next set of books.

The peacefulness of my family life continued through most of my childhood. Yet at about the time when the outer world seemed to be in chaos with war, antiwar demonstrations, civil rights protests and rioting, personal crisis disrupted our idyllic existence. One evening during the fall of 1967, my parents left my sister JoAnn and me alone at home. Usually when my parents had to be away in the evening, we went with them, or one of my older brothers, John or Ray, stayed with us. However, on this night my parents were going to the hospital to visit my Aunt Sadie, who was critically ill from a stroke she had just suffered. My brother John had left home for the air force, and Ray, the only other sibling still at home, was playing in his senior year of high school football. JoAnn was fourteen and I was eleven; by today's standards of latchkey and otherwise independent children, we were certainly old enough to be left alone for a few hours. Yet this was the first time that I remember we were left alone. Since our closest neighbors were miles away, we felt fairly isolated and we imagined that every dog bark foretold some terrible misfortune about to befall us. We teased each other, laughed, and did our normal sibling squabbling about whose turn it was to wash and whose to dry. Upon finishing our homework and chores we waited for our parents to come home with some news of our aunt.

As the night wore on, the time when we were sure our parents should have been home passed. Our joking and bickering ended and real fear crept in. At midnight the dogs began to bark to warn of a car's approach. We quickly hid in our parents' closet until we could be sure that it was really our parents and brother. By this time, we were convinced that the dreaded stranger would arrive before our family. We knew our parents would not knock. Tom Barnett's knock on the door sent us into a small panic. But the news the neighbor brought was even worse. Our parents and Ray had been in an accident and had been taken to the hospital.

Thus began the winter of 1967: Aunt Sadie was in the hospital suffering from a stroke from which she would soon die; my father and mother and brother snatched away without warning in the middle of the night; and my brother John enlisted in the armed forces as a private during the escalation of the Vietnam War.

My mother came home from the hospital within two weeks of the accident. Her major injury was a broken collarbone. After her return home, the household returned to some semblance of normalcy. My father's injuries, however, were more extensive and severe, including a collapsed lung and a shattered right arm. He had to be taken to the hospital in Tulsa, over an hour by car from where we lived. From my one visit with my father in the hospital, I remember him covered in bandages and strapped to countless sustaining and monitoring devices. Even as a child I knew the reason for the visit: that it might be the last time I saw my father alive. The prognosis for his survival was very poor. We were grateful that my father proved the doctors wrong—he lived—but never spoke of the danger of his condition. After what in a child's mind seemed an interminable stay in the hospital, he came home for a recovery that lasted throughout the winter. He was in and out of bed, and my mother, my sister, and I were constantly tending his shattered arm. We bathed and massaged it, hoping to revive it from its now paralyzed state, though I never believed that the therapy was adequate for or scientifically related to his full recovery. Still, he did recover partial use of the arm.

In the meantime, the farmwork, which during winter consisted mostly of feeding the cattle and pigs, continued. During the winter of 1967 the work fell on Ray and my mother. This was a precursor for the following winter. That year, with my father ill again and Ray away at school, the chore of feeding over a hundred head of cattle fell on my mother, JoAnn, and me. My mother was the muscle of the operation weighing 130 pounds. At ages fifteen and eleven, neither JoAnn nor I weighed more than 90 pounds. The winter of 1967 was cold and dismal. Often my body quivered—the response of a frightened adolescent who had not yet learned to express such an intense fear of loss.

Everything in my life and in the world seemed completely upended and uncontrollable. I was eleven years old and for the first time ever I was more frightened by the world than I was intrigued by it. Quietly, I had always soaked up life's experiences. I loved schoolwork; even test taking. In the evening when my chores were completed and before I did my homework, I watched the national news with intense interest. I even enjoyed some, but admittedly not all, of the rigors of farmwork. Now, however, I wanted to retreat.

My life with my family had been more than just the farmwork. My sisters and brothers were my best friends. I rode the bicycle I shared with JoAnn. I played basketball on a dirt court with Ray. On Saturdays when my parents went to town for the family groceries and left us at home, I listened to the 45s that John played for us while Ray and Carlene danced. In the springtime JoAnn and I picked blackberries along the roadsides. In the fall we fished the mud holes together for crawdads—one of JoAnn's favorite activities. Even on the farm there were always sounds and sights that were pleasant, bright, and exciting—the greens of the spring peas, the croaking of the tree frogs, the glimmer of the fireflies that we called lightning bugs.

Yet in 1967 and 1968 everything in the bright world of sunshine, green grass, and purple and yellow flowers appeared to be covered with a gray film. Gone was the brother who entertained us with his love of music, the one who went streaming through our house with its seven-foot ceilings playing an imaginary game of basketball. John was gone—first to an air force base in San Antonio, then to Germany, mercifully not Vietnam, where one of his friends from high school had already died. I wrote him, but the letters he sent home could not take the place of his presence or give any assurance that he was safe from the war.

All around me people seemed to speak in hushed tones perhaps due to the fact that my father needed rest and quiet. I had never been a noisy child but I was even more quiet now, believing that it was the only way to save my father's life. The strain hit us all. My mother was tired and not altogether healed. Each of us carried with us the stress of the injuries and recovery period. Remnants of the stresses remained for months. We could have each retreated into our own hurt, and left alone, perhaps I would have. However, our circumstances did not allow it. We were so accustomed to functioning as a unit that we continued, even in our healing, to do so. Work, church, and school continued. In particular, farmwork had to be done regardless of sickness or death. We continued to attend church. Our neighbors and our community expected it. And Ray, JoAnn, and I continued with school. Our parents' misfortune and the death of our aunt were no excuse for irresponsibility.

By 1968 my world and the world outside my home and family were changing dramatically. The county school board closed Eram as integration began to happen throughout the school system. I would transfer to Morris for junior high school. Even aside from the integration, going to school in Morris represented major change in my early life. Morris was a town—albeit a small town—with paved streets. It had a bank, a feed store, a hardware store, and a drugstore where, if I were lucky, I could buy ice cream while my mother shopped for groceries at Gale's Market. Eram was just a school, standing alone, surrounded by fields of hay.

Though Ray started at the segregated Grayson High School, by 1967 he was attending the newly integrated Morris High School, along with JoAnn. Ray's negative experiences with integration included having to be escorted out of Glenpool, Oklahoma, by local police because the fans there objected to his playing on the Morris High School football team. Amid the racist taunts and jeers his bus was led out of town after his team had won the game.

In my own transfer to Morris, I saw new opportunities—opportunities that were never realized. What I did realize was the signficance of race. My first experience with the tensions of integration occurred in Morris, which, despite the integration of its schools, remained an all-white town. Though not a "sundown" town in the purest sense, no blacks resided in Morris. We bought our groceries there, and went to the post office there, but we did not *live* there. Even as late as 1983, when a black family started building a home on the outskirts of town, arsonists destroyed it before it could be completed.

But even though the social structure set very real lines of demarcation between blacks and whites, my parents insulated us from extreme forms of racism. I often wonder at how they were able to do so, in a society not unlike the Deep South, where so much racial division still remained. By the time I was born my parents had many years, even generations, of experience living and raising children in a segregated society.

Despite the early Supreme Court challenges to Oklahoma's racial separatism and despite the fact that the very first lunch counter sit-in took place in Oklahoma City in 1962, much of the civil unrest experienced in the South escaped Oklahoma. Those of us living in rural areas of Oklahoma watched the movement on television and read about it in the newspapers. As a family we watched and waited in silence, though each member, I suspect, wondered how our lives would be changed by what we saw and heard about. I was at home when the announcement of the assassinations came over the airwaves. In April 1968, as we ate our dinner on a balmy evening, reports of Dr. Martin Luther King's death came on the nightly news. My father spoke of it in knowing terms. It was "predictable," he declared, given the intense hatred King's denouncement of segregation had brought. My mother agreed.

We did not customarily talk of politics at home, and though this tragic event provided a rare opportunity, we did not speak of politics then, either. Nor did we speak of the assassination at all the following day at school. In June, with Ray, I watched the news films of the shooting of Robert Kennedy. Still no discussion from my parents of the politics of our times—the times that would change their children's future. The times were so different than those my parents had known that they knew no language in which to speak about them. My parents' lives were more like their own parents' than the lives of their children. Uncertain of the relevance of their observations, they mostly kept quiet. We never discussed why the family never ate at the lunch counter in Newberry's during our trips to Okmulgee but instead ate our Dairy Queen hamburgers in the car. Or why the rural black folks gathered and shopped at Norman's Grocery Store rather than the larger and newer Neal's, where the whites gathered and shopped. Or why black people were always interred by Dyer's, Ragsdale's, or Brown's funeral homes and never one of the white-owned mortuaries, whose names even today I'm not aware of. The civil rights movement was a remote and abstract experience. In Oklahoma we certainly identified with its goal, but its activities never reached the rural areas except over the television.

There were few incidents of physical resistance to the integration at Morris in my experience. When I arrived there as an eighth grader, Ray and the five other black students in his class had paved the way. Though the black boys had opportunities to mainstream in the high school culture in sports, the black girls' access to the fields of distinction in school culture—cheerleading and homecoming activity—remained limited. None of the black girls were encouraged to participate on the girls' basketball team, which in Morris had a history of state championships. For me it was all the same. I was not athletic, nor did I think myself beautiful in the homecoming queen way. I had a pleasant round face that from age seven was adorned with glasses thick enough to correct my nearsightedness, and that did not seem to change much with age. I looked and indeed was very bookish. I remained that way during high school and college.

Much of the classwork came easy, the rest I studied so intensely at times that my father worried. The time that I spent talking to my friend Pocahontas Barnett on our recently acquired telephone came only after I had completed my homework. Being bookish paid off, however, as I graduated at the top of my high school class, an honor that had been denied JoAnn. When she graduated from Morris High School three years earlier, she was told that even though her grades technically put her at the top of the class, the fact that she had transferred into the Morris system in the middle of the freshman year made her ineligible to be valedictorian. That honor went instead to her friend Clara Ivy, who, since elementary school, had been used to the top spot in her classes at Morris. JoAnn was made salutatorian. JoAnn, who even by then had developed a pretty good temper, did not complain, though she must have been hurt deeply. When I graduated, none of my classmates seemed surprised or disturbed that I was first in the class, least of all the salutatorian that year, my friend Susie Clark. And next year Susie and I went off to college at Oklahoma State University, in Stillwater, together.

I always knew that I would go to college, though only a few of my classmates from high school would. As you can imagine in a family of our size, a good amount of energy was funneled to me, the youngest child. And along with the energy came an equivalent amount of expectation. Fortunately for me, I enjoyed the experience of being taught and learning from my family. My sister Joyce still teases me about reading over and over again the first book I ever owned. She claims she still remembers all of the lines in *Green Eggs and Ham!* This is a testament to her patience with me.

Fortunately, I grew up during a time when social forces were such that I might have a better opportunity to realize my family's and my own expectations. In ways small and large, from school lunch programs to student grants and loans, they enhanced my opportunities for a better life than the one enjoyed by my parents and grandparents. I no doubt have benefited from affirmative action programs, which looked at my race, gender, and background and determined whether I would be admitted. But I am not ashamed of this fact, nor do I apologize for it. Such programs provided me with the opportunity to prove myself, no more, no less. After admission, my success or failure would be determined by my efforts. I do not consider myself either more or less worthy than my colleagues in the same programs.

My parents raised their children to love and leave home because they knew they had no other chance there at a better life. And in just the same order they'd been born, every two years, almost like clockwork, each of my brothers and sisters left home for school or to enter the military. There were few employment opportunities to keep us home. Okmulgee County had, at the time of my birth, a population of approximately 40,000, of which about 7,000 were black. The primary sources of jobs were related to agriculture and were relatively limited. The peanut plant located in Okmulgee, the seat of Okmulgee County, served as the station where most of the local farmers brought their crops for weighing and processing. It provided seasonal work for a few. Work that was dirty and dangerous. Prior to the time of OSHA regulations, several accidents occurred at the plant, one of which, involving the only son in a neighboring family, was fatal. The entire community grieved. As each offered the family condolences, many questioned whether it might have been prevented.

The other notable industry was the slaughterhouse, the success of which was linked to the fact that many of the local residents raised their own beef and pork for food. During the brief period between the time that home curing became unpopular and supermarkets with abundant supplies of meat became popular and accessible, the slaughterhouse prospered. Even the glass jars produced at the local glass plant are, to me, associated with the rural lifestyle. Each rural household of which I was aware used countless numbers of fruit jars from July to September to put up the summer's fruits and vegetables, jellies and jams. Once a flourishing industry and source of jobs, each year the plant employed fewer and fewer individuals. In 1994 the plant closed.

By the economic, social, and cultural standards of most Americans, the family of Albert and Erma Hill was poor. Yet I never knew it, for our lives were rich with family, friends, God, and nature. Even now, as I look back, I do not remember poverty, because we lacked the kinds of hopelessness and despair that choke many of the poor today. As I think of the family that entered the hearing in the Russell Senate Office Building on October 11, 1991, I see not only those present but those who came before us as well. Having lived through our struggles together in a life that was anything but easy, we expected adversity, and we expected to withstand it.

CHAPTER TWO

For months after accepting the admission to Yale and sending in my deposit, I was 110 pounds of nervous energy. I don't recall that my knees shook, but I remember lying awake wide-eyed many nights during the spring of 1977, wondering what it might be like.

In the summer of 1977, just before my twenty-first birthday, I traveled to Connecticut in preparation for my first semester at Yale Law School. I wanted to adjust to living in Connecticut before my classes started. I approached my first year of law school with the mingled anticipation and apprehension of a child about to receive her first bike. I had first become interested in law at age fifteen when I read in JoAnn's sorority magazine that two of the women active in politics and the civil rights movement, Yvonne Burke and Patricia Harris, were lawyers. The images of the marchers and protesters influenced me as well. They were people who knew how cruel the law could be but believed so much in it that they were willing to die for changes in it. The civil rights movement and the people, lawyers and nonlawyers, in it inspired my belief in the law. My family and family friends had instilled in me a belief that I could actually achieve a law school education. But even at age twenty, as I readied myself for school, I had known only one lawyer personally. Nor had I ever spent more than two weeks outside the state of Oklahoma or crossed its border more than twice. For sixteen years of my life, I had not ventured more than 120 miles from our farm, and life in Stillwater during college was almost an extension of my life on the farm. But now the distance offered by Yale was a daunting prospect.

Arriving in New Haven, I knew that my apprehension was justified. New Haven and Stillwater could not have been more foreign to one another. The first thing that I noticed was the cold. May in Connecticut felt more like March in Oklahoma. Not only was the temperature fifteen degrees lower, but it was measured with a Celsius thermometer—sparing me the satisfaction of protesting with absolute certainty just how much colder. In Stillwater I could look from the top floor of my dormitory and see beyond the edge of town to the surrounding pastures, miles across the flats. Neither trees nor buildings nor hills obstructed my view. New Haven, a small town by East Coast standards, stretched into endless suburbs—Woodbridge, West Haven, North Haven—and signs designating the various townships were the only lines of demarcation. In three years in New Haven I never found a vantage point that allowed me to see beyond the city boundaries to the countryside. I felt confined—able to escape only when time and finances allowed me to travel by train.

The Yale campus itself fulfilled my apprehension as well. Even the buildings were different. Ivy really *did* cover the walls of the Gothic-style structures so unlike the red brick buildings of Oklahoma State. And these differences seemed to have everything to do with tradition and expectation. And I feared that my early education at rural schools in Oklahoma and later in college was hardly adequate preparation for the top law school in the country.

I had decided to go to Yale rather than Harvard after visiting both. Yale, the smaller of the two, gave me the feeling of protection and security I needed for two major transitions—undergraduate to law school, public to Ivy League school. But once I got there I discovered that the small size only compensated so much for the inevitable feeling of being an outsider. However much those who direct the educational process perceive it as race and gender neutral, Yale cannot escape its history. (In many respects it does not want to.) It was designed for young white men of privilege and only began to admit women in 1969. From its secret societies to its Whiffenpoofs, men dominated the culture of the institution in the 1970s, just as they had historically. And if we never spoke of class, status, or distinctions in background, it was because they were so clearly taken for granted.

My class at Yale was 165 students from all over the country. I was attracted to students who were making transitions similar to my own, though few, if any, seemed to be bridging barriers of race, gender, class, geography, and education. I recognized my inexperience and naiveté, but was committed to learning all I could at Yale. The summer before, I had vowed to be like a sponge, soaking up everything that the experience had to offer. I valued what I brought to Yale, but I wanted to absorb what it had as well.

My first-year instructors were highly regarded legal scholars. Guido Calabresi was my torts teacher. Geoffrey Hazard taught our section civil procedure, and Robert Bork, constitutional law. Ellen Peters taught me contracts in a small class of about twenty students. The fact that one of these, Robert Bork, had a national reputation in politics as well left no impression. What mattered to me and most of my classmates was that they were known to be leaders in their field and that they were very much in charge of the classroom and of our learning.

At the urging of some of my classmates, I ran for first-year class representative. Surprisingly, I won. This was probably the first and last political office I would ever hold. A strike by Yale custodians and workers in the fall of 1977 left the campus mostly abandoned by students in the evenings. I had made friends with some of the workers who went on strike. Many of them were black and southern. And for a variety of reasons I identified with them much more easily than I did with my professors. They seemed to identify with the black students as well. To show support of the strike, the students agreed to avoid using the Sterling Law Building after classes. We did little else and perhaps there was little else we could do. It was a minor inconvenience for us compared to the workers, whose livelihood was being threatened. This was perhaps the first time that I felt the conflict of being a part of an entity charged with oppression based on class. I had never been so close to the inside before. Clearly, the people with whom I could most readily identify were being hurt. But being on the inside did not give me the power to stop that. Eventually, the strike ended, but for the most part, I never resolved my feelings.

Making friends came surprisingly easy for me in law school. I was so shy that I could hardly look people in the eye, but I still had the habit of smiling whenever I spoke to anyone. Perhaps this helped my classmates feel at ease with me. Despite that, the law school experience was difficult for me psychologically. Legal training, with its focus on "objective analysis," created a dissonance in me that I did not resolve until I started teaching law myself. When I started teaching, I was able to fully explore the analysis rather than simply learn to identify and respond to it. It was then that I realized that what had been proposed as objective was in fact fraught with perspective—the perspective of those who made up the analysis—one that I did not often share. But in law school, rather than question the analysis, I questioned myself. I felt some insecurity, not because of my race or gender, but because my closest friends at the law school all had undergraduate degrees from Princeton, Brown, or Stanford while I had a degree from Oklahoma State University, an "aggie college." And many had had the benefit of travel and culture that were well beyond my means. None of my friends at Yale ever encouraged these insecurities or pointed out the differences, but when it came to hiring for summer jobs, I knew that I was at a distinct disadvantage.

The famous New England fall foliage came early in my first semester. And just as quickly and unexpectedly followed my first bout of severe homesickness. Once again and far earlier than I was accustomed, it was bitter cold. I missed my family, and with the change in the weather, I even began to long for Oklahoma. I had cried when I said good-bye to my sister JoAnn, heaving sobs that lasted well into Kansas, driving north from Tulsa. I consoled myself by calling JoAnn or my mother. Of course I cried again when I got my telephone bill. My family in Oklahoma was experiencing severe stress. Shortly after I began the fall semester, two of my aunts, my mother's sisters, died within hours of each other, one in Arkansas and one in Missouri. I could not afford to travel home to be with my family and attend the funerals. But I wrote to my mother regularly, and she faithfully wrote to me, sometimes twice a week. By the end of the spring semester, I had endured rigorous academic challenges, inevitable second-guessing about my career choice, trying personal circumstances, and one of the harshest winters in the history of Connecticut.

My academic experiences during the second and third years of law school were much more enjoyable. I began to develop a greater sense of what the study of law was about. By the third year I even began to regard the law school environment as intellectually nurturing, not simply challenging. I adjusted to being away from my home and family. I grew socially and personally, becoming less bashful and reserved.

By the end of my last semester at Yale, I had decided to work in Washington, D.C. Though I had an interest in civil rights, I chose to go into a law firm that represented corporate interests, a decision based mostly on financial considerations. I had accumulated considerable debt from college and law school. Moreover, I looked forward to being financially secure myself and being able to offer my parents some of the things they otherwise could not afford. With school behind me, only the bar examination stood between me and the dream of practicing law. Like most of my classmates, I became obsessed with passing. I spent mornings in a review course, afternoons outlining that day's lecture, and evenings studying the next day's material. The sixth week of the course seemed like an eternity. And as the date of the exam approached, I grew more and more anxious and so filled with information and mnemonic devices for recalling it that I thought I might burst.

I moved to Washington in July 1980 just a few days before the two-day examination. Tuesday, July 29, could not come quickly enough. The fact that the following day was my birthday was of little importance. The only important thing about July 30, 1980, was that it would be the last day of the bar examination. On the morning before the examination I was too excited to eat, managing only a few bites. As I sat through the timed segments of the examination, years' worth of information poured onto the pages and out of my head, forever. By the afternoon of the first day, my hands were starting to cramp from writing and tension. It did not help that everyone around me was as uptight as I. That only egged me on. One student walked out and turned in his exam in the middle of the afternoon, apparently giving up. Another left the auditorium-sized classroom and paced back and forth in front of the door for minutes. At the end of the second day, I knew that my endurance was spent and I could take no more. But that didn't matter, as it was over.

I left the room having no sense of whether I had passed or failed. No matter, I told myself, the exam is offered twice every year. I'd take it until I did pass. Each day of the months that followed I thought of it. Then, in November, only a few days before Thanksgiving holiday, the results were published. My name was on the list of those who had passed. But even in all our celebration, the most that I could feel was relief.

I had a circle of friends in place, friends from law school who had also chosen to locate in D.C. These were individuals with whom I developed some of my closest relationships ever, a closeness that still remains. Some took government positions; others went into private practice. My classmate Susan Hoerchner, who moved to Washington in the summer of 1980 to take a job at the National Labor Relations Board, became my confidante, one of the few people I would later tell about my experiences as assistant to Clarence Thomas. Kim Taylor, another classmate, initially chose a Washington law firm but then went to the public defender's office, eventually becoming its director. Sonia Jarvis would come to Washington in 1981 after her clerkship, and for a time we shared a two-story row house on Capitol Hill.

By late fall, Washington was bustling with speculation about the coming change of administration. The Reagan administration would certainly bring new policies that would affect the practice of law in Washington, D.C. I had only voted for one president in my life, Jimmy Carter in 1976. That was the first election in which eighteen-year-olds were allowed to vote. I voted for Carter not so much for his political philosophy, but because he represented a kind of caring and concern about the people of the country that I found alluring. At that point, I had no developed political ideology. I had registered as a Democrat because Democratic candidates appealed to my sense of fairness. Most people in

Oklahoma were Democrats and in some ways mine was a default registration. It never really occurred to me to register Republican.

By November of 1980, too concerned about work and passing the bar examination, I had failed to register to vote in Washington, D.C. By the time election day approached, all of the polls favored Ronald Reagan, whom I mistrusted. The rhetoric he spun struck me as class-divisive. Even though I was enjoying some success having graduated from law school, I could not help but think that many people, family members and friends, who had not would bear much of the economic burden if Reagan was true to his word. Nevertheless, I could not believe that he would be. The events in Iran in the winter of 1979 had taught me that no politician could be. Matters out of their control, like the kidnapping and hostage of Americans in Tehran, ruled much more than any policy they might propose. Ronald Reagan had to be just another politician promising changes that could not come to pass. I had friends who would work in the Reagan administration; I had friends who opposed Reagan. So, with a mixture of apathy and cynicism, I waited to see what would happen.

CHAPTER THREE

Like most of my classmates, I welcomed the end of law school. As is often the case, however, my first work experience was not the "dream job" a Yale degree promised. Wald, Harkrader and Ross was a medium-size, relatively young Washington law firm. Gilbert Hardy, a Yale Law School graduate I'd met in New Haven, encouraged me to come to the firm as a summer associate in 1979. Gil had visited the campus in 1978 and recruited black law students to come to Washington and particularly to his firm. He believed very much in the relaxed, egalitarian philosophy of the firm, and soon after talking to him I began to believe in it too.

In the spring of 1980 I accepted the firm's offer to come on as a permanent hire. My class of new associates included seven women and one man, all from East Coast schools. We got along well with each other and with our colleagues and there was little of the competitive tension that many of my friends at other firms complained about. Though I was by no means rich, my salary allowed me to rent a one-bedroom apartment in a neighborhood near my job, to go out from time to time with friends, and to send an occasional gift to my parents. I felt comfortable with the firm's atmosphere and expectations.

In 1980 Wald's business was growing, and there was plenty of "quality work" to go around. Our offices were in the heart of the business district, just a few blocks away from Dupont Circle, a major transfer point for the city's new subway system. Many days I walked to work from my apartment in Adams-Morgan located about twenty blocks from my job. On my route to work, the characteristic Washington, D.C., brownstones of the residential neighborhood turned into the restaurants and shops just north of the Circle and finally into the modern glass and concrete buildings of the business district. Wald was housed in a modern red brick building with huge picture windows facing onto Eighteenth and M Streets in the city's northwest quadrant.

When the partners expanded to an additional floor, I and four other associates volunteered to take the new offices. Though we were away from much of the intraoffice goings-on, we were content with our separate space. We pretended we had our own mini-firm, though we knew we relied on the people upstairs for our work. My office was near the entryway to the suite and became a popular stopping-off point for my colleagues when they returned from upstairs. We talked about assignments and about the partners for whom we worked; we shared office gossip. The long hours and work pressures sometimes led to squabbles, but they were few and reconcilable. Occasionally, the five of us socialized together. More often I spent my leisure time (weekend evenings) with my friends from law school and one of my colleagues from Wald, the only other new black associate. She and I became good friends, perhaps because of a shared sense of isolation. Until late in our first year there, we were the only black women in the firm, and despite Wald's progressive atmosphere, there were partners who, rumor had it, resisted working with us.

The work I did there had to do mainly with business law. The firm represented major corporations in matters of trade, environmental, and banking law. There were some exciting projects at Wald's, but none were included among my assignments, many of which were in the area of banking law. This was not considered the most interesting or extensive part of the firm's practice, so there wasn't much competition among associates to do it. Nevertheless, I found it challenging, and I was learning an area which I had not studied in school.

One project on which I spent considerable time was a banking law manual. It generated no billable hours, the key measure of accomplishment in the law firm. The project was done pro bono, as a way for the partner with whom I was working to showcase his knowledge of the subject with the hope that that would generate new client interest. It was an admittedly dry subject, particularly for me, for I was behind the scenes and would not be credited with bringing in the clients even if the project was successful. But after weeks of long days pulling together the material and drafting the text, the partner with whom I had been working left the firm, unexpectedly taking the project and my unfinished work with him. I had no clue that he was leaving or even that he was dissatisfied with the firm.

After my main project left the office, I worked on a number of other matters. They were minor and required little ongoing contact with specific partners. Not surprisingly, by the spring of 1981 I had not developed a real niche for myself at Wald. And of course the key to success in a law firm is to do precisely that, as early as possible, by doing well in important projects with successful partners or significant clients. In my first year at Wald, Harkrader I had done neither.

There was no overt discrimination to account for my failure to establish myself early on, but on some level, I began to question whether I would ever truly long to do the firm's work. Some of the work was intellectually stimulating, but I felt very little personal investment in it or in the process by which I might ultimately become a partner. And though there were those who made me feel welcome, there were others whose skepticism showed. I did not fully understand its impact on me until years later, when I heard my colleagues ponder aloud whether a certain minority candidate would "fit in" on the faculty, or whether a certain woman was enough of a "team player," or that "there was just something about" a certain Jewish candidate that someone "just couldn't put a finger on." I would watch, listen, and voice my disappointment as these ill-defined intangibles became more important than the very attractive tangible qualities of a candidate.

I never dealt with blatant discrimination at the firm. But there were rumors that, despite some positive reviews of my work from some partners, others preferred to work with the white associates. Some thought I was "too shy"; others "too aggressive." And though I worked on some good assignments, many were pro bono. I did not receive the "choice assignment," but rather was assigned to work with partners like the banking expert, who was thought to be difficult. Certainly, no other partner stepped in to take me under his or her wing or to teach me about functioning in what was for me a completely new environment. Though there was nothing that would rise even close to the level of a discrimination lawsuit, a response which would never have occurred to me, I confronted prejudice nevertheless. The kind so ingrained as to be unconscious but whose cumulative effect can be as devastating as anything made blatant. In the end, the goal of "making partner," the aspiration of all associates who remain in a large law firm practice, seemed an empty one. Had I understood that I could attain it, I might have been encouraged to stay. But the experience left me somewhat insecure, and I was uncertain that I wanted it or that I could reach it.

I decided to explore opportunities outside private law firms, including positions in the federal government. In the spring of 1981 I spoke with Gilbert Hardy about such a change. Gil by now had become a good friend. We lived in the same apartment building and sometimes walked to work together. Each of us was at a crucial point in our career. He was on the verge of making partner, and I was trying to establish myself as an associate. Gil and I talked about the disappointments of my first few months. He shared my curiosity about other areas of the law, but was invested in the firm (and eventually did make partner). It was in this context that Gil first mentioned Clarence Thomas, a personal friend of his from Yale Law School. Thomas, who was working on Capitol Hill in Senator Jack Danforth's office, was anticipating an appointment by the Reagan administration. Though I had been in Washington for a few months, I knew little of Danforth and nothing of Thomas.

One of Ronald Reagan's chief pledges had been to cut government, and as evidence of his sincerity, the new administration instituted a hiring freeze. Washington is a town that reflects the government in place, and in 1981 organizations and law firms there were taking a similarly conservative approach to hiring. Shortly after deciding to leave Wald, I realized the poorness of my timing. A few weeks after my conversation with Hardy, however, he invited me to a small gathering in his apartment. Gil lived only a few floors below me, and I had been there on other occasions. But it was on this visit that I first met Thomas, who was living with Gil temporarily, having separated from his wife. Our conversation was brief. He seemed enthusiastic as we talked about his upcoming appointment and what he thought he might be able to accomplish. He struck me as sincere, if a little brusque and unpolished. In fact, he seemed almost the opposite of Gil, who was naturally charming, often soft-spoken, and almost boyish. "What an odd pair to be friends," I thought to myself. But Gil and I had become close, and I trusted his judgment. Nevertheless, I expressed skepticism about the administration, in light of Reagan's rhetoric about the poor. The idea that benefits would "trickle down" to the poor if the rich were assisted by tax breaks and the like struck me as foolish. How were we to know that the wealthy would not just keep the benefits of the government's efforts for themselves? Thomas was as enthusiastic as I was skeptical, insisting that much of the rhetoric during the campaign and Reagan's first few months in office would not be administration policy. Thomas had been assured that he would determine the policy of whatever agency he was appointed to. He further assured me that he had a strong commitment to civil rights, which we discussed at some length.

After that meeting I heard nothing from Thomas for weeks. Eventually when he contacted me, we had one or two further conversations about his appointment. From those conversations I realized that we had differences, but Thomas assured me that he was open to new ideas. By the time Thomas offered me a job as his assistant, he had learned that he would be appointed as assistant secretary for civil rights in the Department of Education. I knew a little about that office from a seminar I had attended there between college and law school. And based on that seminar, which involved issues of education at traditionally black colleges, I was very interested in the work. Calculating all of the career risks and the personal risks I could think of, I decided to go work for Clarence Thomas. Perhaps this would be the dream job I had hoped for.

In an informal exit interview from the firm, I met with Robert Wald, one of its founders, who had worked in government himself. I admired his attempt to create a law practice that could be more humane and honorable. And the structure of the Wald firm was, in fact, more egalitarian and less divisive than firms where my classmates from law school worked. But I could not pretend to feel engaged with my work. Wald seemed genuinely sympathetic to my concerns when I explained my reasons for leaving the firm and my interest in government service and civil rights work in particular. And having checked my employment record, he also assured me that the firm would be happy to consider my application if I ever decided to return to private practice.

In October 1991 John Burke, a former partner at Wald, told the Senate Judiciary Committee that he had had a conversation with me regarding my future at the firm and had encouraged me to find other employment. He also alleged that he had worked with me on numerous projects. This conversation never took place, though Burke may believe it did. The firm record is very clear. I worked with Burke on only one small matter. When I was at Wald, he was a relatively young partner who had no general responsibility for the supervision, hiring, or firing of associates. He did work fairly closely with my friend, the other black female associate, who left Wald soon after I did. Perhaps she was the woman Burke advised to find other employment. He had no such discussion with me. Moreover, the record is also clear that in my first year at the firm, my performance was evaluated as acceptable by those with whom I *did* work. And Burke evaluated the limited work I did for him as acceptable.

Perhaps because I was so ready for a change or perhaps because he was so persuasive, Thomas convinced me that the work I would be doing for him would promote the goals of civil rights. He promised a challenge, but seemed to welcome innovation. I believed in the enforcement of civil rights laws, and to reassure myself that I was making a positive choice, I told myself that those who cared about civil rights should not abdicate its issues to those who did not. There would be no hope if the current administration's civil rights agencies were filled with opponents of civil rights.

At all times, I considered myself to be working for Clarence Thomas, not the Reagan administration. It was Thomas who had inspired my allegiance. The fact that he was black was certainly a major factor in my decision to work with him. He even spoke in terms of black solidarity and the need to hire someone black whom he could trust in civil rights matters. To calm whatever misgivings I had about the administration, he encouraged me to think of myself as his "personal assistant." The position was one that was directly supervised by, maintained by, and related to him, not to Ronald Reagan. President Reagan, he claimed, was uninterested in what was to occur in "his shop."

Loyalty to him, not to the administration, was what Thomas encouraged, and it was typical of persons in authority on Capitol Hill and in appointed positions with the government. Perhaps Thomas himself had learned it from Senator Danforth. This brand of loyalty requires that assistants report their actions directly to their supervisors. Any questions or complaints must be addressed to supervisors. When things go wrong, the supervisor is alerted immediately and a responsible party is identified. And, just as surely, when things go right, the supervisor gets the credit. None of this was very different from the practice of law, except there the client's concern was the most important factor. Client matters, hours billed, and revenues brought in were what drove the practice, not the personalities of the partners or a sense of loyalty to them. Perhaps the primary difference between the private and government arenas was that in the latter, personality was often put before substance. Politics followed closely behind personality as a secondary concern.

According to Thomas, no one was to be trusted. Because I was one of two personal assistants, I had only one colleague, and he encouraged me not to trust even her. As the personal assistant to an appointee, I was expected to protect him from his higher-ups as well as from career government workers. And I was expected to keep Thomas' secrets, personal and work-related, no matter how disturbing. I might have disagreed with Thomas in private (as I often did), but in public I needed to put on a good face for other appointees, those who were working in the agency when I arrived and those who would remain there when I left. Whether an assistant in government "worked out," was retained or promoted and enjoyed the continued patronage of the supervisor, or gets "blackballed" depended more on personality than quality of work. It was the nature of the workplace. Had I failed to fulfill the unwritten duties, I would have been fired or shunted away to do irrelevant work. There was little choice in the matter. In staying, I balanced my concern for the issues and my ability to voice objections directly to Thomas against a flawed work environment that I was powerless to change.

In August 1981, shortly after his appointment, I went to work with Clarence Thomas. When I arrived, I did not know of the unwritten duties. But as his special assistant, I quickly learned. My youth and inexperience showed, but I caught on fast. I had just turned twenty-five and was only one year out of law school, with no government experience, but Wald had prepared me for the long hours it would take to gain the knowledge I needed. Uncertainty and apprehension appropriately describe my first few weeks, but I was excited too. And for the first time my work offered the potential for making a positive professional contribution in an area I cared about personally.

I had the support of my friends from law school who lived in Washington. Kim Taylor, who had recently left her job at a firm for a position in the local public defender's office, was as enthusiastic about my leaving the private sector as she had been about her own move. Even those politically opposed to the stated policies of the administration were sympathetic to my wanting to get out of the law firm environment for more personally satisfying work. One classmate, Roger Clegg, was working for the administration. Our mutual friend Mike Debow, who was even more disenchanted with private practice than I, would later take a government appointment. Both were enthusiastic about my move—for political reasons as well as for reasons having to do with the substance of the work. My parents, however, objected—not so much on political grounds as because of their work ethic. My parents had been very proud of the fact that I had secured a job with a law firm right out of law school. They could not understand why I would leave a good, well-paying job so soon after starting it. And they were concerned about the risk involved in changing positions.

I spent much of my time at the Office for Civil Rights looking at current research on the educational development of minority children. The office was the chief enforcement agency for combating race and gender discrimination in education under Titles VI and IX of the Civil Rights Act of 1964. The caseload of the Office for Civil Rights consisted of claims of race and gender discrimination in the provision of education and educational facilities. I was assigned mostly special projects and did very little casework.

One of my projects was to review and monitor the progress of the *Adams* litigation, a case that had begun as a lawsuit against the secretary of education, Joseph Califano, in 1972. The suit involved questions of the continued viability of the historically black colleges in several states, most of them in the South. The discriminatory manner in which states had funded these institutions led to the lawsuit. The plaintiffs, who were black, claimed that these states promoted an illegal dual system of education by maintaining historically black colleges alongside historically white colleges. Yet the ultimate goals of the suit were unclear.

The obvious response to such a claim was to dismantle the system and merge it into a unitary one. Many blacks objected to this remedy because it would result in the discontinuation of the black colleges, whose place in black communities was respected and appreciated. The challenge to the continued existence of the historically black colleges, the primary avenue of higher education for African Americans prior to the desegregation of white colleges, met political opposition.

Another approach to resolving the suit was to ensure equality of treatment by bringing the schools to parity fiscally, programmatically, and with regard to physical facilities. The Carter administration had pursued a response that attempted to achieve parity in the funding of the historically black colleges, which had suffered from years of neglect at the hands of state government. The Reagan administration continued that policy. Thus, the goals of those involved in the *Adams* litigation—the colleges themselves represented by students and college presidents, the state governments and the federal government—ranged from full integration of the entire system into a unitary system to maintaining but enhancing the programs at historically black colleges. The results were as diverse as the range of goals. Some of the black colleges became more integrated, as did their white counterparts; others remained the same. Some historically black colleges gained programs and funding improvements; others did not.

Oklahoma was one of the *Adams* states. Elreatha and Carlene, two of my sisters, had attended Langston University, the historically black school in Oklahoma. In June 1977, the summer after I graduated from Oklahoma State University, the Department of Health, Education and Welfare had held a conference on *Adams*. I was invited to attend, along with students from other *Adams* states, to comment on the role and future of the historically black colleges in the event that the dual system was abolished and a unitary system established. I had advocated the position that the colleges ought to be enhanced. I knew that tradition and programs were such that Langston had very little chance of attracting a large number of white students in Oklahoma, in particular because it was located in a sparsely populated rural area. To allow its demise based on market demand would be the equivalent of punishing the very people, the students and administrators, who had borne the burden of discrimination. Thus in 1981, when the *Adams* cases came up in the Office for Civil Rights, I was particularly interested.

Despite the fact that our office worked closely with the presidents of the traditionally black colleges, there was tension. For the first time I had to confront the antagonism between the administration and members of the black community. The mistrust was perfectly understandable given the administration's antagonism toward some of the civil rights decisions which the black community supported. Yet, in the *Adams* case, though understandable, it was not altogether warranted. The office was attempting to take what I thought was the right position. In my project we did our best to maintain a good working relationship with the college presidents. We knew and understood the mistrust and hired a consultant, Linda Lambert, to act as a liaison. She later became a friend who helped me to understand the dynamics of the relationship between the plaintiffs, the black college presidents.

My chief concern with administrative policy of both the Carter and Reagan administrations was that there was too little willingness to move programs located in the traditionally white colleges to the black colleges. The office also pushed for the continued fiscal and academic viability of those institutions. What the project ultimately achieved is subject to disagreement. The *Adams* states have been released from the court order under which they operated. The historically black colleges remain. Some have new missions and programs. Yet many in the *Adams* states question whether the changes brought about under the *Adams* order have created parity in the system or maintained the system in a less dramatically inequitable form.

I even had an opportunity to make some overtures to those in the civil rights and women's rights communities. This was a particularly sensitive effort. Telephone calls to civil rights agencies and gender rights agencies yielded mixed results in part because, still relatively new to Washington, I had few connections in those communities, and many of the people I spoke to distrusted the overtures. We managed to establish a meeting with representatives of the NAACP-LDF, the NOW Legal Defense Fund, and the Lawyers Committee for Civil Rights, but there was little follow-up. For political reasons, many associated with the administration wanted the assistant secretary's office to limit such contacts. Nevertheless, since the office had a history of working with such groups, I was happy to try to maintain something of those relationships. I saw them as providing a necessary link between what had occurred in the past and what I hoped would be accomplished in the future. I knew that the administration would do very little to promote busing as an alternative, but Thomas assured me that we could take an aggressive role toward enhancing the quality of predominantly minority schools and ensuring gender equity in programs.

The staff of the Office for Civil Rights reflected the same conflicting emotions that troubled those outside in the civil rights community. Many of the staff were committed to the vigorous enforcement of civil rights. In varying degrees, former administrations had been committed to this ideal as well. Yet the ideal was in conflict with the rhetoric of the new administration, and the conflict was even more profound because the administration had chosen a black man to carry out its policies. The people who had been working at the Office for Civil Rights took a wait-and-see attitude, showing deference to Clarence Thomas because he was, after all, the appointed head of the office. More important, as a black man he presumably shared the race struggle that they were engaged in professionally and in some cases personally as well.

Nevertheless, Thomas was known to be a conservative—albeit a black conservative. This concept was new in the political mix of the Washington civil rights community in the 1980s, and many did not know what to make of it. The deference granted to Clarence Thomas because of his race was balanced by skepticism. And the civil rights community, including many people at the Office for Civil Rights, wondered how Thomas could be committed to both civil rights and the rhetoric of the Reagan administration. As Thomas' assistant, I met with the same skepticism. I had one other problem. Because I was a young, single black woman, the rumor mill speculated that I had been hired for both my race and my sex. Aware of this, I stuck to my work, made only a few friends in the office, and kept counsel with friends outside the office about Clarence Thomas. For me the work was what mattered.

One project on which I spent a good deal of time was an article I ghostwrote for Thomas on the state of minority education and academic achievement. The article explored the role of the historically black school in the academic achievement of black students during Jim Crow. Though it recognized the decline in black achievement scores in the years following the 1954 decision in *Brown v. Board of Education,* it fell short of blaming busing and school desegregation. Instead, I cited economics in general, and in particular the deterioration of the economic base of inner-city schools, as the reason for the decline in standardized achievement test scores. The article was published with Clarence Thomas as author.

In 1983, when I left his employ, Thomas expressed disappointment with the article because it did not support the conservative conclusion that the government should spend less time and effort on desegregation. Thomas respected commentators who had reached such conclusions. He even cited outstanding segregated black schools to support his conclusions. No doubt he was dismayed that his only published journal article at the time did not reflect that point of view. However, I had given him drafts of the piece. And at the time I wrote it, he expressed no disagreement with the tone, nor did he refuse to have it attributed to him.

It was clear to me that Thomas and I disagreed on the importance of the *Brown* decision and its role in the continuing protection of the civil rights agenda. This, more than any other disagreement, stands out in my mind. His position was based on William Julius Wilson's theory that race as a barrier to equality had diminished in significance relative to economics. Thus, the issue of blatant racial constraints was of minimal concern. Economic development was the key. I believed that race still stood as a significant barrier to the advancement of blacks and other racial minorities, despite the outlawing of overt racial classifications and distinctions made on race alone. Economics was secondary. Moreover, I knew that being poor could be debilitating for anyone, but I was certain that the combined impact of racism and poverty was often devastating. Though I had emerged from a poor rural background well educated and now comfortably middle-class, I knew that I was the exception. And I knew that race, poverty, and gender could not be actuarialized out of the combined impact. There was no scientific way of measuring the ratio of racial disadvantage to gender disadvantage to economic disadvantage.

I assumed that Thomas and I operated in an atmosphere of mutual respect, ideological disagreements notwithstanding. I voiced my views when I could substantiate them, carefully balancing my opinion about how to accomplish objectives against the fact that he was in charge. I suspected that some of my ideas were unpopular with people in the Reagan administration (later at the EEOC one appointee, Armstrong Williams, indicated his distrust of me to Thomas). And though I had social acquaintances who worked with the administration in other offices, I was never in the inner circle of appointees. Nor did I seek it out. I committed to what I believed in and wanted only to do the job that I had been hired to do. I had no intentions of advancing in the administration. At twenty-five, only two years away from an environment that practiced respect for different ideas, I believed that I could work on projects that would serve both the administration and the goals of equality.

But the atmosphere of mutual respect soon began to erode. At the time, the erosion seemed gradual, but now I realize how quick it really was. Though I was not a political appointee and, as a Democrat, would not pass the administration's litmus test, I was one of the few people in the office whom Thomas had himself hired. Moreover, I was a close friend of Thomas' friend Gilbert Hardy. Thomas identified me as an insider and the career office staff as outsiders. He began to confide in me about personal and political matters as they related to his work at the Office for Civil Rights. And despite our differences, he appeared to view me as a potential political protégée. I gathered from our discussions that he expected to mold me to his views. He also appeared to see me as a sympathetic sounding board for his personal problems. In college, while briefly considering a career in psychological counseling, I had developed my listening skills.

At first neither my role as listener nor as protégée interfered with my ability to do my work. As he continued to tell me about his difficulties with his marriage, his child, and even about his problems growing up black in Georgia, I convinced myself that this particular time in his life would pass and that work would become the focus of our relationship. I considered these things confidences and still do. In time, however, and precisely when I cannot say, Thomas began to pressure me to see him socially. But for our professional relationship, the requests might have seemed innocent. Still I declined, explaining each time that I did not want to mix my personal life with my professional life. I had just taken the position as his assistant, and the work was important to me. I had friends from school with whom I socialized and had begun to meet others as well. I was dating two or three men casually, but even if I had not been, I would not have considered dating Thomas. I suspect that the fact that he was my supervisor was most important to me, but because of several other considerations as well, I was not attracted to him. Sure that I could keep it all under control, I concluded that I should be able to handle the situation, maintain my integrity, and keep my job. But I was fooling myself.

Notwithstanding my rebuffs and protestations, Thomas continued from time to time to suggest a closer relationship. Perhaps his experience on Capitol Hill led him to believe that his position entitled him to personal as well as professional access to his staff. Perhaps my rejection of his requests was a challenge to his authority. For whatever reasons, gradually his confessions about his life became more personal, more graphic, and more vulgar. I have no more details of his comments to add to my testimony. I believe, then and now, that what I said was sufficient to establish the ugliness and inappropriateness of the statements made by Thomas. What I describe here in this book attempts to put them in the context in which they occurred. As I said in the statement I sent to the Senate on September 23, 1991:

> . . . *Clarence Thomas would call me into his office for reports on education issues and projects or, if his schedule was full of outside appointments, he would suggest that we go to lunch together at one of the area government cafeterias. After a brief discussion about work, he would turn the conversation to discussions about his sexual interests. His conversations were very vivid. He spoke about acts that he had seen in pornographic films involving such things as women having sex with animals and films involving group sex or rape scenes. He talked about pornographic materials depicting individuals with large penises or breasts involved in various sex acts. I was extremely uncomfortable talking about sex with him, at all, particularly in such a graphic way, and I told him repeatedly that I didn't want to talk*

about those kinds of things. I would also try to change the subject to
education matters or to nonsexual personal matters like his back-
ground or political beliefs. However, I sensed that my discomfort with
his discussions only urged him on, as though my reaction of feeling ill
at ease and vulnerable was exactly what he wanted.

The second time his conversation turned sexual, I knew that I had
made a mistake in taking the job with Clarence Thomas. Working as his
special assistant put me in a vulnerable position. Yet my only course
seemed to be standing my ground, avoiding the problem when I could,
and focusing on my work. I wanted very badly to believe that the behavior would end if I continued to resist.

I had no idea where to turn for a solution to the problem. It was
1981, I was living in Washington, and I had no close family in the area.
Gil Hardy was too close to Thomas to trust with the information. I had
no powerful political contacts. Clarence Thomas was the most powerful
and well-connected person I knew. I was so politically naive that when I
met Secretary of Education Terrel Bell at a reception, I had not a clue as
to who he was. "Excuse me, but I didn't catch your name," I said after
introducing myself, to his considerable amusement. We spoke briefly
afterward, and I never saw him again. I doubted I could turn to him, and
I was uncertain who in the administration could be trusted. I suspected
that some might do nothing and others might use the information
against me. I had no reason to believe that Reagan appointees would
have any interest in assisting me.

As a novice to Washington, I very much wanted to handle the situation professionally. Thus, I tried to separate my sense of personal offense
from my professional role. After all, that was what I had learned as a
young black woman: do your schoolwork or job and don't take biases or
insults personally. And there was another old dynamic at work. As Clarence Thomas' assistant, I believed my professional role included protecting him. I had listened to Thomas complain that the people in the civil
rights community were out to get him because he challenged the con-
ventional way of thinking. I knew he felt that there were those in the

administration who did not trust him or his commitment to their ideals. I had to consider how my information might be misused by outsiders and by the administration. I had been schooled by Thomas not to trust either, and I worried that anyone who challenged him on the basis of my information might do so at my expense.

In conversations too embarrassing and hurtful to recall, I confided my problem to Ellen Wells and Susan Hoerchner, and at one point intimated to Brad Mims what was happening, though I did not tell my roommate and friend from Yale Law School, Sonia Jarvis. She was experiencing workplace difficulties of her own and was in the process of changing jobs. Ellen knew Thomas from her time as a Senate staffer in Senator Danforth's office. By the time she and I met and became close friends, she had changed jobs. Our friendship was based on an affinity despite any difference in backgrounds. We were both socially reserved, but in the Republican world of 1980s Washington we felt like we were renegades. Together, Ellen and I struggled to discover a way that I might keep my job but avoid the behavior. At one point, we even discussed changing my perfume. Mostly, we talked as though I had control over the behavior, though we both knew I did not.

Of the friends I told, not one suggested that I bring a charge of sexual harassment against Clarence Thomas. No one suggested that I go to the agency with oversight authority over Education or file a complaint with the EEOC. Frankly, neither course of action seemed viable, then or now. All I really wanted was for the behavior to stop. I wanted to do my job. Neither my appeals to reason nor my efforts to dissuade Thomas by laughing off his advances worked. In time I became convinced that this was a game to him, one that he controlled and intended to win.

A few months after the noxious behavior began, Thomas seemed increasingly preoccupied with other matters. The administration had stepped up talk about abolishing the Department of Education and there were rumors about another appointment for him. Thomas also told me that he was involved in a new relationship. As gradually as they had begun, the sexual advances and remarks tapered to an end. We had fewer personal conversations and I assumed that the troubled phase of his life had concluded or that whatever distraction or amusement his offensive behavior held for him had died. I was so overjoyed that I did not question cause or consider that it might just as mysteriously resume. My stomach no longer went into convulsions at the thought of going into the office. And gradually, I was able to interact with Thomas without anticipating some repulsive remark or unwanted suggestion. At last, work became a source of pleasure once again.

At the time, I was developing a conference to be sponsored by the Office for Civil Rights. For me it was a logical extension of the research I had done for the article I had ghostwritten for Thomas. Marva Collins, a teacher with phenomenal success in raising achievement levels in Chicago's urban schools, was receiving national attention. Collins was known for expecting more of her students and had developed a way of communicating that helped them achieve. The kind of toughness her program appeared to promote fit in well with the "self-help" philosophy of the political conservatives in power. I proposed bringing her and others with outstanding teaching records to Washington to discuss their successes and techniques. The conference message would be that minority and poor children can achieve if provided with a proper learning environment. Structuring the program required researching the social science and policy literature on the education of disadvantaged youth. I was thrilled to be able to combine research, which I love, with a practical enterprise. Once again I began to believe that my job gave me just what I wanted and needed out of work.

I worked on this project along with other routine office matters during the winter of 1981 and into the following spring. In the spring of 1982 before the conference occurred, Thomas called me into his office and confirmed the rumors that he had been nominated to chair the Equal Employment Opportunity Commission. He advised me that I could go with him and do the same kind of work there that I was doing at Education. He even indicated that there might be some way for us to continue to be involved in the conference I was planning. Thomas made clear that he would do what he could to protect my position if I decided to stay at Education, but that he had no real control over it. It sounded as though the talk about abolishing the department was serious. In February 1982 David Stockman of the Office of Management and Budget had alluded to administration plans for a "major, sweeping program to hold the deficit down" that included the elimination of the Department of Education. This played into Thomas' decision to go to the EEOC, even though the administration did not hold that agency in high regard either.

As Thomas explained it, the choice seemed to be between certain employment at the EEOC and uncertain or no employment if I stayed at Education. I did not inquire further about his assessment of the situation. Again I was trying to ignore the personal implications in favor of making a purely professional choice. Consequently, I did not ask him about his past objectionable behavior toward me, nor did I seek assurances that it would not be repeated at the EEOC. As far as I was concerned, it was a closed chapter. I relied on Thomas' professionalism and hoped that he, too, had separated personal considerations from workplace responsibilities.

Despite my concerns, I knew that Thomas in an odd way was offering me job security. Putting my misgivings aside in hindsight, even foolishly so, I decided to take the job at the EEOC as Thomas' assistant. I was apprehensive, but I chose to look forward. Again I was attracted by the challenge of learning a new area of policy and instituting some positive programs at the EEOC. In the summer of 1982, as I cleared out my desk at the Education office on Third and C Streets Southwest and moved into the Foggy Bottom offices of the EEOC, I focused on the potential for growth the change offered. The work, the people, even the EEOC offices, were very different from those at the Office for Civil Rights. Whereas the offices for Education had been old, traditional, and utilitarian government office building with beige walls, gray tile floors, and metal furniture, the EEOC office was a newer, modern structure once slated to be a hotel. Still, both were dilapidated. Where the ceiling leaked in the Education office building, the ventilation was poor in the EEOC office building.

Initially, Thomas' office staff at EEOC was quite small; indeed he was understaffed. Along with a childhood friend of Thomas', Carlton Stewart, I was one of only two lawyers and personal assistants at first. Diane Holt had come over from Education and was one of two secretaries. Out of necessity, I became more involved with day-to-day agency administration and did less work on special projects. To keep up with regular commission meetings, I was assigned to review the claims brought before the commission. Thomas had to be briefed on the cases and advised as to the kinds of questions raised and whether the commission should use its resources to pursue the claims. The EEOC, not unlike other federal agencies, was backlogged. To avoid falling further behind, we began a case review immediately after moving in.

There was a good deal of internal and external dissension surrounding the agency. In particular, Mike Connolly, the EEOC general counsel, had appointed himself the administrative spokesperson for the agency. His outspokenness continued after Thomas' arrival and Thomas objected to this usurpation of his and the other commissioners' authority. There were also struggles over which was the lead agency on civil rights matters for the administration. President Jimmy Carter had granted the EEOC that role just a few years earlier. But now Brad Reynolds, assistant attorney general for civil rights at the Department of Justice, was seeking to establish his office as the final arbiter of administrative civil rights policy. Since Reynolds' department decided which cases of discrimination the government appealed, he was in a prime position to designate himself as the authority.

The Department of Labor's Office of Federal Contract Compliance Program (OFCCP) got into the political power play as well. That program was meant to ensure that employers entering into contracts in which the government was a party attempt to include minorities and women in their workforce. The executive orders that served as the basis for such guidelines were hotly contested by some in the administration.

Shortly after I arrived at the EEOC, the OFCCP delivered to the office of the chair a packet of regulations that in essence undermined the executive orders the OFCCP was supposed to implement. Some of these regulations conflicted with existing EEOC policy. One particularly volatile provision limited the amount of back wages a victim of discrimination could receive in damages. Thomas designated me as the point person for our office and gave me control in how and when matters came to him. There was virtually no time to respond before the proposed regulations were scheduled to be sent out for public comment. My expertise was limited, but I got excellent guidance from EEOC staff people, including an attorney, Stuart Frisch. They advised me on problems with the proposals and educated me about the intra-agency and the inter-agency politics as well. Frisch presented the EEOC position to Thomas and he gave his approval. Frisch and I and other members of the staff met with OFCCP officials and, point by point, went over the objections to the regulations which were a thinly veiled effort to gut the government's program to diversify the businesses holding federal contacts.

Eventually, the old program was salvaged and the proposed regulations withdrawn. When they resurfaced and were approved by the commission in July 1983, the summer I left the agency, many of the objectionable proposals had been eliminated. I think I am prouder of this work than of any other I did during my time at the EEOC.

The final factor in Thomas' early struggles at the agency had to do with internal operations. Just before I arrived, the Office of Management and Budget handed the agency a highly critical evaluation. Some of the criticisms in that report could not be ignored; they demanded that the chair respond if the budget process for the following year was to proceed. Thus, when I got to the EEOC, I fell into the thick of things administratively and politically. I spent much of my first few months dealing with crises or near crises. But though my misgivings about the administration were growing, I still felt that I could do good work. Moreover, despite any offensive interaction with Thomas, I still felt some loyalty to him, much of it born out of the portrait he drew of himself as unfairly maligned from both inside and outside the administration. We disagreed on issues, but past EEOC policies and practices were often consistent with my thinking and I had those to fall back on when we disagreed.

The mood in the office left no time for reflection. Until more assistants could be hired and someone put in charge of the staff, I was overwhelmed. I could count on little guidance from Thomas himself, since he was occupied with his own responsibilities. We worked with little organization or structure until Chris Roggerson and by then Allyson Duncan came on as office managers. Both had extensive EEOC experience. Duncan had been a special assistant in the office of legal counsel but left for the chair's office when a new counsel was appointed. The staff once again had some supervision, and lines of responsibility were more clearly drawn. We managed to put out a good deal of work and even to catch up on some of the backlog.

Among other assignments, I was asked to review the EEOC's position on sexual harassment shortly after we arrived at the agency. The EEOC is the government's enforcement agency for claims of sexual harassment in the workplace as a part of its antidiscrimination enforcement responsibilities. Individuals who felt that they were victims of an employer discrimination would file claims with the EEOC. Agency officials investigated the complaints and made recommendations about whether the complaint stated a cause of action under Title VII of the Civil Rights Act.

The administration's rhetoric called for lessening employer responsibility in cases of harassment probably on the assumption that the behavior was private behavior or that it was not harmful to the victim. Whatever the reason, the pursuit was consistent with a pro-business philosophy of the administration. Acutely aware of that goal, I felt as though I had been dipped in a vat of scalding water as I read over the policies and cases pursued by the agency. I was flooded with embarrassment at my own experience. Still, it never entered the discussion as I reviewed my conclusions with Clarence Thomas. I knew then that I would not work for him for much longer, not because of anything that was happening at the time, but rather because of the aftershocks of what had happened in the past.

After studying the issues, I recommended that the EEOC continue its policies, which stated that employers were liable when supervisors sexually harassed employees or when they failed to respond to coworker harassment that was known to them. Imposing employer liability was an effective means of addressing the problem of harassment. When I presented my findings to him, Thomas grumbled and muttered something to himself. And though I could tell that he would have rather not, he accepted the recommendation nevertheless. What I did not know until years later was that Thomas was part of the administration's transition team which had recommended the change in policy to reduce the burden an employer bore for supervisors who harassed their workers.

Turmoil at the Education Department continued. In July 1982 Harry M. Singleton was named to succeed Thomas as assistant secretary for civil rights. Harry Singleton, a friend of Thomas' from law school, was another black conservative who surfaced in Washington during this period. In October *The Washington Post* reported that an internal department report had recommended major personnel cuts in programs that primarily benefited minority and disadvantaged children. The report provoked charges that the Reagan administration planned to use layoffs and budget cuts to get rid of programs that a Congress more sympathetic to civil rights refused to eliminate. In April 1983 Singleton announced a new "loyalty" requirement in the Office for Civil Rights, adding to the sense of uneasiness in the agency. These changes stipulated that all personnel must receive a "critical sensitive" clearance requiring a background check and sign a waiver of privacy for medical records. The theory was that if they carefully screened for sympathy to liberal policies, they could quash disagreement and rid the agency of anyone who might leak material to the press. Some speculated that the new requirement was intended to uncover employees who had leaked information critical of the administration's civil rights policy. Rumors about the abolition of the department, layoffs, and programmatic cutbacks continued throughout 1983 and 1984. I was relieved to be away from it.

With the benefit of hindsight, I see that I might have responded differently regarding my own circumstance. Yet, even armed with information about agency policy, I did not pursue a charge of sexual harassment against Clarence Thomas. At the time, the case results were mixed. Some federal judges in the 1970s expressed outright skepticism about the cause of action, describing harassment as purely personal behavior. Others accepted it reluctantly. It was not until 1986 that the Supreme Court declared that sexual harassment was sex discrimination. In view of the administration's behind-the-scenes resistance to the concept, I saw little hope of having my charge addressed. Nor was it clear how I could raise such a claim, given that I worked for the head of the chief enforcement agency.

Though they were much maligned in Congress and by the Office of Management and Budget, I found the career people at the agency were its greatest asset. I developed a sincere appreciation and respect for what they accomplished in their efforts to combat discrimination, notwithstanding the pervasive criticism of their work. Nevertheless, the chair's office never worked as a cohesive unit, where there was very little leadership exercised. Other factors played in as well, not the least of which was the continual political pressure to change the agency's longtime civil rights policies. My desk was always covered with work. A completed project was quickly followed by one or two new ones. It was not the work I had hoped for, but it was worthwhile, and presented me with a chance to gain substantive legal knowledge.

As fall turned to winter, Thomas once again began to make sexual comments and innuendos, as well as remarks about my hair, dress, legs, and figure. At first I was surprised. I had believed that was in the past. Once again, my negative responses did not stop him. I became completely unnerved about the behavior. My stomach began to tie in knots at the thought of going to work each day. As I disclosed to the Judiciary Committee:

> *Three to five months after I went to work at the EEOC, during the fall and winter of 1982, the sexual references and pressuring about going out socially resumed. These comments were random and ranged from pressing me about why I didn't want to go out with him to remarks about my personal appearance. I remember him saying that someday I would have to explain to him the real reason that I wouldn't go out with him. He seemed very displeased that I wouldn't agree to date him and showed his displeasure in the tone of his voice,*

his demeanor and continued pressure for an explanation. He would comment on what I was wearing in terms of whether it made me more or less sexually appealing and he commented on my appearance in terms of sexual attractiveness. All of this occurred in the Office of the EEOC, usually in his office. Because these comments were random, unprovoked and out of context, I became very self-conscious about being in contact with him and about my appearance.

Thomas never issued ultimatums, but I knew that without some capitulation to his comments or acquiescence to his right to make them, he would have no use for me in his office. He never spelled the message out in words, but it was clear from his tone and his actions. Though he had not expressed any dissatisfaction with my work, he began to give significant assignments to others. When he was not being suggestive, he was being gruff or difficult. He complained whenever I asked him to approve or sign off on a project. He stopped promising me that I would one day work on special projects. Though I detested the task, I even did some speech writing for him, with limited success. I hated doing the work and I was not any good at it.

The pressures of working in an intensely political environment I could withstand. They were part and parcel of the Washington experience. In fact, I saw them as instructive challenges. But the sexual undertones and overtones on the job were now more than I felt I should have to contend with. One night in January 1983 I went to the hospital emergency room with severe stomach pains. Sonia was asleep, and I left her a note to explain. My doctor ultimately concluded that the pain was stress-related. None of the other likely causes checked out. Immediately after the Sunday hospital stay, I began to look for another job.

Almost by chance, I was asked to interview for a position at the O. W. Coburn School of Law at Oral Roberts University in Tulsa, not far from where I grew up and where my parents still lived. The request to interview for the job came during a trip I made to the university to give a presentation on the agency's enforcement areas. Thomas had taken me and Bill Ng, an attorney and another of his assistants, who did part of the presentation as well. I still recall that on that fateful trip to Oklahoma Thomas had wanted me to sit with him in the rear of the airplane. I told him I preferred to sit up front because the smoking allowed in the rear in those days bothered my allergies. Of course that was only partly true. I could not bear to spend any kind of time in such close proximity to him.

My interview at Oral Roberts went well. After it was over, the dean of the law school, Charles Kothe, told me all that was left was to check my references. Kothe was clear: he made the decisions at the law school, and the job was mine if I wanted to accept it. I had not planned to return to Oklahoma; I had not planned to go into teaching. I would leave behind me in Washington a budding relationship with a young surgical resident for whom I cared very deeply. But the opportunity to leave the employ of Clarence Thomas and to be nearer my family was most compelling.

I had my misgivings about the law school at Oral Roberts. In an effort to attain accreditation, the school had gone through one lawsuit against the American Bar Association and another lawsuit was a possibility because the school was only provisionally accredited. Without full accreditation, the school would likely close. I gave some thought to the conservative ideology of the school, but having just come from the Reagan administration, I felt prepared to deal with conservatives. Moreover, Oral Roberts was not as engaged in political activities as were his counterparts, Pat Robertson and Jerry Falwell. The religious aspect of the school did not dissuade me either. I had grown up in a religious home, was well grounded in my beliefs, and had no sense that they would interfere with my duties or vice versa. I decided to go to Oral Roberts University to escape the harassment and be near my aging parents. It was not the best of all possible alternatives, but it was hardly the worst. I was settling.

I returned to Washington and asked Thomas for a reference. "I take you on a trip, and you end up getting a job offer," he said only half-jokingly. I can only assume that he gave me a favorable reference, however, because in May 1983 Oral Roberts University made me an official offer to start teaching there in the fall. I finished any outstanding work and left the EEOC as soon as I could afford to, living off savings and withdrawing money from my federal retirement fund in order to get out as quickly as I could.

My family was overjoyed that I would be returning to Oklahoma, though not everyone was thrilled that I would be working for a religious university. Still, my parents had none of the same reservations about my job change this time, since it involved moving closer to them. I had never spoken to them about the difficulties I had on the job, unable to bring myself to mention them, out of either embarrassment or a sense that my parents would be pained to hear it and helpless to do anything.

After I gave notice that I was leaving, Thomas asked if he could take me to dinner. I resisted, explaining that I did not think that it would be appropriate. He promptly countered that the dinner was simply a professional gesture offered as a matter of courtesy, not a social overture. In the hope of maintaining some level of professionalism, I took him at his word and consented. So, on the last day of my employment at the EEOC in July 1983, Clarence Thomas and I went out to dinner. We went to a restaurant near the EEOC office directly from work. Our conversation concerned my performance at both Education and the EEOC. Thomas said he was pleased with all of my work with the exception of the article on minority education and a speech I had written for him at the Office for Civil Rights. Finally, he made a comment I will always remember. He said that if I ever told anyone about his behavior toward me, it would ruin his career.

He did not attempt to explain his inappropriate conduct, nor was he in any way apologetic. Showing little or no concern for how the behavior had impacted me, this comment was typical of the self-centered view he held of his own behavior. I only wanted to block the whole situation out of my mind—to move on with my life and forget about it. I did not care that he was thinking only of himself (expecting no more from a man who had behaved as he did), for at that point, I was only thinking of *myself*. I thought how dangerous it is to put your trust in an individual whose personal political aspirations outweigh his sense of right and wrong. Recalling his conversations about the hurt he experienced as a youth, I tried to consider what kind of pain he might have experienced to bring him to this point. Yet I knew that the only thing for me to do was flee. I told him that I simply wanted to leave the EEOC. The dinner ended and with it most of the respect that I had for Thomas.

CHAPTER FOUR

I cried throughout most of the airplane trip from Washington to Tulsa. I wept for what I would leave behind. My choice was not a happy one. It was a horrible one, not so much for what I was going to as for the reasons I was leaving. Looking back on that tearful journey from Washington, I think of my grandparents, who wept as they left Arkansas for Oklahoma. They, too, were tired of fighting against overwhelming odds. Like them, I did not suspect that the trouble I was leaving might be matched by more racism and sexism. I only knew that I was going home.

Rising above the experience proved easier once I was out of the agency. I'd gained back five of the pounds I lost during my last months at the EEOC. Once I was no longer under his supervision, I began to bifurcate my feelings about Clarence Thomas psychologically. I was able to think of him as a former employer and even a personal acquaintance with whom I could continue a congenial relationship. I separated that from his mistreatment and I equated this reaction with professionalism. Even so, I removed his name from my résumé and avoided reference to him when possible. On one occasion when an application form requested references from a former employer, I asked him for a letter of recommendation. He agreed, but none was forthcoming. And I never spoke to him about it again. When asked by a local group to get him to speak in Tulsa, I made the call.

During my first year at Oral Roberts, Charles Kothe became a professional consultant to Thomas. Kothe had been working on employment issues for the Reagan administration and had a warm admiration for Thomas. He had even written a biographical story about Thomas as a model of "bootstrap success." Thomas seemed to think that Kothe could help him make contacts with "old line" Republicans. That they worked together meant that my escape from Thomas could not have been complete. Kothe expected that I would be gracious and work with Thomas as well, and Thomas expected that I would help him to maintain the relationship with Kothe.

At Oral Roberts University, working on some equal employment research projects, I called Thomas' office on occasion. His records suggest that I called him eleven times from 1983 to 1991. I do not recall talking to him eleven times because the calls were of little personal importance to me. They had a purpose—to further my work. My sense of professionalism, which some may describe as opportunism, allowed me to divorce my personal feelings from my work interests. That, in retrospect, was a mistake. But the reality was that Thomas was a part of my work history no matter how I might handle it. Though I had dealt with the situation as I best knew how and had chosen not to rely on him in future employment endeavors, I had performed well as his assistant, and I refused to let his bad behavior cheat me of every benefit of my good work. The balance was difficult, maybe even impossible, to maintain, but I tried.

Teaching was at first a little intimidating, but later became fun. I had to overcome a basic shyness and reserve about speaking in front of groups of people. Once in law school, I'd been chosen to present a gift to one of our first-year teachers, Guido Calabresi. I managed to get up in front of the class and make the presentation but I spoke so softly that not even he heard the remarks I made. The courses I was now teaching, employment law and commercial law, were never so much the issue as my reticence about standing in front of the room.

At Oral Roberts O. W. Coburn School of Law, I was the only female as well as the only African American faculty member. I had the support of most of my colleagues on the very small faculty, but it became evident that I did not have the support of all of the students. The ideological and conceptual problem I posed for some of them was acute. I am certain that, as a black woman, I challenged their notion of authority. In response they challenged me. For a handful of them, any statement I made in class, no matter how basic, was open to challenge. One particular student vacillated between refusing to respond in class when asked to do so and responding sullenly. A group of male students protested my assignment to teach commercial law on the basis that I was unqualified to do so. They were supported by one of the other faculty members, Roger Tuttle, who also questioned my qualifications and hiring. The school was relatively small—the largest class had approximately sixty students. Because of its size, rumors and accounts of incidents traveled fast among the student body.

The school attracted some good students, but others would have been deemed marginal by most admission standards. I believe that many resented my background and the fact that I had a degree from Yale Law School, often regarded as the best law school in the country. The conservative racial and gender politics and even prejudices of many in the student body went a long way to convince them that I did not belong in front of the class in the role of their instructor. They supported their personal biases with much of the popular rhetoric of the day that decried affirmative action and hinted that blacks who had made it into schools and professional positions during the 1970s and 1980s did not deserve to be there. Some expressed their resentment overtly. Others were cordial and respectful. A few were downright vicious and spread obscene rumors about me, perhaps unhappy with the grades they received in my course. Yet to say that my time at Oral Roberts University was consumed by hostility would be to exaggerate the impact of a few. I had many friends among the staff, students, and faculty at Oral Roberts. And many there remain friends and supporters today.

I left Oklahoma in 1977 as a student. Returning in 1983, I was an adult. I bought a Tudor-style house on a half-acre lot on a quiet street in the hills of North Tulsa. Its large country kitchen and living room made it the perfect place for the family to gather on my first Christmas home.

My brother Albert and sister Elreatha lived only a short distance away, and JoAnn and Alfred just a little farther. By now she was JoAnn Fennell, married to Jerry, with three children. Eric, her oldest, whom I'd adored as a five-year-old when I left Oklahoma, was now an adorable eleven-year-old. Jonna, her daughter, was a six-year-old armful of energy, and Jerry, Jr., the youngest, was a round ball of joy and affection. We did everything together—birthdays for the kids, weekend trips to our parents' house, shopping for Thanksgiving turkeys and Christmas trees. We even belonged to the same church, the Antioch Baptist Church, which was a stone's throw from my house. As in our childhood, the church was a center of our social activity. My cousins Sandra and Ruth attended Antioch as well, and we all belonged to the same mission group. Under the influence of my nieces and nephews, I became "Auntie Faye" to the children (and some of the adults) in the church. Personally, I was still pining for the man I'd left in Washington, and I returned to see him on two occasions. I started seeing other men and eventually got into a steady relationship.

For three years my relationship with my parents and siblings, nieces, nephews, and cousins flourished. I became a member of the community, active in professional and charitable organizations. I became a member of the committee on minority involvement of the Oklahoma Bar Association, an officer in the Tulsa Black Lawyers association, and a member of the Tulsa Women Lawyers group. I applied to serve as a Big Sister in the local Big Brothers/Big Sisters program, but due to a larger number of Big Sisters than Little Sisters I was not matched. Still, because of my interest in the program, the board of directors asked me to serve as a board member, which I did.

After three years, my time at the O. W. Coburn School of Law came to an unexpected end. The university administration decided to sell the law school to Pat Robertson and CBN University in Virginia. Each faculty member was advised that he or she would be considered for a position at CBN but I declined to be considered, choosing rather to stay in Oklahoma.

In the fall of 1985 I interviewed for a position with the law school at the University of Oklahoma. The school offered me a position there for the fall of 1986. The school is in Norman in central Oklahoma, and though relocating there was not ideal, I would still be able to reach my parents or the rest of my family and friends in Tulsa within two hours.

The academic atmosphere at the University of Oklahoma was certainly superior to that at Oral Roberts. There was a strong sense of collegiality as well. Faculty members frequently socialized together. In Tulsa my friends were drawn from my neighborhood and community activities, but in Norman my social world was filled with other faculty. It was a comfortable arrangement. I had once again moved to a place where I had an established social base. My colleagues on the faculty of the law school had a reputation for being friendly and encouraging social interaction. I soon began the task of establishing my teaching and research, the latter of which had been somewhat neglected at Oral Roberts, which did not offer tenure and hired teachers on a year-to-year basis. Research was rarely emphasized or rewarded.

In 1988 I was promoted from assistant to full professor. I also served on various committees and boards, including the faculty administration committee, Committee A. The faculty voted to give me tenure in October 1989, and in 1990 the campus tenure committee and the Board of Regents confirmed the vote.

My career progress at the university was rapid but not always easy. When I first arrived, there was considerable student unrest over faculty hiring. One matter in particular seemed to stir student resentment. The faculty had refused to hire a very popular white male professor in 1988, not too long after the period when I was hired. He and I did not teach the same subjects and were at considerably different levels of experience. In short, we were neither comparable nor in competition for the same job. Nevertheless, some students insisted on comparing us and argued that I had been unfairly hired over him.

Once again I was the only African American faculty member, only the third in the history of the school, and the first African American woman to teach there. And once again I was the youngest faculty member. I did not socialize with the students in general, though I was the faculty sponsor for the Black Law Student Association and went to some of the meetings of the Christian Legal Society. The common complaint was that I'd been hired simply because of affirmative action. In the intensity of the law school environment, any perceived error in my teaching or attitude toward the students was viewed as evidence of my incompetence. Rumors about student reactions to my calling on them in the classroom included comments such as "You don't have to answer a nigger," or "That nigger doesn't know anything." One administrator told me that he relied on "hall talk" from the students in evaluating my first year of teaching.

Yet despite some of the same resistance I had encountered at Oral Roberts University, the University of Oklahoma was a place where I could be productive and make a contribution. I felt more a part of the national academic community at Oklahoma, shedding some of the isolation I'd experienced because of the religious ideology rightly or wrongly associated with Oral Roberts University and its provisional accreditation. Some academics had shunned me because of my association with the school, assuming that it was established for the purpose of promoting an indefensible, conservative political agenda. Their somewhat misguided ideological view of the school was a product of the politics of the times.

My involvement with other law teachers, particularly minority law teachers, was a great help to me. When I moved into my office at the law center, waiting for me on my desk were notes and newsletters alerting me to the experiences of other African American faculty who had faced hostility from students. These stories, many from seasoned teachers and experienced scholars, helped me to understand my experience at Oral Roberts and to prepare for what I was to experience at Oklahoma. They also showed me that I would have to overcome the experiences without much assistance from my white colleagues. But by the end of the spring semester of 1988, in my second year teaching at Oklahoma, the students began to accept me as a faculty member. I did not change significantly, but I learned to meet some of their expectations without compromising mine. I took on a tougher and more detached demeanor and a more rigorous approach to classroom exchanges. What I had exhibited as concern had been interpreted by the students as weakness. To some extent, I had to stop showing that I cared about the students. Out of this new approach, I developed a reputation for being demanding. Yet one class of students who admitted that they'd started the year hating me gave me a box of candy on Valentine's Day. Once again, I'd had to detach myself from the hurtful offenses I suffered. But in this case, a certain level of detachment paid off.

I kept developing my teaching and research, now focusing on contract and commercial law. In the spring of 1989 I taught my courses on an accelerated schedule and went to Europe to do research in German commercial law and practices. I was also able to attend the meetings of the international law body UNIDROIT, which was in the process of drafting international principles of contract law. The assembled international experts looked twice when I first appeared at their sessions, but the United States delegate, Alan Farnsworth, and the organization's director, Michael Bonnel, were quite encouraging. I was gradually accepted into the group, one of a few women and the only black woman present. These meetings enabled me to follow the development of the body of law from near its beginning to its end in 1994. That same year I taught a commercial law course in the University of Oklahoma's summer program at Oxford University. Though I occasionally taught a seminar or course in civil rights law, my intellectual and professional life was headed in another direction. Still, I continued to sponsor the black student organization and helped with the formation of the Coalition of Minority Students, an umbrella group that included Asian, Hispanic, Native American, and African American student organizations.

I was so immersed in my experiences at the University of Oklahoma and my interest in commercial and international law that by 1991 I had successfully overcome my experience with Thomas to the point of disregarding it. I had for all I knew put it behind me for all time. As painful and unfair as it was, the Thomas episodes, like the racist hostility at Oral Roberts and later at Oklahoma, were something in my life that I'd had to rise above in order to move forward. I refused to wallow in these experiences or punish myself because of them. I rarely talked about them.

Perhaps wrongly, I wouldn't even try to make those responsible for the behavior accountable in any way. In that sense, I share some of the responsibility for its perpetuation. For my own benefit, however, I only wanted to move beyond it. It was not that I ever forgot what had happened, or even that I work very hard to forget; I had simply convinced myself that what mattered was my right to not cling too tightly to the hurt, and to move on with my life.

CHAPTER FIVE

Norman, Oklahoma, and Washington, D.C., have one thing in common: dreadfully hot summers. In Washington the humidity hangs in the air like a thick clear fog, routinely threatening thunderstorms. The result is a lush green environment that is mildly oppressive by August, the hottest month. In Oklahoma, however, summer begins in May. The humidity hovers, only rarely turning into rain. And by summer's end in Oklahoma, grass and shrubs are parched and withered.

I do not like the heat. By mid-July I am out of sorts. I pant from air-conditioned home to air-conditioned car to air-conditioned office in the morning, and in the evening I reverse the routine. I wonder how I managed all those un-air-conditioned years in the fields and at home. I remember how I looked forward to visits to my cousins, whose big cooler bellowed water-saturated air into their family room. I delighted in the temperature of that room until it was time to go home, where the only respite was the night breeze through an open window.

The summer of 1991 was a difficult one for me even before the temperature reached one hundred degrees. I was suffering from a medical condition that seems to run in my family. My uterus was covered with tumors that caused me considerable pain and discomfort. Each day I would rise to moderate pain that increased as the day wore on. I have an even stronger aversion to medication than to heat—even over-the-counter medication—but some days the pain was such that I would take the anti-inflammatory pain relievers my doctor prescribed. Since these had side effects, I would try to manage without them when I could.

On the morning of July 1, 1991, like most lawyers in the country, I waited in anticipation of the president's announcement of his choice to replace Justice Thurgood Marshall on the Supreme Court. The White House had circulated a number of names as potential nominees. Political commentators, in the business of speculating about such things, were predicting that President George Bush would name a Hispanic judge to succeed Justice Marshall. Prominent among the possibilities floated were Judges Ricardo H. Hinjosa and Emilio M. Garza, both of the Fifth Circuit Court of Appeals, and Judge Ferdinand F. Fernandez of the Ninth Circuit, all Reagan appointees with solid Republican credentials. Judge Jose Cabranes of the Second Circuit was the only Carter appointee under consideration, and Judge Clarence Thomas of the D.C. Circuit Court of Appeals was the only African American. Two white women, Judges Edith Jones of the Fifth Circuit and Pamela Rhymer of the Ninth Circuit, were reportedly on the list too, along with two white males, Kenneth Starr, the solicitor general, and Judge Patrick Higginbotham of the Fifth Circuit.

The New York Times reported that television journalists were declaring forty-three-year-old Judge Garza the front-runner. Compared to some of the others under consideration, Judge Garza had limited experience on the court of appeals, having been appointed early in 1991, from a federal district judgeship he had taken in 1988. However, he had more overall federal judicial experience than Thomas, also forty-three, who had only been appointed to the court of appeals in 1990.

Amid all the speculation, President Bush maintained that race was not a consideration in his deliberations. He insisted that he would "go for the best-qualified candidate." Many observers, including Justice Marshall himself, commented that race would undoubtedly be a factor in the president's selection of the successor to the first and only African American on the Court. Having heard and read the reports of the journalists, I mentally dismissed the idea that President Bush would choose Clarence Thomas to fill Marshall's seat. Following the cue of the media (perhaps for the last time in my life), I awaited the announcement of the country's first Hispanic Supreme Court nominee.

Early in the day, I went to the university to prepare the examination for my contracts class, which consisted of about thirty students, a relatively small number that made teaching more enjoyable than usual. Despite my interest in the nominations, my thoughts were elsewhere— about thirty miles away in the Oklahoma City office of a gynecologist I was yet to meet. At midmorning I left the law school for the drive to my appointment in the city. Like too many doctor's visits, this one was frustrating and disappointing. My new gynecologist, chosen primarily because my health plan covered his fees, speculated that a hysterectomy was inevitable but said he would treat my condition with painkillers until the discomfort became unbearable. I reminded him that the internist who had referred me thought that immediate action was in order. He responded with a smile, "They tend to overreact. They don't see as many of these as we do," and added, "I treated one woman whose tumors were the size of a seven-month fetus. Yours are nowhere near that big." Somehow I was not reassured. Finally, he suggested that he had spent far too much time answering my questions, and that was the end of my visit. Never mind the time I had spent in the examining room waiting for him. I returned to Norman praying that I could find a gynecologist who'd be both responsive to my condition and covered by my health plan. By midday I had completely forgotten the president and the Supreme Court.

Late that afternoon, back at the law school, I got a call from David Margolick of *The New York Times*. Through him I learned that President Bush had selected Clarence Thomas as his nominee to the Supreme Court. I was caught completely off guard. I had spent most of the day waiting in an examination room. All morning, whenever I thought about the nomination, I assumed that Garza would be picked. I was guarded in my comments to Margolick. Whether honestly or as part of a journalistic ploy, he seemed dissatisfied. He told me he was doing a "psychological profile" of the nominee, and I responded that I was not qualified to give such a psychological analysis of Thomas or anyone else.

Margolick neither quoted me nor referred to our conversation in his article, which appeared a few days later. But his call made me wonder: if, on the very day of the nomination, a *New York Times* reporter knew that I had worked with Clarence Thomas, who else might know and what might that mean in terms of future inquiries? I did not mention Thomas' conduct toward me to Margolick. In fact, I had not mentioned it to anyone in years, until later that evening, during a conversation with my friend Karolyne Murdock, whom I had come to know in 1988 when we were both serving as members of the board of directors of the Women's Resource Center. This local organization offered counseling services for rape victims, sponsored group sessions for marital and family crises, and provided shelter for victims of battering and other forms of domestic violence. Karolyne, a bank vice-president with over twenty years in banking, and I, the commercial law teacher, had hit it off immediately. I was very impressed by the professional demeanor and the financial expertise that she brought to the board. Our friendship was based partly on our common concern for community issues—Karolyne followed her membership on the center board with a membership on the board of a local child advocacy group—and partly on our mutual love for movies. On July 1 it was the movies that brought us together.

Karolyne and I drove from her office to the local theater to see *Batman*. At first we focused on our work weeks. Then we talked about my visit to the doctor. Despite the news from Margolick, my health concerns were by far the greater distraction. But on the way home, Karolyne asked my opinion of the Thomas nomination, unaware that I had worked with him. She wanted to know what I thought both as a member of the legal profession and as an African American. When I told her about my experience with Thomas, her response was immediate. "You have to disclose this information, don't you?" Oddly enough, as I think about it, this was the first time someone had suggested that I should raise a complaint about the behavior. I wish my reaction had been so certain. "I'm not sure what I'll do," I said. She looked concerned but did not push.

That evening, for the first time in several years, I spoke with Susan Hoerchner. Upon hearing about the nomination, she had instantly recalled our conversations about Thomas' behavior. As far as she was concerned, Thomas was a complete scoundrel. She reacted as someone witnessing the pain of a friend. She had not forgotten. She did not suggest that I go to the Senate or anyone else with the information. She simply expressed her dismay that inexcusable behavior had seemingly been rewarded.

For years I had spent considerable time and effort convincing myself that what happened to me no longer mattered. For the first time I was forced to consider that it *did* matter—that the behavior was not only an offense to me but unfitting for someone who would sit on the Supreme Court. I had paid little attention when Thomas was nominated to the D.C. Court of Appeals. He had been confirmed before I had any real idea what was occurring. In February 1990, when Thomas was before the Judiciary Committee for that nomination, I was preparing to go to Europe. Now it suddenly hit me that the behavior I knew about was no longer simply a personal concern, that the Supreme Court mattered to me as an attorney and as a citizen, and that I had a responsibility to provide the Judiciary Committee with relevant information. At the same time, it occurred to me that this nomination was a political move, despite George Bush's declarations to the contrary. The depth of the political force behind the nomination would not be revealed until weeks later, but even then I knew politics was an inescapable factor. As the controversy over the nomination emerged, my course of action became even less clear.

I am by nature a cautious person, and on July 1, 1991, I had not had a chance to weigh all the factors. Moreover, even if I decided to disclose my information, I was not sure whom to contact. At the time, I was convinced that my name would surface in a thorough Senate investigation. I relied on the process to find me instead of interjecting myself into the process. In retrospect, this may have been my way of deferring responsibility for making a decision. I reflected on my experience, and I waited to hear from the Federal Bureau of Investigation or the Senate Judiciary Committee. The wait lasted from July to September.

Much of the spring I had been preoccupied with trying to get the correct prognosis and treatment for the condition. In late summer, after seeing several doctors, I found a female gynecologist who had had the same condition. She discouraged me from simply taking pills to alleviate the pain and recommended exploratory surgery. She performed the surgery in July 1991 and confirmed the condition but could not determine the tumors' size or location. The surgeon recommended their removal, with the possibility that a hysterectomy would become necessary. I was thirty-five years old, and for the first time, being without children and single weighed heavily upon me.

Surgery was unavoidable and I knew it, but I also knew it might alter my life forever. I had never had a burning desire to have children. And I looked at JoAnn's children with the sense that they were partly mine. But now that it seemed I might never have them, I had to stop and think seriously about whether I was willing to give up that capability.

Meanwhile, I tripped through my house along trails from the kitchen to my bedroom, the only two rooms that had not been overtaken by a renovation project that had begun in mid-June. I wondered how the enclosure of a deck outside could absorb so much of the space inside. Each day the workers left me a new coat of plaster dust, a final reminder that they had control of my space. It seemed impossible to find a place to work at home, though I kept trying: there was no work space in the galley kitchen; my bedroom was too small for a desk; and my study was cluttered with dining room furniture.

Though it was summer and classes were over, I had plenty of work to do. I had agreed to be the faculty representative in the office of the provost, a year-long assignment that involved splitting my time between the law school and the main campus. I was to teach as well as to work on special projects for the provost, including updating the faculty handbook. In addition, I was preparing for the American Bar Association annual meeting which was being held in Atlanta in August, and would feature events focusing on minority involvement. I had become active in the ABA Business Law Section, and in particular with the Uniform Commercial Code Committee. As chair of this committee's membership subcommittee, I was organizing a reception for local attorneys who might consider joining us. Packing for my trip to the bar association meeting was a challenge. I had to find clothing that would accommodate my protruding stomach (the tumors had by now grown to the point that my waist was two sizes larger than my hips) and the heat and humidity of Atlanta in August.

Atlanta was the perfect site to encourage greater participation by African Americans in the ABA. There also seemed to be more white women than usual. I saw more former classmates and old friends than I had ever seen at an ABA meeting before. Events were well attended, and presentations were well received. Everywhere, conversation turned to Clarence Thomas, the first black man to be nominated to the Supreme Court since 1967. And everyone at the meeting seemed to take particular care in assessing his abilities. In accordance with its standard practice of reviewing the qualifications of judicial nominees, the ABA was considering its rating of Thomas.

After one session, I ran into a friend from law school, George Jones, who was one year ahead of me and one of the most thoughtful and analytical law students I knew. Jones believed that the Thomas nomination should not be challenged because he would serve the black community better than any of the potential white nominees. I found the nomination questionable because of Thomas' lack of experience. I thought the black community would fare better challenging the nomination, even at the risk of a white replacement. The conversation left me disheartened. I knew that many in the black community would not want to "give up" Thurgood Marshall's seat to a white justice, no matter what.

At the same session, I also ran into Carlton Stewart, who had been at the EEOC with me before he was transferred to the commission's Atlanta office. Carlton was ecstatic about Thomas' nomination. He and Earl Grayson, who was with him, both gushed their support for Clarence Thomas and mentioned scornfully that a local NAACP group had been censored by the national office for supporting him. I allowed that the nomination was a great opportunity for Thomas. Stewart and Grayson were two friends elated by their buddy's personal success. Merit did not seem to enter into their response. After my conversation with Jones, I realized that it was senseless to argue the nomination with such diehards, and I changed the subject when a law student approached us to talk about teaching as a career. Later, at the hearing in October, Stewart and Grayson would claim that I said the nomination was "wonderful" and spoke of it in "glowing terms." I did not. Their own enthusiasm undoubtedly colored their recollection of the conversation.

At that ABA meeting I revealed to only one person my doubts about Thomas' ability to carry out the responsibilities of an associate justice of the Supreme Court. Over lunch in an Atlanta hotel, I confided in Cathy Thompson, a classmate from Yale Law School. Cathy and I shared similar backgrounds that separated us from others in our class at Yale. Both of us had attended state colleges not known for their sophistication, yet both of us had done well and made many friends among our more "urbane" classmates. Cathy grew up in North Carolina and had returned there to a successful legal practice. By the time we met in Atlanta, we were eleven years out of law school. As we had lunch at the swank Hotel Nikko, we both felt quite successful. She had served as president of her state bar association, and I was a tenured faculty member at the only state law school in Oklahoma. We were two small-town girls who had beat the odds.

Cathy and I hadn't seen each other since the American Bar Association meeting in 1989. We spent most of our lunch catching up. The nomination of Clarence Thomas came up, as it inevitably did that week. Cathy knew I had worked in Washington but not that I had worked for Thomas. Either by nature or by experience, Cathy is a matter-of-fact, pragmatic person. She listened calmly, though I could tell that she was shocked by what I told her. Mostly, I described how Thomas had pressured me for a social relationship, deliberately omitting the graphic details, to spare myself as much as her. Those details seemed inappropriate in any context, and certainly at an ABA lunch. I was near tears even disclosing what I did. Talking to Cathy, I felt that she could have been me, that my experience might well have been hers, and maybe even had been in one form or another.

After lunch neither of us knew what to say. We left feeling a little less sophisticated, and a little less secure about the trappings of "success." My career had been less about success than survival. Success was simple for me. It meant having work that I found meaningful, being intellectually challenged, and doing the work well. I had not set a goal of attaining a particular status within a certain time frame, as some of my peers had—partner in a major firm or full professor at a top twenty law school by age thirty. My goal for success was modest and unstructured. Yet at each turn I was hampered by obstacles that turned me away from success and drove me down the path of mere survival. I tried to remind myself that despite the obstacles, I had achieved more than my grandparents could have imagined.

A few weeks after I returned from Atlanta, another member of the press contacted me. At the urging of a relative who worked at *The Washington Post,* I spoke with Sharon LaFraniere, a reporter who was doing a profile on Thomas. She seemed to be focusing on Thomas as a boss, but she also mentioned some rumors she had heard about his strict upbringing of his son. I declined to comment on the latter. About the former, I contributed that while Thomas could be a demanding supervisor, I thought his professional expectations of his employees were consistent with his responsibilities. This time, when asked what I thought of Thomas' views on civil rights, I was more critical than I had been in my conversation with Margolick. LaFraniere's story, which ran on September 9, 1991, read:

> *Anita Hill, a former special assistant to Thomas at the Education Department and the EEOC, was particularly disturbed by Thomas's repeated, public criticisms of his sister and her children for living on welfare. "It takes a lot of detachment to publicize a person's experience in that way" and "a certain kind of self-centeredness not to recognize some of the programs that benefitted you. I think he doesn't*

understand people, he doesn't relate to people who don't make it on their own."

At a conference for black Republicans in 1980, Thomas had said of his sister, "She gets mad when the mailman is late with her welfare check. That's how dependent she is." Political commentators had cited this remark as a key to Thomas' rise in popularity with the conservatives of the Reagan administration. Ellen Wells, who has since changed party affiliations, attended the conference. She recalls that Thomas painted his sister as an odious, unworthy individual who had chosen slovenliness over industry and fraud over honest work. Moreover, according to Thomas, his sister had schooled her children to do the same. When I spoke to LaFraniere, I did not know that Emma Mae Martin had gone on welfare in order to care for an ailing aunt and was now self-support-ing, working two jobs. Thomas' characterization of her had just stuck with me for years. I had even mentioned to Thomas himself how unduly harsh I thought it. He shrugged off my reaction. Had I known the truth about his sister, I would have been even more critical of Thomas' indif-ference to her situation in the early 1980s. But most detestable was Thomas' willingness to malign his sister as a ward of the state to further his own political ambitions. That demonstrated a level of duplicity of which even I would not have believed him capable.

Once again I chose not to go into the details of that experience with LaFraniere. Like Margolick, *The Washington Post* reporter seemed to me to be missing the point that the significance of the nomination was what it would add to the jurisprudence of the Court. While neither expressed any hostility toward Thomas, both seemed to be pursuing a line of ques-tioning that relied primarily on personal opinion with little attention to Thomas' record. I was certain that opinion would be mixed. It is hard to imagine anyone getting to the point of being nominated to the Supreme Court without a number of vocal supporters. But from my observation of him and his own early assertions about his lack of popularity, I knew that there were many who would be critical too.

The debate over the merits of the Thomas nomination continued throughout the summer. The American Bar Association gave Thomas its lowest rating ever, reflecting a lukewarm if not chilly reception to the nomination in the legal profession. The Leadership Conference for Civil Rights, a coalition of 185 national organizations, opposed the nomination forcefully, stating two grounds: that Thomas "let his personal opinions interfere with his constitutional and statutory responsibilities to enforce civil rights laws" and "demonstrated a consistent hostility to many of the Supreme Court's most fundamental civil rights decisions."

Though President Bush had declared that race was not a factor in his selection of Thomas, the White House chose to focus on Thomas' personal background in pointing to his qualifications for the post. All but ignoring his judicial record, the White House spun a tale about his childhood poverty and his triumph over discrimination. One Thomas proponent remarked that his hard work and self-discipline sent a message that it is possible for blacks to succeed in American society. Much of the media coverage followed suit, tracing Thomas' history to the small town of Pin Point, Georgia, where he had spent a portion of his youth, through his education at Holy Cross and Yale and his nomination to the Court. Some of the coverage mentioned his comments about his sister, but few saw the irony in the contrast between the choices he had in life and those of his sister.

After a fire destroyed his mother's home, Thomas and his brother, Myers, were sent to live with their grandparents in Savannah. Martin, their sister, remained in Pin Point and lived with an aunt. Both Thomas and his brother graduated from private school. Martin graduated from public school. "I had the opportunity to go to college if I wanted to, but I made the choice," she told an interviewer. "I took care of the older people." While Thomas was in law school, Martin survived by working two minimum-wage jobs. Later, when her aunt suffered a stroke, Martin quit work to care for her. Her husband had abandoned the family in 1973, and she and her two children lived on a monthly public assistance check of $169. By 1991 Emma Mae Martin had returned to the work-force.

Yet the media stories about Thomas rarely called attention to the different opportunities and expectations for him versus his sister, namely the educational opportunities and the freedom from caring for the el-derly that were his and not hers. Inequities that can be reasonably attrib-uted to her gender alone went undiscussed, as did the programs that enabled him to enter the best schools. Even Thomas' early job with his mentor, Jack Danforth, seemed to come from Danforth's own style of affirmative action. As the story goes, Danforth, who was attorney general of Missouri at the time, sought recommendations from Dean Guido Calabresi of Yale for a black law student who might want to work in his office. Yet in 1991 the press coverage focused on Thomas' own efforts rather than the social programs that had benefited him throughout the 1960s and 1970s. Thomas contributed to this shift in the discussion when he contrasted himself with his sister, condemning her lack of initiative and extolling his self-initiative and resourcefulness.

Nowhere was the discussion of Thomas' nomination more intense and divisive than in the African American community. Some polls said that 52 percent of blacks supported Thomas' nomination. In retrospect, though that figure was used by Thomas supporters, it seems incredibly low given that one would expect some measure of support from African Americans for another already prominent African American. Blacks who supported the nomination seemed split into two camps. One line of thought suggested that any black nominee would be better than any white nominee because a white nominee would mean losing what was seen as the "black" seat on the Court. Others thought that Thomas would be better than a white nominee because his background and the circumstances of his upbringing would make him empathetic to poor blacks. Despite what his detractors described as his dismal civil rights record, this camp believed that he would change once secure in a lifetime appointment. (At his confirmation hearing, Thomas suggested the same when he distinguished his early positions as those of a political appointee rather than those of a jurist.) Both groups believed that he should be given a chance.

Thomas' critics in the black community maintained that his views were so antagonistic to the well-being of the community that his race was secondary, even problematic, as it would lend credibility to an anti-civil-rights agenda. Some were convinced that the community would be better off with a conservative white person on the Court than with Thomas. One black congressman argued that the question should not be Thomas' "skin color" but rather whether he was "going to be on our side in the dark of night when the chips are down." Christopher Edley, who would later testify against the nomination, said that only Thomas' color accounted for his selection over Starr. And more than a few pointed to what they called President Bush's cynicism in declaring that Thomas was the "best man" for the job. Thomas' supporters in the African American community accused his detractors of being elitists; African American critics accused his supporters of putting skin color over principle. In nominating Judge Clarence Thomas to succeed Justice Thurgood Marshall, Bush created a situation in which the community would lose whether the nomination failed or succeeded.

The divisive nature of the political debate surrounding the nomination made it even more difficult for me to think about coming forward. I had no desire to become embroiled in the drama that was unfolding in the African American community or the political community as a pawn for either side. In fact, one friend, a Washington attorney and law school classmate to whom I mentioned Thomas' behavior, bluntly advised me, "Don't get involved. It wouldn't be worth it."

I didn't get involved. Instead, I continued to wait for a call from the investigators. I struggled with the information that weighed heavily on me and my inaction in the face of it, and as the humid days of August stretched on, I prayed for some direction.

CHAPTER SIX

By midafternoon on August 19 the temperature in Norman threatened to reach one hundred degrees. My first class of the fall semester was about to begin. Outwardly, it was a typical beginning to a fall semester. As always it seemed too hot for fall, too hot to begin the school year. But despite the intense heat, more than two hundred students of the incoming class entered their first year, primed with anticipation. Their energy was contagious and the intensity of their enthusiasm and anxiety eclipsed the summer heat. Happy to be back in the classroom, I found myself ignoring the weather altogether. But some matters I could not ignore.

When Shirley Wiegand, my close friend and colleague on the faculty, returned for the school year, we charged back into our exercise routine—five-mile walks three times a week. Our feet slightly slowed by the heat, we recounted at full speed and in detail our respective summer experiences. After we had covered all the personal grounds, I finally asked, "Did I ever tell you that I worked for Clarence Thomas?" "No, you did not," she said. The pace of our conversation slowed as I confided in her.

I told Shirley that I did not know what to do. Together we approached the situation as we had been trained—as attorneys, even law professors. True to our profession, we discussed the situation in a series of what-ifs. First, we discussed how I would go about raising the issue if I decided to proceed—to whom I might speak, how much I would disclose initially, whether my statement should be written or oral. Second, we tried to consider what might happen and who might be affected if I raised the claim. We reached no conclusions, and our intuitions fell far short of what was to come. Prepared to respond to an inquiry, but by no means eager to answer, I kept waiting for the call from someone in the government doing a background investigation of Thomas.

On the afternoon of September 5, 1991, the first call came. Gail Laster, counsel to the Judiciary Committee's Labor Subcommittee, which was chaired by Senator Howard Metzenbaum, reached me in my office at the law school. I did not ask her how she had gotten my name and telephone number. I assumed that she had employed the same resources David Margolick had. My conversation with Laster began casually, almost pleasantly. I was not teaching on the day of the call and thus was a little more relaxed about spending time on the telephone. We recalled that we had been at Yale at the same time and had friends in common. Kim Taylor, whom I had known since law school, had supervised Laster at the D.C. public defender's office. After some catching up on what each of us had done since our time in New Haven, Laster turned the conversation to the purpose of her call.

"Do you know anything about allegations of harassment at the EEOC?" she asked.

I responded with a question: "Do you mean allegations that Thomas harassed women at the EEOC?"

"We have heard rumors to that effect," she said.

My immediate thought was that other women had complained and their stories had gotten back to the committee. Because Laster did not ask if I had been harassed, I assumed that she was referring to claims by other women. I knew nothing of such claims, but I did know that Thomas was capable of harassing behavior, so I told her that she should follow up on the rumors. But though I could not imagine how she might have known about my experience, in fact Gail Laster was referring to me.

While I had been wrestling with what to do and preparing for the new semester, my name was traversing the political circuit of Washington, D.C. Peter Fleming, the special investigator who was later assigned to determine who leaked my statement to the press, pieced together the story from his research. Not until May 1992, when I read his reports, would I find out what had led Gail Laster to telephone me. According to Fleming, "In July, Nan Aron, director of the Alliance for Justice, a public interest group in Washington, heard a rumor that a woman claimed that she had been sexually harassed by Clarence Thomas." I did not know Aron, nor was I familiar with the Alliance. Yet through bits of information they had, individuals at the Alliance identified me as the source of the story and obtained my office telephone number. Nan Aron passed this information, including the general nature of the allegations, to William Corr, chief counsel to the Judiciary Committee's Subcommittee on Antitrust, Monopolies and Business Rights, also chaired by Senator Metzenbaum, Laster's employer. Aron told Corr that there were other people who might be aware of Thomas' harassing conduct.

Corr delegated Gail Laster to investigate Aron's information. Whether Gail was chosen because we knew each other, because she is a woman, or because she is black is uncertain. Laster sought further details from Aron about my identity and location but first contacted two other women who had worked with Thomas. Allyson Duncan, his office manager at the EEOC, indicated her support for the nomination and said she knew nothing about rumors of harassment. Neither she nor Judy Winston, who had worked at Education, mentioned any knowledge about inappropriate conduct by Thomas.

Sometime during the week of August 19, at a staff meeting, Laster reported to fellow Metzenbaum staffers the results of her work on the Thomas nomination, which also included follow-up on matters besides the information brought to the senator's office by Aron. Laster described her conversations with Winston and Duncan and said that she had not yet spoken with me. After discussion, the staff determined that she should contact me.

By September 5, when Gail Laster called me, I had given up the idea that FBI agents in charge of investigating Thomas' character and fitness for the Supreme Court would contact me. I was once again busy trying to juggle my own schedule. The immediate needs of more than one hundred students in my two classes, as well as various projects in the provost's office, captured my attention. Yet in the back of my mind, I wondered what more I should have done—what more I *could* have done—to let the Senate Judiciary Committee know about my experience. The committee was set to open the confirmation hearing on Thomas on September 10. Until September 5 I said nothing. Even then I responded with caution.

After I advised Laster to investigate any rumors she knew of, she explained her tentativeness in approaching me about the question of harassment, still without indicating that she had information about me personally. She said that she didn't want to be part of any attempt to discredit Thomas based on racist sexual stereotypes about the behavior of black males. For the moment both she and I were caught in the complicated politics of the nomination. Each of us wanted to fulfill our responsibilities to the process, but neither wanted to be instruments of racism. We put concerns about gender bias aside because race was the issue at the front of everyone's mind. I agreed with Laster that she ran the risk of catering to racism, but I still suggested that she investigate what she had heard. I sensed that Laster was not the one who should be investigating the claims. She was very conflicted about them and seemed too vulnerable to accusations that she was engaging in racism. My sympathy for her position would soon turn to empathy, when I was subjected to the same criticisms. But at the time, my feeling that she did not really want the answer to the question she had asked contributed to my not being more forthcoming with her as well.

Despite her mixed feelings, Laster contacted Kim Taylor shortly after speaking with me. They discussed my conversation with Laster and its background. Taylor did not know about the experience I had with Thomas, but she knew me. On the basis of that knowledge, she advised Laster to be more direct if she wanted clearer answers. However, I did not hear from Laster again. After speaking with Taylor, Laster consulted with her boss, James Brudney, chief counsel to Senator Metzenbaum's

Labor Subcommittee. Brudney had graduated from Yale Law School the year before I did. I knew who he was but we did not socialize together. Brudney had already been advised of her contact with me and had authorized the call to Taylor. He recognized both names from our time at Yale together. After talking to Laster, Brudney instructed her to "discontinue" her investigation. I can only speculate that he thought she had too little information to move forward with an investigation.

On September 6, without knowing about the conversation between Laster and Taylor, I was pondering whether to call Gail Laster back. But before I had a chance, Ricki Seidman of Senator Ted Kennedy's staff telephoned me. Seidman was the chief investigator for the Senate Labor and Human Resources Committee, which was chaired by Kennedy. In late August, Bonnie Goldstein, Senator Metzenbaum's investigator, who also got my name from Nan Aron's organization, had passed the information to Seidman to follow up. Seidman contacted the Alliance for Justice office and spoke to Goldstein's contact, George Kassouf, who informed her that he had not spoken to me directly but was relying on other sources.

When she telephoned me, Seidman at first spoke in general terms about the Thomas nomination. When she turned the conversation to sexual harassment, I told her about my conversation with Gail Laster of the Metzenbaum staff. Seidman continued the conversation and then asked directly, "Do you have any comment on rumors that Thomas sexually harassed you while you were at the EEOC?" It occurred to me that the whole inquiry was based on rumors. In a city like Washington, that could mean anything. Seidman had not told me the source of the rumors or given me any indication what the committee might do in response. "I will neither confirm nor deny the information at this time," I told her. We then talked more generally about victims of sexual harassment, and the conversation ended with Seidman's promise to contact me again on Sunday, September 8.

This was the second call I had received in two days about Clarence Thomas and sexual harassment, and I could no longer deny that the committee knew something about Thomas' behavior and knew that I was its target. I had been thinking about coming forward all summer, but had decided to wait until the investigators came to me. When that had not happened by the end of August, I had assumed it would never happen. So when the first call came, I was not prepared. And when the second call came, I was taken aback that two separate inquiries were being made. At that point, I needed to talk things over with someone I trusted. I went to Shirley Wiegand and another woman on the law school faculty, whom I had not confided in before, Leisha Self.

Our conversation was intense and gloomy. I was agitated and my two colleagues equally apprehensive. I did not detail the behavior, but they immediately understood its nature. Together we began to formulate a plan for moving forward. Their advice was to make the disclosure but only after receiving assurances about the procedure the committee would follow in investigating the charges. Of the three of us, only Wiegand had experience litigating Title VII claims. Self had some experience in labor law generally. None of us were experts on sexual harassment. We decided that any statement and investigation must be kept confidential. Despite our legal experience and sense of obligation to the legal process, our skepticism about the politics involved counseled caution. And that is how I attempted to proceed, with caution.

Ricki Seidman contacted me again on Monday, September 9. By then I was ready to go forward, but I insisted that the information not be made available to the press. Seidman assured me that the committee could accommodate my desire for confidentiality. During that conversation I told Seidman about Thomas' pressuring me for dates and about his discussions of pornography. I indicated that the conduct was not isolated, but avoided any further specifics. I said I recalled one person who could corroborate the general nature of what had occurred, but I was hesitant because I did not want to bring Sue Hoerchner into the matter without consulting her first.

On the morning of Tuesday, September 10, I sat in the small bedroom I had converted to a den, and watched Joseph Biden, chair of the Senate Judiciary Committee, open the Thomas confirmation hearing. I felt numb. The sight of Jamal, Thomas' son, reminded me how much time had passed since I left Washington. I'd still lived in Washington and worked for Thomas when I first met Jamal, then a child; now as the hearing unfolded he sat behind his father a fully grown young man.

I had kept my secret for all those years—enough for a child to become an adult. I had not counted the years, and had been fully prepared to go on keeping the secret. Now I would do so no longer. I was not happy about what I felt I had to do ten years before—keep quiet—nor was I happy about what I must do now—speak out. There was no joy, no sense of righteousness or vindication. At best, I felt some small relief, as if a certain pressure had been released—like the unbuttoning of a shirt collar. I had carried the burden of the secret for so long that I trained myself to ignore its existence. The shame I felt should never have been mine, but I had taken it on by my own silence. Now, having finally made the choice to relinquish the burden, to tell the secret, to admit the embarrassment, it was almost as if nothing had happened. In a moment of calm, after I turned off the television set, I realized the significance of what I was about to do, and I prayed that I could see it through.

That same Tuesday, September 10, James Brudney of Senator Metzenbaum's staff contacted me. Ricki Seidman had informed him of her conversations with me and had suggested that as a former acquaintance he might be an appropriate contact for pursuing the matter. From the beginning of our conversation, I expressed three reservations about going forward. First, I did not want to testify in a public hearing. The nature of behavior to which I had been subjected was embarrassing and personal. It was something I chose not to discuss publicly. Second, I wanted to know what kind of process the committee would use in investigating the charges. I was sure that if the committee, without an independent investigation, simply went to Thomas and asked him about the truth of the allegations, he would either deny them or reduce them to a "misunderstanding." He could bluff and bluster his way around the charge if he thought it was simply my word against his but would be less able to simply deny them if he knew that the committee had conducted an investigation. He had told me that my disclosure would "ruin" him. I knew that he would not take it without some resistance, and if there was no further investigation, the committee would feel safe to dismiss my charges. Finally, I was hesitant to go forward without some indication whether other women had reported similar behavior. I suspected there were others but had no way to prove it. What I did not know was that the women the committee had contacted thus far had denied that anything in the nature of harassment had occurred.

Jim Brudney asked for details of the behavior. The details, he said, would help me to be more clear and certain about my recollections as well as to demonstrate the seriousness of the matter. I gave him the details of the topics Thomas discussed, the language he used, even some of the graphic scenes he had described. It was enough to convince Brudney of the seriousness of the conduct. I was still hesitant to go forward after we talked. None of my uncertainties had been addressed. Brudney simply did not know what process the committee would follow, although he suggested that a closed executive session of the committee, away from the media, might be possible.

Brudney reported our conversation to Senator Metzenbaum, who told him to refer me to Senator Biden as chair of the committee. According to the report of the special investigator, Brudney never mentioned my name to Senator Metzenbaum. The next day, September 11, Brudney spoke with Harriet Grant of Biden's office. He identified me by name but informed Grant that I did not wish to testify publicly. That same day Brudney called me again to say that I would have to contact Grant if I chose to go forward. On the morning of September 12 I called Grant; she was out, but I left a message with my name and daytime telephone number. That afternoon I talked to Harriet Grant for the first time. This was my first official contact with the committee. It occurred a week after Gail Laster's call and several weeks after Senate staffers had first heard about the charges.

For me, the hour or so before a lecture is a time of reflection. I spend it organizing my thoughts and focusing on the main objectives of the day's lesson. On the afternoon of September 12 Harriet Grant returned my call forty minutes before my class was to begin. I had been concentrating on how to communicate to first-year students the difference between an offer to contract and an offer to negotiate a contract, but when I picked up the phone, I lost all focus.

Grant and I talked for about thirty minutes, as I recounted Thomas' behavior and expressed the same concerns I had expressed to Brudney. I also tried to encourage Grant to investigate whether there were other women who had had similar experiences with Thomas, convinced that the committee would dismiss allegations by one person. In this and in a second conversation with Grant on the same day, I stressed that at all times I wanted to follow the proper and most effective procedure for getting the information before the committee. Her emphasis throughout the conversation was that I would not be advised of the committee's procedure and that the handling of my complaint was the committee's prerogative. However, she did explain that according to procedure, the next step would be to inform the nominee about the charges.

I knew that approaching Thomas without some preliminary investigation would be fatal to my claim. And I suggested to Grant that going to Thomas at this point in the process would not be helpful in determining the truth. I thought of the resources the White House had employed in pursuing the nomination thus far, and I knew they would not stop simply because I had raised a claim of impropriety. A feeling of betrayal started to set in as I sensed that this was simply a move to make me go away. The Senate staff had brought me into the process, but the committee was not going to take any responsibility to follow up on the investigation. As in my conversation with Ricki Seidman, I told Grant that a friend could corroborate my account, but again did not offer Susan Hoerchner's name because I still hadn't contacted her.

On Friday, September 13, and again on Sunday, September 15, Jim Brudney telephoned me at home. In a tone that seemed more embarrassed than disappointed, he informed me that the committee had decided not to investigate my charges, apparently because of my request for confidentiality. Somehow Grant had interpreted my desire to avoid a public hearing as a request for total anonymity. At no time had I made such a request. I assumed that everyone who knew about the charges knew my name. After all, Senate staffers had initiated the contact with me. Brudney interpreted the inaction as a misunderstanding of my request for confidentiality. I interpreted the inaction as either disbelief in the charges or unwillingness to investigate them. I was convinced that the decision not to pursue the investigation reflected the committee's indifference to the behavior I had described.

Nevertheless, on Monday, September 16, I contacted Susan Hoerchner about using her as a corroborating witness. Having been brought into the process, I was not willing to be dismissed so easily. Hoerchner reached Grant on Tuesday and expressed a desire for confidentiality as well. She was particularly vulnerable to publicity as an appointed judge in the California administrative law system. But as in her conversations with me, Grant failed to give Hoerchner a sense of how the committee would pursue an investigation of our statements, leaving Hoerchner with the same feeling of uncertainty I had.

On Thursday, September 19, I telephoned Harriet Grant to clear up her misunderstanding about my intentions: "I do not want the matter abandoned. What I want is for the committee to have the information." All along I had assumed that my name would be used in their investigation. I pressed Grant for information about my options. I wanted to know how the committee intended to proceed. Who would make the inquiries? Whom would they contact? How would the information be processed, and who would get it? None of these questions had been answered. They remained unanswered. "I cannot give you information about how your statement will be handled," Grant said. "That is up to the committee."

I was somewhat incredulous. The committee expected me to make a statement and to involve another person but would not give me any idea how, when, or even if they would use the information provided. It occurred to me that I bore all the responsibility and risk, and the committee none. Had I been thinking clearly, I probably would have abandoned the matter at that point. Instead I became more determined. I suspected that I would have been treated differently had I had political contacts, money, title, or any other indicia of power.

On Friday, September 20, after consulting with her supervisor, Grant informed me that if I proceeded, my charges would be given to the FBI to investigate. I said that I was willing to talk to the bureau but questioned Grant once again about what would happen under this proposed process. "The FBI will need to interview you and your corroborating witness. Then they will talk to Thomas and anyone he names." Grant refused to say more. Instinctively, I was still skeptical about what might unfold, and I told Grant that I wanted to consider my options further before talking to the FBI. The entire matter confused me. I felt as though I had been drawn into a maze and left to find my way out alone.

In the meantime, I had contacted Susan Deller Ross, a professor at Georgetown Law Center and director of the school's gender bias clinic. Jim Brudney had referred me to Ross as an expert in sex discrimination who was respected as such by members of the Senate. According to Brudney, Ross had testified before the Senate on a number of occasions and thus had some understanding of Senate procedure as well. In telephone conversations over the next few days, she listened to my story and explained to me the current status of sexual harassment law. She and Brudney were the first persons to whom I had given a detailed description of the events of 1981 and 1982. Even when I confided in friends years earlier, I had not given them the graphic details of Thomas' lewd remarks. I was grateful for the contact with her. Unlike the committee staffers, she seemed to care about my welfare. Just when I was beginning to doubt that my experience mattered, she reassured me that in her professional opinion it did.

Between September 18 and September 20, Sue Ross and I struggled with how to proceed. Neither of us expressed any malice or desire for vindication over Clarence Thomas. Our focus was merely on the obstacles the Senate seemed to be raising to hinder me from coming forward.

On September 22 I called Ross to discuss Grant's suggestion that the committee would bring in the FBI to handle the investigation. I did not know whether the FBI had any experience in investigating this type of charge. Sue Ross and I were both skeptical about how an agent might hear and present the information. Perceptions of the injury of sexually harassing behavior vary from individual to individual. Between males as a group and females as a group, definitions of harassment vary widely. Whether an FBI agent could report the behavior as I had experienced it concerned Ross as much as it did me. She suggested that I prepare a written statement to be sent to the committee, relating the experience in my own words.

Over the weekend I decided to move forward—to agree to the FBI interview, but on the condition that my own statement accompany the report that would be given the committee. When I spoke to Grant and informed her of my decision, she assured me that my statement would appear along with any FBI report.

On the morning of Monday, September 23, I rose early. I had tossed and turned in my bed all night, checking the clock periodically. At 5:00 I could stand it no longer. Getting out of bed was a relief; my sleep had been so fitful that I felt as though I hadn't had any at all. The details of the events that I was soon to recount in my statement to the Judiciary Committee were turning over and over in my head. When I finally sat down to write, I spent four hours composing and typing a four-page statement.

At first my account was clear. I was calm. However, as I recalled and articulated my experiences, I became more and more tense and upset. The nine years that had passed began to fade, and I was reliving some of the behavior as if it had just happened. My writing became less and less cogent. The end document contained several typographical and gram-matical errors. But I was so happy just to get through it that when I finished it, I did not reread it. Nor did I ask anyone else to read it for errors. I was too embarrassed by its content. If I had not sent it in to the Senate as it was, I might never have sent it at all.

The house had been quiet all morning. I wrote my statement without any interruption or distraction. But as I was leaving, the telephone rang. A stranger on the other end of the line introduced herself and said that she worked in the building where my doctor's office is located. "You hit my car in the parking lot of the medical building," she said, and men-tioned the date of one of my visits to the doctor.

"What are you talking about?" I asked, genuinely puzzled.

"I had a friend with the police department trace your tag number," she said.

Though no visible damage had been done to her car, she claimed that the collision had caused a misalignment of her wheels. I did not recall any such collision and was sure none had taken place. Nevertheless, I gave her the name of my insurance agent and asked her to contact him. "I am too distracted and too busy to take care of this myself."

She insisted that she wanted to handle the matter without going to my insurance company. "I would be willing to settle with you for a new set of tires," she declared.

"Look, I don't have time to discuss this now. I'd rather you talk with my insurance agent and let him take care of it," I snapped back. The conversation ended.

I drove the mile or so from my home to the university, printed out the statement, and had it notarized by Sheryl Waters, a notary public in the law school office. I called Harriet Grant to inform her that I was ready to send her my statement. She told me she would wait by the fax machine so that only she would receive it. I went to the law school fax machine in the library on the first floor of the building and telefaxed the statement to the number Grant gave me.

Finally, I had disclosed what had happened. After years of not mentioning it, or mentioning it only in the most general terms and even trying to forget the matter, I had recounted, in detail, the experiences to which I had been subjected nine years prior. But though I understood it was all far from over, I had no idea of just how tumultuous the next few weeks would be.

CHAPTER SEVEN

Monday, September 23, 1991, was like no other day in my life. As hard as I try, I cannot liken it to any occasion or event I have experienced before or since. Harriet Grant had advised me to send in my statement quickly. The hours I spent composing and writing it seemed to fly by. She'd also told me that the FBI would be contacting me to set up an interview. And the hours between her call and the FBI contact and then the visit by the agents were interminable. Half the day my heart raced; the other half I sat watching the clock, waiting for something to happen.

FBI Agents John B. Luton and Jolene Smith Jameson arrived at my home at 6:30 in the evening. Naively, I had not asked anyone to be there with me, and later I regretted it. I apologized for the disarray in my living room as I showed them in. The work that had begun in the summer was still progressing, although I was now able to use my living room furniture, albeit crammed into a small space in the front of the room. I did not take notes, and neither they nor I recorded the conversation.

Under what was described to me as standard procedure, Agent Luton asked most of the questions, and Agent Jameson took notes. Luton explained that the notes would be used to file their final report. Neither of them said anything about their experience in investigating this type of complaint. I offered the agents a copy of my statement to accompany their report, but they informed me that they already had a copy. I told them about Thomas' descriptions of pornography, the pressure for dates, the discussions of his sexual activities.

After I answered specific questions about Thomas' behavior, Agent Luton asked if there were other details that I would feel comfortable relating to them. I declined to add anything further. He suggested that I might feel more comfortable giving details to Agent Jameson alone. I again declined to add to the information I had provided. I thought that what I had said was more than enough to convey the nature of what had happened. I still did not trust their role in the process. Moreover, their inquiry was not a demanding or probing one. It was professional but relaxed.

I did add the comment Thomas made on the evening of my "exit interview" over dinner: that if anyone ever learned about his behavior toward me, it would ruin his career. I had mentioned the comment in my statement and when I spoke with Brudney, but it had not come up during the FBI questioning. I remember precisely what I said to the agents because I could not forget Thomas' own words. Nor could I forget that the tone of his words had been neither apologetic nor re-morseful. The only regret he expressed was that his behavior might appear improper to others. Thomas made it clear that he expected me to keep my mouth shut. Agent Luton would remember the comment differently—he claimed I said Thomas had threatened to ruin *my* career—and it would be reported differently. In statements circulated to the press by Republican senators, the FBI would allege a "discrepancy" between my testimony about Thomas' remarks at the hearing and what I told their agents.

Before they left, Agent Luton asked me a question he felt compelled to justify. He asked if there was anything in the way I dressed or carried myself that might have led Thomas to believe it was appropriate to talk to me about pronography or to make otherwise suggestive remarks. Agent Luton said that by asking the question he was in no way suggesting an answer. In fact, he said that while he was certain that I had not dressed or acted inappropriately, he felt obliged to ask. It was difficult to know whether the agent was catering to the myths about sexual harassment or simply anticipating the defense against my claims. I answered that I had dressed then, as I did at the present time, rather conservatively, and certainly in a way appropriate to an office setting.

The agents ended the session by informing me that my corroborating witness would be contacted and that I would undoubtedly hear from them again with follow-up questions. Follow-up contact, Agent Luton explained to me, was inevitable, and I should expect it. We chatted briefly after the interview, which lasted approximately forty-five minutes, and I showed them the work I was having done on my house.

The agents' questions were not as direct as those Jim Brudney had asked a few days earlier when he sought the details of Thomas' behavior. In responding to the FBI agents, I spoke specifically to their questions but did not elaborate or volunteer more information. I was much more uncomfortable talking about the matter to two strangers face-to-face than I had been on the telephone to Jim Brudney. Though Brudney was only an acquaintance, I knew and trusted him and his role more than I trusted the FBI agents. And again, the information I provided was enough to begin their investigation, had an unbiased and careful investigation been the goal.

There was no follow-up to the interview. The next time I heard from Agent Luton was in the spring of 1992, when he called to get a reference for a law student who had applied for a position with the FBI. "Is a reference from me going to hurt or help the student given the fact that you contradicted my hearing testimony?" I felt compelled to ask. Luton said that the agency took into account all of the references it sought out. He added, almost condescendingly, "I told you that the process wasn't going to be easy." I had not expected it to be easy, but I certainly had not expected the FBI to become actively involved in the harm that was done.

On Tuesday FBI agents visited Susan Hoerchner at her home in Whittier, California. Their conversation lasted approximately one hour, and she told them what she remembered of my account to her of my experience. She never heard from the FBI again either.

I continued to get what I characterized as the "runaround" from

Harriet Grant of Biden's staff. "No, I did not promise to circulate your statement with the FBI report," she said when I called to ask if that had been done. "No, I can't tell you how your statement was handled," she added.

My frustration was mounting, but so was my resolve. I called two friends, Sonia Jarvis and Kim Taylor, to ask whether they knew someone on the committee staff who could give me some information. I tracked Sonia down in California, where she was attending a Stanford alumni weekend. She and Kim, another law school classmate teaching at Stanford, suggested I talk to Charles Ogletree, who was at the same function.

Charles Ogletree is a professor at Harvard Law School with an outstanding reputation for his skills and integrity. He had worked in D.C. for ten years in the public defender's office, trying criminal cases. We spoke, and I gave him the substance of my concern that my statement had been mishandled. Though I did not know it, Ogletree passed the information to Laurence Tribe, a Harvard colleague, one of the country's leading authorities on constitutional law and an adviser to Biden. Nor did I know that on September 27 Tribe contacted Biden staffer Ron Klain to impress upon him the seriousness of my charges. "A group of women law professors on the West Coast are concerned about the statement," Tribe is reported to have told Biden. Again unknown to me, the senator responded by delivering my statement to all of the Democrats on the Judiciary Committee.

Senator Paul Simon telephoned me after reading the statement and the FBI report. "You cannot maintain confidentiality if the information is circulated to the entire Senate. It is bound to get to the press," Simon informed me. At this point I had no idea what measures had been taken to investigate my claim. And I could not trust the press to handle the matter properly, since I had no idea what information might be available. And still no one on the committee advised me of what was happening or had happened with my statement.

That same day the committee voted on Thomas' nomination. Seven members favored the nominee. Seven voted against him. But by a vote of

13–1, the committee voted to send the name forward for full Senate consideration, to take place on October 8.

Days passed and I heard nothing. I did not know about the exchange between Tribe and Biden. I did not know which of the senators, aside from Senator Simon, or their staff members had the FBI report or my statement. I assumed the committee had abandoned the matter, and I was angry. All along, I had been skeptical, expecting very little from the process and feeling powerless to demand more. Sue Ross and I put the matter to rest—nothing more would be done and I would never know just what had happened.

On Thursday, October 3, Nina Totenberg of National Public Radio called. Hers was a voice I had heard many times over the radio. Her stories on legal issues often interested me. By late that week, she had pieced together much of the story. I refused to discuss the matter with Totenberg at that time. On Friday, October 4, acting on a tip that a "certain law professor" had information that might threaten the nomination, *Newsday* reporter Timothy Phelps called me. I had spoken to Phelps before, when, earlier in the summer, he had contacted me about Thomas' association with South Africa and rumors that he had been sympathetic to the apartheid government. I had confirmed Thomas' connection with Jay Parker, whom Phelps had concluded was an agent of the White government, but offered little more. Phelps seemed professional, more issue-oriented than many in the press. Now, contacting me again during the first week of October, he was just as professional and courteous. From at least two sources, he had matched my name with information about allegations of sexual harassment. Immediately, I telephoned Charles Ogletree for advice. Certain that *Newsday* had some information, but perhaps not enough to go forward without my cooperation, Ogletree advised me to say nothing unless they proved that they had my statement.

Both reporters had recounted to me so closely what had transpired to date that I was sure they had the statement or would soon, regardless of my actions. At some point during numerous telephone calls, I told both

Phelps and Totenberg that I wanted proof that they had the document. And while Totenberg exhibited either feigned or real exasperation with my reluctance, Phelps seemed to understand and called to suggest a deal. His Senate source would give him the information for me to confirm, if I gave the source my permission. I refused. On Saturday afternoon a frustrated Phelps called with details about my statement. I confirmed only the details he had and refused to provide more. Phelps' story ran on Sunday, October 6, in the morning edition of *Newsday,* but the presses ran on Saturday, and the story went out over the wires that evening.

Totenberg telephoned after Phelps on Saturday and read the opening paragraph of my statement, confirming what I already knew. The press wanted the story badly, and there was nothing I could do to stop them. If she had it, eventually so would others. So, from my office, I granted a taped interview with Totenberg to air on Sunday morning.

For the remainder of that Saturday, I telephoned family to inform them about the story. "Did you send a statement to the Senate? Is the story true?" my mother asked. This was the first she had heard of it. Afterward, I located my nephew Eric, who had been doing high school recruiting for the college on campus that day. He knew about the FBI's visit. "The press has the story," was all that I could say. "How did they find out? Are you all right?" he wondered. For the next few weeks his innocently confused look would haunt me. We were best of friends, and I knew that this would hit him nearly as hard as it did me.

Despite being consumed by the events of the day, I tried to go about my regular routine. That evening, in tax professor Mark Gillett's van, a group of my colleagues and friends went together to a yearly law school minority recruitment dinner. I sat with one of the law school alumni, Melvin Hall, and some potential students. I ate my dinner quietly, thinking about but never raising the matter. Returning home in the van, I told the group to expect the NPR report the following day. I gave them the substance of the story but few details. Their mood was quiet, concerned. No one knew what to say or what to expect. Even I could not predict the storm that was about to overtake the law school's usual calm.

Tim Phelps' story in *Newsday* alerted other members of the press. And starting after midnight, a reporter from CBS called my home every half hour. I gave up the idea of sleeping and got out of bed about 3:00 A.M. I knew that before long, especially once the story aired on public radio, other reporters would find my home. Deciding to check into a local hotel, I dressed and went to the supermarket to buy microwavable food, wanting to be prepared to stay in the hotel room throughout the next day, or longer if necessary. I called Eric to let him know where I would be. Around 7:00 Sunday morning, I drove to Shirley Wiegand's house. Together we listened to Nina Totenberg's report on National Public Radio. Shirley decided that she should go to the hotel and get me a room using her name and credit card.

All that Sunday, I tried to develop a plan to deal with the situation. None came to mind. Eric was my messenger, shuttling back and forth between the law school, my house, and the hotel. "The press is everywhere," he told me. "Some are staying at this hotel." Pointing to the law school logo on his sweatshirt, I warned, "Change clothes before you come back. Someone might spot you." My words made me acutely aware of my predicament and the futility of remaining in the hotel. I could not believe any of it.

I was anxious, but not yet desperate. Eric and I prepared for our classes. Because I assumed that my schedule would continue uninterrupted, I even made an appointment to meet with my minister from Tulsa about a project he was working on later that week. Shirley came over to visit me late in the afternoon. I had a map of the hotel grounds, and from telephone calls coming into the law school, she provided the numbers of the rooms where press members were staying. Together we avoided journalists and went out to a track for our regular walk. It was a cool, crisp autumn evening, the best time of the year for one. And I needed to be out of the hotel room, if only temporarily. The press was so focused on sexual scandal that later certain reporters suggested I had spent the evening in a tryst with Shirley Wiegand—no doubt easier for some than admitting that I had simply eluded them under their very noses.

By Sunday evening I knew that I could not avoid the chaos that was to come. It was as if all summer long I had only been putting off the inevitable. My colleague Rick Tepker prepared a statement announcing that I would hold a press conference in the law school on Monday. I could barely read it, so unreal was the entire situation to me. Nevertheless, I signed off on it. I watched a local news report claiming that I had returned home that evening but fled upon seeing the press. The report had footage of a car driven by a black woman with black female passengers pulling into the driveway. Later I learned the occupants were law students playing a prank on the press. I ate dinner and went to bed. Amazingly, I managed to sleep for several hours.

For weeks and months after the hearing of October 1991, professional news analysts and commentators attempted to explain the intense anger that erupted because of the proceeding. In retrospect it is difficult to understand how the various emotions intensified so rapidly during the confirmation hearing. In a relatively short time, anger, confusion, disappointment, distrust, and more anger reached a boiling point, as people around the country focused on their televisions or radios to try to comprehend the spectacle which the process became. The hearing combined a variety of potentially volatile elements—gender, race, power, sex, and yes, politics—which when combined and subjected to the glare of television caused a mild explosion.

Memories of behavior which women had once had to "grin and bear" or at least go out of their way to avoid came back to us, and it no longer seemed right to dismiss them. By going back and looking at the entire record of the proceeding and the press accounts, one can begin to recall how the scene was set for the response. In fact, put in context, the intense emotional response was predictable, even natural.

I woke early Monday morning and returned home from the hotel just before daybreak to find one remaining crew of reporters camped on my neighbor's lawn. They quickly crossed the street to mine. One member of a crew of three or four journalists carried a glaring light that blinded me so that I could not see the faces of those approaching. Live microphone in hand, a female reporter introduced herself by saying that she wanted to ask me a question about my statement to the Senate Judiciary Committee. "I won't answer anything until you get that light out of my eyes," I said. After a brief discussion among themselves, the crew obliged, and I proceeded to tell the reporter nothing she didn't already know. "Yes, it is true that I sent a statement to the Senate. Yes, there will be a press conference today."

I went into my home, concluding that the only purpose of the exercise was to capture me when I was not expecting to be photographed, a form of "ambush" journalism relying on the theory that a surprise visit might elicit some telling response or reaction more newsworthy than a formal interview. Apparently, the statement I had issued the previous day explaining that I would be giving a press conference was not adequate. The competitive nature of the industry required "extemporaneous" reporting. Privacy—my own right to enter my home without intrusion—meant nothing compared to the potential "news" the ambush might elicit. I did not rush into my house to avoid the crew, but frankly, I was very annoyed that I could not go home in the early morning hours without being confronted by reporters. After all, the story had not changed while I slept. This crew's approach promised that the thoughtful handling the story had received from Phelps and Totenberg would be a thing of the past. In its wake would follow the familiar kind of careless, untrustworthy journalism I had dreaded from the beginning. The crew dismantled their equipment and left my neighbor's lawn. It was barely 7:00 A.M.

I had watched news conferences before, but never expected to participate in one myself. As I dressed that morning, I realized that I had no idea what I would encounter. The people who would be helping me were novices. Already, Dean David Swank's office was swamped with telephone inquiries, and the press corps swarmed the hallways like locusts. The media attention was focused on the law school building. And to quell the uproar, Dean Swank announced that the press conference would take place as planned. As a matter of consideration for students, staff, and faculty, who were in a state of bewilderment about the entire situation, the law school location made sense. But this choice created a different uproar. "You've got to send her someplace else," objected the university administrators. "What about the local Holiday Inn?" one official demanded. David Swank held his ground: "She is a member of this faculty. I will resign before I turn her away." Later, public officials excoriated him for his stand.

The conference was initially scheduled for 10:00. CNN asked that it be postponed for an hour so they could carry it live. We agreed. I saw no point in appearing unreasonably uncooperative with the media. Besides, a delay gave me more time to brace myself.

I drove to the law school by myself and crossed the fifty or so yards from the parking lot to the law school building. Two of my colleagues, Associate Dean Teree Foster and Rick Tepker, spotted me and met me on the walkway, sparing me from having to step into the turmoil alone. Inside the building the scene was surprisingly calm. Most of the press had gathered in the classroom where the conference was to take place. I went to the dean's office to discuss the procedure with Foster, Tepker, and Swank. Though we were used to evincing self-confidence in most situations, our inexperience showed. And the press statement issued the day before would later be described as amateurish. No doubt it was one of the first Rick Tepker had ever written. But we were all amateurs. There were none of the high-paid professional "handlers" to which Senator Alan Simpson would later allude with disdain. I did not even know what the term "handler" meant until later that day when advised by the press.

As I walked down the crowded hallway to classroom 2, familiar faces offered reassurance. The circumstances were so unreal that friends seemed out of place. I saw Dr. Thomas Hill, the academic adviser for the athletic department, whom I had known since he arrived at the university in 1988, and Beth Wilson, a friend and the affirmative action director for the university. In a small gesture of support that I will not forget, Beth wrote her home number and a note on a bank deposit slip: "Call me if you need anything."

Students, staff, and my colleagues filled the classroom, along with the press. Eric was there with a college friend. Everyone except the press stood and applauded as I entered the room. The Student Bar Association, the Black Law Student Association, and the Minority Coalition presented resolutions supporting me. This at once bolstered my resolve and overwhelmed me with dismay. They did not deserve this massive intrusion of cameras and reporters; none of us did.

Yet I was in a classroom, a place where after some struggle I had finally come to feel at home. And my statement came more easily for that fact. Though this was one of the rare occasions on which I would receive a standing ovation in the classroom, it was only one of many at which I would be pummeled with questions, a fact I tried to remind myself of as the reporters' questions began. But somehow the familiarity of the setting only heightened the surreal quality of the press conference. I could not comprehend that it was actually happening. When I think back on it, it is as though I am standing behind myself viewing the whole thing from over my shoulder.

"One or two more questions," Dean Swank announced. Each reporter tried to make sure that hers or his was the last. In the statement, as in responding to questions, I tried to urge upon the press that in sending my statement to the Senate I had responded to the inquiry of a Senate staffer, that I was not acting to raise a sexual harassment claim but out of my sense of responsibility to the nomination process, and that I felt the Senate had an obligation to resolve the matter, since some of its members had already responded to the reports of my charges by impugning my integrity. This was the first time I asked for a public resolution, but at that moment I knew that if there was none, I would certainly live under the shadow of the accusations of fabrication forever. Even with a public resolution, the shadow might well continue for years. Without a chance to address publicly the allegations of those who called me a liar, I would spend my entire life addressing them privately. I wanted the matter resolved "so that all of you nice people can just go home," I concluded. We all laughed nervously.

After what seemed an hour-long press conference, I went to the dean's office. Ovetta Vermillion, the dean's assistant, informed me that Tim Phelps was in the waiting room. She showed a man into the office whose face I had never seen but whose voice I recognized immediately. As he introduced himself, he seemed genuinely sorry for the way things had evolved in the thirty-six hours since his story ran in *Newsday,* or perhaps I wanted so badly for someone to feel remorse for the turmoil that I mistook what was only fatigue in his eyes. At the same time, I was sure that as a journalist he would have liked to get the "scoop" for his paper, and he didn't get it. I was not trying to be evasive. I just had nothing to tell him, nothing more than I had said at the press conference.

Finally back in my office, I sat exhausted at my desk. I wanted at least to try to respond to the telephone calls I'd received that morning and to finish preparing for classes. Later in the day, a stereotypically arrogant ABC news correspondent interviewed me for the evening program. He seemed to see the story as an inconsequential Washington political scandal. Dan Rather interviewed me for the *CBS Evening News.* To my surprise, he conducted a sincere inquiry into the situation. It would be too much to say that I was pleased with the interview, but I was relieved that someone seemed to understand the real-life elements of what was occurring. After confronting incredulity and lack of sensitivity throughout the day, I was refreshed by Rather's appreciation of the issues. And despite the seriousness of both the day and the subject matter, the interview provided its moment of humor. Throughout the whole thing, a fly buzzed around my head, seeking perhaps its own fifteen minutes of fame. When it was over, I was sure that no one would remember anything I said, only the fly I was trying to ignore.

As friends and family members telephoned me from around the country, the question first and foremost on their minds was "What is going to happen next?" I had no answer for them. "All I can do is wait to hear from the Senate," was my only response.

Over dinner with Eric and Shirley, I discovered that the stress of the day had not taken away my appetite. Though I only now appreciate it fully, this was the last time I would eat in a public restaurant with some sense of anonymity. After dinner I went home alone to a ringing telephone and an answering machine full of messages, some worse than I had anticipated—death threats and threats of rape or sodomy. People felt free to leave the most cruel and revolting messages imaginable. Yet not all the messages were of that kind. Many, mostly those from women, were words of encouragement. Some were delightful, like the one from two "older women," as they described themselves, "friends, one black, one white," who wanted me to know that they were behind me and were praying for me. Amazingly, that one message of support undid the damage of all the threats.

Halfway through the playback, the tape jammed and I lost the remaining messages. This was symbolic to me in the days to come of the many things that had seemed to go wrong in the past few days. But the broken message machine did not stop the telephone from ringing constantly. After talking to my mother, I turned off the ringers and went to bed.

CHAPTER EIGHT

Unlike its reaction to my confidential statement, the Senate's reaction to a public airing of my claim was swift, and in some cases outright hostile. This kind of resistance did damage and disservice in a number of areas. Of course, the immediate denunciations of my claim and their unsupported comments about my character harmed me personally. But they also misinformed the public about the issue of sexual harassment and disparaged the right of a private citizen to become involved in matters of public significance. And Senate efforts to press the nomination at all costs threatened the integrity of the nomination process itself.

Because both Democrats and Republicans acted irresponsibly, their behavior said less about party politics than politics in general. It was politics in general that showed its face in the arrogant statements of the senators. Their resentment that public pressure had forced them to change their internal policies was clear. And to many around the country, even those who did not identify with the harassment experience, the Senate's attitude suggested that their own experiences might well be dismissed if the Senate found those experiences unpopular or unpleasant. They saw a Senate out of touch with the lives of its constituents. Those who knew firsthand or related to the harassment issue recognized that it was the senators' resentment at being accountable to the public that had caused them to attack me. The side of public life that the people witnessed during the hearing was contemptible but true. And nothing painted the unpleasant picture more vividly than the senators' own words.

One of the first reactions to my statement that I heard was from Arizona Senator Dennis DeConcini, who said the following during a press conference on the afternoon of October 7, a short time after my own press conference was ended.

> *If you're sexually harassed you ought to get mad about it, and you ought to do something about it and you ought to complain, instead of hanging around a long time and then all of a sudden calling up anonymously and say "Oh, I want to complain." I mean, where is the gumption?*

Later, more than one person would ask me, "Did you hear what DeConcini said?" Each person who asked seemed more incensed than the last, and none of them seemed to care that DeConcini was a Democrat. As one woman put it, "Here is a man who probably never had to face discrimination in his life telling women how they ought to react to being sexually harassed. 'Where is the gumption' indeed?"

I can't count the number of times since October 1991 that I have been asked, "Why did you wait ten years to raise charges of sexual harassment against Clarence Thomas?" To which I must first say that I wasn't waiting from 1983 to 1991 to raise charges against Clarence Thomas. I was living my life. I was involved in the day-to-day struggles that everyone who lives and works and cares about their families and friends has. I had a full life of which Clarence Thomas was no longer a part. Moreover, the question misconceives what I was attempting to do in disclosing the information. I did not see the response as an effort to get relief or redress for the behavior. I was supplying information about how Thomas conducted himself in his professional role.

Perhaps a different question, and I believe a better question, is "Why didn't you bring charges of sexual harassment immediately after you left the EEOC?" To understand the muteness of my response, one must understand that I wanted most of all for the behavior to stop. That was my chief objective throughout. I found a way to make that happen by removing myself from the situation. Even in hindsight I am convinced that there was no way to stop the harassment decisively except by leaving. What were the precedents? There was a woman in the District of Columbia who sued Department of Corrections officials for harassment she experienced in the late 1970s. She is still attempting to obtain relief for her harm despite the fact that she won her suit years ago. I also recall one of the very first sexual harassment lawsuits ever filed. The woman involved in this case, Paulette Barnes, was an African American suing her supervisor in the Environmental Protection Agency, complaining that he stripped her of all job responsibilities after she rejected his sexual advances, ultimately abolishing her position altogether. I know of a third woman whose career as a doctor was stalled for over ten years because as a resident she complained about a doctor's harassment. I also know of countless women who changed college majors or professional careers and sometimes even relocated to other cities in lieu of confronting their harassers.

These were my options. I assessed the situation and chose not to file a complaint. I had every right to make that choice. And until society is willing to accept the validity of claims of harassment, no matter how privileged or powerful the harasser, it is a choice women will continue to make. I do not believe that in the early 1980s I lived and worked in a society, either in Washington or in Tulsa, that would have supported my right to raise a claim of harassment against the head of the EEOC. And given the state of the law and what occurred in 1991, I do not believe that a complaint would have stopped what was happening. For years I made the choice to remain silent about my experience and to push on in my life. I made that choice, like many other women, because I thought that it was my only choice. Even today most women choose to keep to themselves the slights, innuendos, harassment, and abuse they experience—because they are women. I hear from former students, now young lawyers working with seasoned professionals and struggling to maintain their dignity and their jobs in this kind of ongoing balancing act. I hear from middle-aged and older women who believe that their silence has allowed them to survive both economically and socially. In the world according to Senator DeConcini, all these women are sorely lacking in gumption. Yet they function in a world that encourages them to question their own reaction and to stop being "so sensitive" to the pain of their experiences. That alone takes a lot of gumption.

DeConcini also misrepresented the sequence of events that led to my statement to the Senate. No one contests that my first contact with the Senate came at the initiation of Senate staffers; it was a point I sought to stress at the press conference and one that was not debatable. Therefore, not only did I not make a call to the Senate and say that I wanted to complain, but there was never any anonymity. The Senate staffers called me and thus always had my name and my location. By the time of the hearings they had ample information about my background. Even Senator Simpson, in a rare display of probity on the matter, allowed that at least some Democrats on the committee had my name as early as September 23.

What is more important, DeConcini's remarks reveal that he based his dismissal of my charges more on how he thought a woman should respond to harassment than on whether he believed that Thomas had actually harassed me. At one point in the days preceding the hearing, DeConcini said, "I don't say it didn't happen. I say there is another side." Very often the responsibility for ending discriminatory behavior, in whatever form, is placed on the target of the discrimination, rather than the person who carries it out or those in a position of authority to stop it.

In his comments DeConcini described how a victim of discrimination should feel and act. First that person should "get mad," and then she should "complain." If she does not, according to DeConcini, nobody should care, even when a lifetime appointment to the nation's highest court is at stake. In other words, those who do not react in the way prescribed by DeConcini deserve no attention from those who should be concerned about the problem. In focusing on the target's reaction instead of the behavior of the harasser, DeConcini failed to understand that most harassment victims experience a variety of emotions in the face of harassment; anger is just one of them. And different people deal with harassment in different ways. Some women internalize the anger; others deny it.

Filing a complaint in response to harassment is only one way of "getting mad." As I said, it is one that many harassment victims feel would be fruitless. Only 3 percent of reported harassment incidents end in a formal complaint. DeConcini proposed this reaction as the only valid course in response to harassment, though it is one that few harassment targets ever take.

In addition to revealing real ignorance about the harassment issues, DeConcini's comments reveal a good deal of arrogance. Given the negative reactions to charges of sexual harassment, telling women that they should angrily complain, without any consideration of the effectiveness of the complaint mechanism, is tantamount to telling them that they should subject themselves to further abuse.

DeConcini was not a trial judge responding to a plaintiff attempting to bring a claim in federal court ten years after events occurred. He was a member of a committee reviewing the entire record of a nominee for a lifetime appointment. The committee had spent the last few months reviewing Thomas' life as far back as his childhood in Georgia. No one on the committee prevented Thomas or his supporters from bringing in character evidence dating back nearly forty years. Moreover, the committee had spent hours discussing Thomas' role as assistant secretary of education and chair of the EEOC. Thomas' performance in those capacities and his role as a member of the Reagan administration were chief topics of the first round of the confirmation hearing, during which the committee had also received and discussed evidence of Thomas' improprieties in handling expense and travel reimbursement. There were claims that he was reimbursed by the government for what was essentially personal business relating to his membership on the board of his alma mater, Holy Cross University. No one objected that the material was outdated. Nevertheless, when the topic of his conduct in official positions turned to sexual harassment, DeConcini and many other senators balked at the idea of hearing it.

DeConcini and some of his colleagues apparently had a double standard for receiving information, depending on the nature of the information. The committee seemed willing to exclude "old" information on sexual harassment while considering "old" information on practically anything else. If the Senate is unwilling to view evidence of sexual misconduct with the same openness as it views evidence of other types of improprieties, victims of sexual misconduct, most often women, will face trouble when they attempt to inform Senate committees of such behavior, whether in an information-gathering session for legislative purposes, a confirmation hearing, or a disciplinary proceeding such as the Ethics Committee hearings on harassment allegations against Senator Robert Packwood. The double standard casts harassment as "personal behavior" rather than behavior that reflects on professionalism.

DeConcini's willingness to let harassers and those with the power to end harassment off the hook is not shared by the courts. One issue of litigation in the sexual harassment arena is whether an employer is relieved of liability after taking steps to end discrimination in the workplace. Courts scrutinize the employer's sexual harassment policy to determine if it is adequate and evenhandedly enforced. The courts have concluded that it is not enough for an employer simply to say that sexual harassment is prohibited. The employer must establish a procedure under which targets of such behavior can come forward and state a claim without fear of retaliation, and the procedure must provide for the fair investigation and resolution of the complaint should the complainant prevail. The employer does not relieve himself of responsibility for ridding the workplace of harassment by declaring that the target of the behavior should get angry. Nor does the duty to an aggrieved employee end simply because the employee failed to avail herself of the employer's grievance procedure. The employee may still file a lawsuit.

In his press conference DeConcini essentially claimed that the Senate had no duty to investigate my charges because I had not filed a complaint against Thomas ten years ago. DeConcini should not have been allowed to sidestep his responsibility to me, or more important, to the American public, with such a bold assertion, which ignored one critical fact. The responsibility of the Senate Judiciary Committee to investigate the character and fitness of nominees to the Supreme Court is comprehensive in scope and time. It is by no means limited to formal complaints filed against the nominee, nor to events of two, three, or even ten years past.

During the hearing, when Senator DeConcini questioned me, our exchange would prove quite revealing. "And the fact that you admit that, in retrospect, maybe you should have done something, you have concluded that it is all someone else's fault; none of it is your fault." What was supposed to be a question became a statement—an accusation. "Yes," I responded. If he meant that the harassment was not my fault, certainly my answer was yes. And if he was referring to the circumstances that brought me before the public, my answer was still yes. I had no say in how his committee had handled my statement, and certainly no part in the leak to the press. "Is that your frame of mind?" DeConcini's dissatisfaction with my response was obvious in his tone. "That is my frame of mind," I answered. Clearly, DeConcini wanted to blame me for what was happening in 1991 because I failed to file a complaint ten years earlier, but I held firm. The hearing was no more my fault than the harassment itself.

On Monday afternoon a group of women requested a meeting with the Senate majority leader, George J. Mitchell of Maine, to discuss a postponement of the Senate vote on the confirmation. The group included black and white women from academic and political backgrounds. Their objective was to persuade Mitchell to delay the vote and allow time for a thorough investigation. They were asked to wait until the senator was available, and one of them finally had to leave because of a prior commitment. The meeting with Senator Mitchell was perhaps more frustrating because of the long wait that preceded it. "My hands are tied. I can't do anything," Mitchell declared. Despite his perceived power as majority leader, he would take no responsibility for the action the Senate was about to take in voting to confirm Judge Thomas to the

Court. The schedule for the vote was set, and according to Mitchell it could not be changed. Yet later when Daniel Patrick Moynihan of New York, the senator in charge of the Senate Calendar, threatened to call a week's recess, Mitchell exerted his authority, reminding his colleague that he, not Moynihan, was the majority leader. Senator Mitchell's inaction opened the door for the Republican senators to go on the offensive.

Unconstrained by any sense of senatorial decorum, Senator Alan Simpson appeared on ABC's *Nightline* that evening. He brought with him telephone logs that Thomas supporters had retrieved from his garage, hoping they would kill my claim. More numerous than the eleven calls I had made to Thomas' office at the EEOC in the ten years since I left my job were the calls and remarks that had been blacked out, removed from any public scrutiny. Yet no one questioned Thomas' selection of what the committee would see. Simpson implied that I had "pursued" Thomas. The campaign that began with DeConcini's "blame the victim" remark continued with Simpson's labeling me the aggressor in my relationship with Thomas. And the anticipation of a second round of the Thomas confirmation hearing, which might have been seen as an opportunity for responsible consideration of my claim, seemed instead to provoke greater irresponsibility among some senators. The press appeared to relish their remarks, calling upon senators from the Judiciary Committee in particular.

When Senator Simpson appeared on *Nightline* on October 7, armed with Clarence Thomas' telephone logs, he raised another question I have been asked countless times since: "Why did you keep in touch with him?" To which I must say that I was not threatened by Thomas as a person. I was threatened by the power he had held over me as an employer. That threat ended when I left his employ. Tellingly, so did the behavior.

By no means were Clarence Thomas and I good friends. I did not invite him to my home during the time we worked together. I spent five weeks in Washington during the summer of 1987 without contacting him or his office. My telephone calls to him had each had a work-related purpose. Some commentators have described them as "opportunistic," suggesting that I was seeking something I had no right to expect, though I had worked for Clarence Thomas for two years and had performed my job conscientiously. When I called upon him or his office for information, or to pass along a legitimate request, I did so on the basis of that performance. Never would I have considered those solicitations opportunism. I received no personal gain. Besides, I had not been the one to behave inappropriately. So why should I later allow his behavior to deprive me of a job benefit I had rightfully earned?

Part of the answer to the complex question of why I stayed in touch has to do with the idea of control. By pretending that my departure from the EEOC was cordial, I denied to myself the significance of the harassment. But by staying in touch subsequently, I regained something I hadn't been able to maintain working for Clarence Thomas: professional decorum.

In 1992 I met a retired man who had gone to fight in World War II and left his young bride, his high school sweetheart, at home. She worked to support herself while he was away. When we met, he appeared to be as in love with her as when they were newlyweds. During the hearing he asked her jokingly whether she had ever been harassed, fully expecting she would say no. To his surprise, she said she had been harassed, in fact by their high school principal for whom she worked while he fought in Europe. But he had revered the principal, now a good friend, and rather than cause tension between the two, she kept quiet. Throughout what they both described as a happy marriage, filled with love and open communication, she had denied her own pain to spare his respect for a man who was his "role model." Paradoxically, I am both consoled and saddened by the fact that so many others do the same. I wonder if something in our training tells us to "forgive and forget" or "let bygones be bygones," or any of the other clichés that allow us to deny our hurt.

In stark contrast to Senator Barbara Mikulski, Senator Simpson was exasperated by the prospect of reconvening the confirmation hearing. In a profoundly crass statement, following his *Nightline* appearance Simpson broadcast his ignorance about sexual harassment and the purpose of the upcoming hearing. The tall Wyoming native, who projects a "cowboy" image despite his gray flannel suit and conservative necktie, warned of the treatment I could expect from the Senate:

> *It's a harsh thing, a very sad and harsh thing, and Anita Hill will be sucked right into the—the very thing she wanted to avoid most. She will be injured and destroyed and belittled and hounded and harassed, real harassment, different from the sexual kind, just plain old Washington variety harassment which is pretty unique in itself.*

I looked for some sympathy in Senator Simpson's words. I found none. I took his message as an unfriendly warning, something just this side of a threat—an attempt to dissuade me from coming forward.

In distinguishing sexual harassment from "real harassment," Simpson's statement suggests that the former is tolerable, if not excusable—that it is mild or harmless, or at least less harmful than the "real" kind he had apparently experienced or inflicted as part of the politics of Washington, D.C. According to Simpson, being "injured and destroyed and belittled and hounded" is a consequence of "real harassment," not sexual harassment. Perhaps because Senator Simpson never experienced sexual harassment, and is not likely to, he did not perceive it as real, injurious, or destructive. What *was* real to Simpson was "plain old Washington variety harassment." The pity is that Simpson could not extend his understanding of Washington-variety harassment to sexual harassment to see that both have the same basis—abuse of power—and the same aim: self-gain through devastating or demoralizing the target.

Nor did Simpson's personal experience with Washington-variety harassment relieve him of his responsibility to attempt to relate to the experience of the thousands of his constituents who understood well that sexual harassment is real harassment. Although Simpson apologized after the hearing for his choice of words, he could not take back the twin message they sent: that sexual harassment is not real and that complaints about sexual harassment should be met with "real harassment." I will not count the number of times, even before the hearing, that I have been threatened with sodomy, rape, assault, and other forms of sexual and nonsexual violence. Some of the callers have used almost the same words: "Now you will know what real harassment is like."

Senator Alan Cranston of California summed up the danger of Senator Simpson's dismissive assessment of my claims in the debate on the postponement of the hearing:

> *I am appalled at statements being made that these are not serious charges because they involve verbal, not physical, abuse. I am appalled at the stunning admissions of a lack of sensitivity to the problem of sexual harassment. What has a majority of this body been saying to all the women who are subjected to sexual harassment? Who have been, are now, or will be subjected to sexual harassment?*

Needless to say, Simpson's views on "real harassment" did not suggest that he was approaching the hearing with anything like an open mind. And if there was any doubt on that score, his reference to my claim on the second day of the hearing as "sexual harassment crap" extinguished it. Simpson's statement played over and over in my mind during the next few days. I contemplated the prospect of experiencing "real harassment." The statement became self-fulfilling—almost a call for the Republican senators to sink to the level of Simpson's vision of the proceeding. Simpson set the tone for the hearing and his colleagues followed him. Ironically, their view of "real harassment" Washington style was quite similar to what many women who complain about sexual harassment in the workplace experience as well.

Tuesday, October 8, 1991, began early with an interview by the *Today* show's Katie Couric. Even after the ABC and CBS interviews of the day before, the experience of being broadcast around the country lacked a sense of reality for me. Nevertheless, I approached the interview in the same way that I had approached my contacts with Senate staffers. I was simply trying to communicate information that was relevant to the process. I had no established agenda, and I expected to be treated fairly and honestly.

Just before questioning me, Couric had questioned Senator Arlen Specter of Pennsylvania, a former prosecutor and a member of the Judiciary Committee, who remarked that he had "looked Judge Thomas in the eye and questioned him. He denied these charges. Given the lateness of the allegation, the absence of any touching or intimidation, and the fact that she moved with him from one agency to another, I felt I had done my duty and was satisfied with his responses." I told Ms. Couric that Specter had not bothered to look *me* in the eye and that he had done nothing to follow up on my statement personally. With the exception of Senator Simon, whose call had come in just before the leak, no one, not even the chairman of the committee, had bothered to talk to me.

Senator Specter was the third member of the "fact-finding" tribunal, after Senators DeConcini and Simpson, to declare that he did not believe my statement about Thomas' behavior.

Specter claimed that he had reached his conclusion about my claim when Thomas looked him in the eye and denied the allegation. To consider this method in perhaps the most positive light, Specter was demonstrating that he was sufficiently self-impressed to believe that Thomas could not mislead him and that he, Specter, would know if Thomas tried. A more cynical interpretation suggests subterfuge: by posing the question to Thomas, Specter gave the appearance of an inquiry but was in fact playing a game whose outcome he already knew.

Specter's readiness to rely on the word of the very man accused of harassment seems inconsistent with the instincts he must have had as a former prosecutor, yet it is typical of cases involving sexual misconduct. Women who accuse men, particularly powerful men, of harassment are often confronted with the reality of the men's sense that they are more important than women, as a group. Consequently, the man's word is often lent more credence than that of his accuser or even observers. An example that has received some media attention springs to mind.

In January 1990, Edward A. Brennan, chair of the board of the United Way of Americans, received unsigned letters on UWA stationery accusing UWA President William Aramony of having an illicit sexual affair with a teenager and of misusing UWA funds. Shortly thereafter, Brennan met with the sixty-three-year-old Aramony, who told him that the allegations were unfounded. Brennan was convinced of Aramony's truthfulness and in turn convinced the board. Neither Brennan nor the board called for any further independent inquiry, and Aramony continued as UWA president until his resignation in 1992.

However, in September 1994, in a 182-page indictment, a grand jury charged that Aramony had diverted hundreds of thousands of dollars from UWA before he left the organization, and that he had used some of the misappropriated funds to support a relationship with a young woman who was seventeen years old when their affair began. The indictment also included charges of sexual harassment stemming from accusations that Aramony told certain female employees that they would "get nowhere in UWA" if they rejected his sexual advances.

Brennan, like Senator Specter, had an impressive record. While he headed the UWA board, he was also chair of Sears, Roebuck. Yet neither Brennan nor Specter is so talented that he is beyond being deluded by other intelligent or powerful men. Moreover, neither seemed to appreciate the high stakes involved in the particular situation or the lengths the accused would go to defend himself. In both cases the stakes involved placing or keeping an individual in a position of power and authority and preserving the trust of the public.

That otherwise very impressive men are capable of misleading friends and the public, and even of lying under oath about their sexual improprieties and poor judgment, has become all too familiar news. Ben Chavis of the NAACP lost his position as that organization's director because the board learned of his use of NAACP funds to settle a sex discrimination and reportedly a sexual harassment claim. In the face of highly incriminating tape-recorded conversations, President Bill Clinton's first-term secretary of HUD, Henry Cisneros, is under investigation to determine whether he lied to the Federal Bureau of Investigation regarding "conscience money" he paid to a woman with whom he had formerly been romantically involved.

Two lessons can be gleaned from these situations. Though not all men misrepresent such episodes of their lives, many are evidently capable of doing so. What is even more apparent is that it is often impossible, particularly with a cursory inquiry that involves questioning only the person accused of the misconduct, to determine the truth of a matter with certainty.

But beyond the initial assessment of the situation in which each found himself, parallels between Mr. Brennan and Senator Specter diverge. Brennan chose not to pursue his own investigation, but appears to have cooperated with a grand jury conducting an independent investigation of the charges against Aramony. Specter, on the other hand, approached the "fact-finding" hearing already sure of his own conclusion. Similarly, in many cases involving sexual harassment, employers marshal their efforts behind a conclusion that charges are false without pursuing a genuine investigation or inquiry beyond taking the word of the alleged harasser. In addition to doing little to stop an individual from repeating unwelcome behavior, this sends a signal to others, potential harassers and victims alike, that the behavior is protected. Moreover, institutionally, the person bringing the claim becomes the party in the wrong. These are dangerous messages to convey to the public when, even by conservative estimates, no fewer than 40 percent of workingwomen will experience sexual harassment.

When women began to say that the senators "just don't get it," they meant among other things that they did not understand the impact their comments regarding me had on *all* women's claims of sexual harassment. Clearly, they were so intent on confirming Thomas that they were willing to sacrifice not only me but other women as well.

According to accounts of the hearing, the Republicans designated Specter "chief prosecutor" in an event the administration viewed as "The People v. Anita Hill." Perhaps Specter was chosen because of his prosecutorial skills and because he went into the hearing convinced that I was not telling the truth. Accounts suggest that he himself had a political stake in destroying me as a credible witness, now seeking the favor of conservatives who'd been outraged by his opposition to the nomination of Judge Robert Bork and his generally liberal position on "women's issues." All of which suggests that Specter had no intention of participating impartially in a fact-finding hearing. His conduct during the hearing only confirmed this. And Senator Cranston's message was lost on Arlen Specter as he and his Republican colleagues planned their strategy for the hearing.

After the *Today* interview on Tuesday morning, I tried to keep to my teaching schedule and to ignore the discussions taking place in Washington. I soon concluded that I had carved out an impossible task for myself. Though campus security had to escort me through the press barrage on my way to class and later that evening to my home, I did meet with my class that afternoon. It was important that I do so for two reasons, one altruistic, one selfish. First, I wanted my students to be disturbed as little as possible. Second, the classroom was the one place where my life still felt real to me; outside, it was all press conferences and television and newspaper interviews.

The two parts of my life came together on Tuesday afternoon. Though my students and I didn't discuss the day's events in class, they were on our minds. And as I concluded my introduction of the Material on Warranties in Contracts for Sales of Goods, Ovetta Vermillion interrupted my lecture to let me know that the Senate had voted unanimously to postpone the confirmation vote on Thomas and hold a hearing on my claim. I finished my lecture.

Afterward, I attended my second press conference. This time, following my own instincts, I declined to answer any questions except to say that I would cooperate with the committee and preferred that the matter be resolved in the hearing. To a disappointed press, anxious to get started on their own analysis of the content of my charges, I refused to say more. This was not a matter to be tried in the media and reduced to twenty-second sound bites.

The members of the Senate, however, thought differently. In addition to Senator Specter, who had concluded that no harassment had taken place and that my statement must therefore be false, Specter's colleague

John Danforth, Thomas' friend and mentor, stated that he had asked his friend if the allegations were true and that he believed Thomas' denial.

Earlier that afternoon a group of women legislators from the House side, including Representatives Patricia Schroeder of Colorado, Eleanor Holmes Norton of the District of Columbia, Barbara Boxer of California, and Louise Slaughter of New York, appeared at the regular luncheon of the Democratic senators. In a scene reminiscent of *The Wizard of Oz,* in which Dorothy Gale and her friends seek an audience with the Wizard and are turned away at the door, the congresswomen were told to go away and come back later, when Senator Mitchell had finished his dessert. In the meeting that followed, Mitchell advised the women to focus on Democrats like David Boren of Oklahoma, who had pledged to vote for Thomas, and try to enlist their support for a delay. Mitchell himself still seemed to want to avoid an active role in addressing this increasingly volatile issue. His reluctance would later provoke one woman to observe, "So much power and so little leadership."

CHAPTER NINE

The sentiments expressed in the senators' comments fell far short of demonstrating any responsibility to the confirmation process or to the upholding of the law. Instead Senator Orrin Hatch attacked the law governing sexual harassment itself, saying that it is "so broad that a person can accuse someone at any time and ruin their reputation."

The scope of the law of sexual harassment was alternately exaggerated and reduced by the senators in the days before the second round of the hearing. In contrast to Specter, who in effect limited the law to sexual assault or battery when he cited "the absence of any touching or intimidation" as a reason for disregarding my claim, Hatch perpetuated the idea that the law gives anyone license to challenge an individual's reputation on virtually any grounds.

Senator Hatch's baseless assessments tapped into a growing sentiment of distrust of civil rights laws. The law governing sexual harassment, found in Title VII of the Civil Rights Act, is undoubtedly the law to which he was referring. The Supreme Court recognized sexual harassment claims as valid in 1986, and the EEOC has promulgated specific guidelines for the investigation and evaluation of harassment claims. Federal law provides sanctions against a party who files a frivolous lawsuit. Statistically, the rate of frivolous sexual harassment claims is the same as for other types of claims: only about 3 percent. When investigators dismiss harassment complaints after a thorough investigation, they most often do so because of insufficient information as opposed to a conclusion that no harassment existed or that the claim was unfounded.

Hatch's statement harks back to an oft-quoted and equally erroneous statement made by an English judge who said that an accusation of rape is easy to make but difficult to disprove. A litany of facts about the crime of rape shows the total lack of merit in that claim. Many women who are victims of rape or sexual assault do not even discuss the matter with close friends because of the social stigma attached to being raped. Only one of ten rapes that occurs in this country is reported to law officials, making rape the most underreported crime. Convictions in rape trials are the most difficult to obtain of all criminal convictions, and sentencings for sex crimes the most lenient among sentencing for violent crimes. In 1995 a Pennsylvania court found that the prosecution had not proved the elements of rape, though it successfully showed that an intruder had broken into the complainant's home, thrown her to the bed, and assaulted her. The complainant resisted throughout, constantly saying, "No." The court based its findings of insufficient evidence on the fact that the assailant did not force the act upon her with a gun or a knife. In 1990 the jury acquitted two of five defendants in a notorious New York case involving the sexual assault of a woman whose assailants drugged her during the encounter. One juror, polled after the verdict, explained that his vote for acquittal was based on his belief that the nineteen-year-old plaintiff was a "scorned woman."

Sexual harassment is also an underreported offense. As I have said, only 3 percent of the incidents of sexual harassment culminate in a formal complaint being filed against the harasser. And by most accounts, employers rarely sanction those who are found to have harassed an employee or colleague. The same kinds of explanations offered for dismissals in rape cases are offered to dismiss sexual harassment claims.

Hatch's complaint described the law as overly broad. Senator Specter erred in the opposite direction, basing his decision to ignore my claim partly on the mistaken assumption that sexual harassment law governed only touching or threats. Under Specter's reasoning the only time sexual harassment is cognizable is when it includes sexual assault or battery. Since 1986, when the Supreme Court decided its first sexual harassment case, all courts have recognized not only the "quid pro quo" form of sexual harassment but the "hostile environment" form as well. Quid pro quo harassment is the equivalent of sexual extortion. A supervisor informs an employee that retaining her job or gaining promotion or raises is contingent on complying with sexual requests. Hostile environment harassment does not require the explicit threat of being dismissed, but can exist where the supervisor's or fellow employees' persistent unwanted sexual requests, comments, suggestions, or other conduct pervades the workplace, making it antagonistic or otherwise hostile. The law has never required unwanted touching as a prerequisite to a claim of sexual harassment. And underlying the recognition of the hostile environment form of sexual harassment is the assumption that certain workplace conditions can produce a level of intimidation even though the harasser does not assault the target or threaten retaliation for not acceding to sexual requests.

Whereas Hatch's overstatement lumps false and legitimate claims together in the minds of potential claimants and the public, Specter erroneously elevates the burden in a sexual harassment complaint to some tortious or criminal act, so that individuals who have not experienced physical contact or outright coercion at the hands of their harassers may wrongly conclude that they have no cause of action. Both statements are unfortunate reflections of the senators' ignorance, passed into the public domain as wisdom. Such flawed analyses from the mouths of public officials are worse than unfortunate on the eve of a hearing in which they are charged as fact finders. After all, since Congress is responsible for passing the legislation aimed at ending racial and gender discrimination in the workplace, the public assumes that members of Congress have some knowledge of those laws. Thus, the public is likely to be swayed when a senator espouses a position on the limits of the laws' protection. Faulty information, negligently or purposefully spread for partisan reasons, is particularly harmful when its source is a person in public trust.

As Tuesday, October 8, wore on, pressure mounted for a delay of the

Senate vote on the Thomas nomination. Once the Republican senators realized that a hearing on my claim was increasingly likely, the negative rhetoric escalated. The generalized comments and misrepresentations about sexual harassment turned into personal attacks on me. Like the rhetoric of the day popular in today's political campaigns, the pro-Thomas rhetoric was based more on aspersions to me than enthusiastic arguments for the candidate.

As the Senate debated a postponement of the vote, Senator Hatch displayed his ignorance of the issue of sexual harassment as well as his hostility to my claim. "She isn't some young, high school secretary," he said. "She's a Yale law graduate interested in civil rights and these issues and an expert on them." Over the course of the two preceding days, Hatch had declared my claim a political ploy. He had even accused Senator Metzenbaum of leaking the confidential FBI report to the press, though he later apologized for this unsupported accusation. While declaring that he took sexual harassment seriously and was sympathetic to its victims, Hatch had decided days before my testimony that my statements about my experience were untrue, apparently, at least in part, because I was too old and/or too educated to be sexually harassed.

When Senator Hatch said that I was not "some young, high school secretary" but "a Yale law graduate," his information was not faulty, but the conclusions he apparently drew from it were. First, Hatch may have meant that harassment is directed only at young women whose education does not include a college degree. In fact, women of all age groups and educational levels are victims of sexual harassment. And though I was twenty-five when I worked for Clarence Thomas, well within the range of twenty-two to thirty-five whom harassers tend to target, women in their forties, fifties, and sixties are also sexually harassed. Nor does a woman's education or profession exempt her. Dr. Frances Conley, a neurosurgeon at Stanford University, left her position there after years of experiencing sexual harassment and other forms of sex discrimination. One of the most patently offensive incidents occurred when one of her male colleagues fondled her under the operating table during a surgical procedure she was performing. In a 1989 survey, 52 percent of the women engineers polled reported that sexual harassment was the greatest frustration of their work. By suggesting that only high school secretaries are subject to sexual harassment, Hatch painted a picture of harassment victims that was misinformed and patronizing. He promoted a myth that excluded most of the workingwomen in the country from his sympathy, since most who experience harassment do not fit Hatch's description.

Hatch may also have been implying that lawyers, particularly those who graduate from Yale, are more likely to raise complaints about harassment than other women. Again he was wrong. While lawyers often defend the rights of others, there is no evidence that they are more forthcoming in complaints about violations of their own civil rights. I know of only one major case in which a woman lawyer brought a claim of sex discrimination against her employer, *Hishon v. King and Spaulding,* in 1980.

Most sexual harassment cases do not involve women lawyers as plaintiffs. Yet one should not conclude that sexual harassment does not exist in the profession or that women lawyers are not its targets. In a 1991 survey conducted by the American Bar Association's Committee on the Status of Women, four of five women lawyers said that they had experienced or witnessed incidents of sexual harassment in their workplace. Surveys from around the country support this finding. And women versed in civil rights law are no more likely to bring claims than other women lawyers. In 1994 a group of female attorneys with the NAACP, the oldest civil rights organization in the country, complained publicly for the first time about a pattern of gender bias that had existed in the NAACP for years. Their allegations included harassment-related charges as well as charges that women were not paid comparably to men in similar positions and were not promoted at the same rate as men. Despite their familiarity with civil rights law, these women did not sue to complain about violations of their civil rights. For years they attempted to deal with the matter internally. There is no factual basis for Hatch's implied assertion that women lawyers either are not victims of discrimination or are more likely to complain immediately.

Hatch may have been making an even more troubling, if veiled, assertion in his statement from the Senate floor: that well-educated older women do not deserve sympathy even if they *are* harassed. While women in these categories may be in a better position to complain about sexual harassment, they are still subject to the social and legal constraints that compel other women to remain silent. As court cases and empirical studies show, neither education nor professional achievement nor age insulates a woman from the attacks on character often waged if she raises a sexual harassment claim.

Hatch's misguided observation reminds me of a comment attributed in 1981 to Phyllis Schlafly of the conservative Eagle Foundation, who claims that men hardly ever ask sexual favors of women from whom the certain answer is no. Virtuous women are seldom accosted by unwelcomed sexual propositions or familiarities, obscene talk, or profane language. Accordingly, since virtuous women so seldom experience harassment, the numerous claims must be raised by women without virtue and thus society should not be concerned about it.

Stretching the imagination to assume that Schlafly is correct about the experiences of the virtuous woman does not resolve the problem. Schlafly still misses the point that the law is in place to protect a victim's civil rights, not her virtue. The issue of virtue has no bearing on the question of the law's application. Similarly, my age and education had no bearing on whether the behavior Thomas engaged in was offensive. After all, we do not require that a man who complains about a mugging show that he is a good person or even that he acted sensibly to prevent the mugging. Nor should we care in the case of a mugging whether the victim has other resources. We ask only that he show that he was mugged. Very often we conclude that he was by simply taking his word for it. Hatch and Schlafly reduce the issue of harassment to the question of who is most likable rather than whether there has been a violation of a person's civil rights. Schlafly stacks the deck by declaring that victims lack virtue. Senator Hatch did likewise by implicitly limiting the right to complain to young women with only a high school education.

Unfortunately, it is true that society is often less sympathetic to victims of sexual harassment who in its assessment ought to be able to take care of themselves. Hatch played on that lack of sympathy and missed the point altogether that the issue of the hearing was not sympathy for me but whether an individual who had engaged in harassing behavior should be appointed to a lifetime term to the country's court of last resort. Here again, context is important. If the character and fitness of the nominee are the central issue, the age, education, or profession of the complaining witness should not matter. For even if society is willing to say that it does not care about a particular category of harassment victims, it still must care about the qualities of a person who is to be appointed to the Supreme Court. In the debate about whether to delay the confirmation vote, Senator Jim Sasser of Tennessee reminded his colleagues of their "most profound responsibility to advise and consent" and their obligation "to the character of the judicial branch." The comments emanating from Washington in the days leading up to the hearing show that some in the Senate had lost sight of both.

Barbara Mikulski, Democrat of Maryland, also forcefully reminded her Senate colleagues of the message they would send to the American public if they decided to proceed with the vote. In clear terms, she warned them about wielding the Senate's power to attack a woman and pointed out the irony of wielding that power in the context of a claim about sexual harassment—behavior that is itself about the abuse of power.

> *What disturbs me as much as the allegations themselves is that the United States Senate appears not to take the charge of sexual harassment seriously. We have indicated that it was not serious enough to be raised as a question in the Judiciary Committee. We did not think it serious enough to apprise the Senators themselves that this was an allegation. . . . And then over here we have Professor Anita Hill. . . . She has come forth with pain because reliving this situation has indeed been extremely painful for her. If we do not give full airing to this, she will always be the woman who made these allegations. And*

now, we face the fact that even yesterday, Professor Hill was attacked on the Senate floor with unprecedented venom. A woman was attacked on the Senate floor with unprecedented venom when she was herself talking about being a victim. We owe it to Professor Hill not to attack her on the Senate floor, but to submit her to a line of question about the events that she alleges to see if, in fact, they are true. . . .

To anybody out there who wants to be a whistle-blower, the message is: Don't blow that whistle because you'll be left out there by yourself. To any victim of sexual harassment or sexual abuse or sexual violence either in the street or even in her own home, the message is nobody's going to take you seriously, not even the United States Senate.

While the senators displayed a lack of empathy with the experience of sexual harassment from the point of view of the target, they showed that they were well versed in the diversionary tactics used to attack individuals who raise claims of sexual harassment and to avoid any scrutiny of the alleged harassers. In the days before the hearing, senators denigrated my claim maliciously and with total disregard for its validity. Senator Strom Thurmond called the claim the "rantings of a disgruntled employee who had been reduced to lying." Senator Danforth called it "garbage" and "sleazy," expressing his concern for the sanctity of the U.S. Senate: "we can't have this body known as the trash dump of American politics." Senator Hatch described the charges as "trumped up." President Bush and his staff got involved as well. Marlin Fitzwater, veteran journalist and White House spokesperson at Kennebunkport, called the charges an attempted "smear," and the president summed up the attitude of the entire lot when he declared that he was "not in the least concerned" about the charges.

Surprisingly, the Senate voted unanimously to delay the vote on Thomas and hold a hearing on my claim. But during the debate Senator Danforth had given the speech that most likely compelled his colleagues to do so. He revealed that Judge Thomas himself wanted the hearing held to "clear his name." In hindsight I think the Senate's consent to the hearing was quite cynical. I believe that the Republicans who voted to hold the hearing did so because they felt that the idea of a public hearing would be so threatening that I would withdraw my complaint, or that even if I did appear they would be able to destroy me.

The tone was set for the hearing by many irresponsible and insupportable accusations. Hostile senators primed the public to despise my claim and the law from which it arose. The press contributed by publishing the misinformation with little attempt at balance. A 1992 *Columbia Journalism Review* study showed that the press coverage was biased in favor of Thomas, with his proponents quoted three times more often than those who favored a hearing on my claim. Thomas' family life and personal background were explored quite positively by the press for weeks prior to the leak. Before the hearing the press gave little attention to my background. *The New York Times* carried a major story about me featuring a photograph of my parents, but it was the only paper to do so. Only after the hearing did the press explore my background, and then only to prove or disprove this or that theory about my charges. With nothing to contradict them, hostile senators could portray me in any manner they chose. Once the hearing started, those same senators could paint my claim as bizarre or aberrant and therefore incredible, since credible information about sexual harassment was also absent from the press coverage.

The hearing had not started, but already five members of the Judiciary Committee had blasted my claim publicly. Despite the many errors in their statements, the press continued to pay great deference to the senators. Peter Jennings described them as "profoundly intelligent men." No member of the committee expressed a belief in the veracity of my claim. Those who did not actively campaign against it preferred to remain neutral.

I realized that I would go to Washington for a hearing but had only the sense from the statements of Senators Simpson, DeConcini, and Specter of what reaction to expect. David Boren, the Democratic senator from Oklahoma and a graduate of the University of Oklahoma School of Law, had not returned calls from Dean David Swank, who had begun calling him on Monday, October 7. Surely by now Senator Boren knew the reason for the call. But in an unmistakably political move Boren had already declared his support for Thomas, even before the Senate Judiciary Committee concluded its first hearing evaluating Thomas' competency for the position. Yet, neither Boren nor anyone on his staff has ever discussed any matter related to the hearing with me. Interestingly, on my subsequent return to Oklahoma, Lyle Boren, the senator's father and a former politician, made a concerted effort to contact me, calling the law school more than once until he reached me. The elder Mr. Boren, now deceased, apologized to me and told me of his embarrassment at his son's position during the hearing.

David Swank had also contacted Senator Don Nickles, Republican from Oklahoma, who *did* return the call, though he supported the Thomas nomination as well. During our conversation on Tuesday, October 8, he seemed uninterested in my claim. He talked instead about the difficulty of traveling from Oklahoma City to Washington, D.C. He also invited me and my family to visit his office for a tour if we were "out sight-seeing during your trip to Washington for the hearing." At the time, I declined his offer, and I rather doubt that I will be asked again. It was clear that despite the fact I was a voter in Oklahoma, I had no representation in Washington from either Boren or Nickles.

During the evening of October 8, I received a telephone call from Senator Joseph Biden, who formally informed me of the hearing. It was to be a public hearing that would convene "as early as Friday." This left me less than seventy-two hours to prepare. "Harriet Grant will help you with the witnesses," Biden said.

"How many witnesses will I be allowed to call?" I wanted more specifics than I had gotten from the committee before.

"Anita, I mean Professor, I assume that in addition to your testimony we will hear from Ms. Hoerchner," he responded. "You both will be subpoenaed by the committee. I strongly recommend that you contact someone who can talk about sexual harassment. I understand that Judge Thomas plans to call two coworkers as well as women who worked around him," he added.

Thomas seemed much more organized than I. I asked how the hearing would be conducted.

"Well, at this point the only thing we can do is to conduct an open hearing," he said, almost as if I were to blame. "I give you my word that I acted only to protect your confidentiality." He began to outline the measures he had taken to ensure that the press would not get my statement. But by now the leak of my statement was of little consequence to me. I had to begin the business of preparing to present my testimony to a hostile panel of senators.

"The only mistake I made, in my view, is to not realize how much pressure you were under. I should have been more aware," Senator Biden confessed over the telephone line. ". . . Aw kiddo I feel for you. I wish I weren't the chairman, I'd come to be your lawyer," he added when I told him I had not secured legal counsel. I fought the urge to respond as I furiously took notes of our conversation, hoping for some useful information. Little concrete information was forthcoming. As he closed the conversation, I could almost see him flashing his instant smile to convince both of us that the experience would be agreeable.

Though Senator Biden had offered members of his staff to assist me, including Grant and Ron Klain, past experience suggested that the staff would not be very helpful. That meant that I had to contact Sue Hoerchner myself and prepare "character witnesses" for a hearing that might begin fifteen hundred miles away "as early as Friday." Again, where process was concerned, I was at a complete disadvantage. And after making some telephone calls with very little result, I gave up. The whole thing was overwhelming. The only good news of the evening came when my brother Ray called to say that he would be in Norman the next day and would travel with me to Washington.

CHAPTER TEN

I woke early on Wednesday, October 9. I had no particular plan for the day or for the next few to follow. Though I had been getting advice from Sue Ross and Charles Ogletree, I had not approached them to represent me at the hearing. As I was not a member of the Oklahoma bar, I had very few contacts among lawyers in Oklahoma. I had long ago left Washington, and though I kept my bar membership there, I knew few practicing lawyers there either. I had no idea whom to enlist in such a situation. Nor could I even think of an analogous situation. This was not a sexual harassment claim, which would be brought in court. But I was not just a witness giving testimony to a neutral Senate committee; the campaign against my testimony had already begun. And though I had not been formally indicted, effectively I had become the accused.

At dawn I was sitting in my kitchen with my head in my hands, trying to gather the energy to move. I did not even have reservations to travel to Washington. When the telephone in front of me rang about 6:00 A.M., I took only seconds to answer it. On the other end was Emma Coleman Jordan, a professor at Georgetown Law Center, whom I knew from my work with the Association of American Law Schools. Professor Jordan, a black woman, was then president-elect of that group, and an outstanding scholar of commercial and banking law.

In her calm, take-charge fashion, Emma snapped me out of the near trance into which I had fallen. "Do you have legal counsel?" she asked.

"No, I don't," I said. Though my response must have shocked her, she remained calm. The hearing was to convene in forty-eight hours, and I had not even spoken to anyone about representing me. She told me that she had been in touch with several other law professors around the country and that they had proposed a list of people who would be good legal counsel in this situation. One of the people she spoke to was Professor Judith Resnik of the University of Southern California, whom I knew in passing from my days at Yale, where she had been on the law faculty. Judith Resnik had contacted John Frank, an Arizona lawyer whose firm would volunteer his time and the time of another lawyer to provide me representation. Frank, a constitutional scholar with expertise in the Supreme Court nomination process, had testified in the hearing on Judge Bork's nomination but had not been involved in the Thomas confirmation hearing to date. He also had Yale connections, having taught constitutional law there.

I did not know any of the people on the list, but Jordan assured me that she would see to it that they were all contacted about their availability. Unlike me, Jordan, along with other women who were concerned that the Senate conduct the hearing fairly, had developed a plan. That telephone conversation—I refer to it as the telephone call that saved my life—gave me the energy to move into action. I took down the names and told her I would get back to her with any thoughts I had. I quickly got dressed and went to the law school to ask my colleagues if they knew any of the lawyers on the list.

Chaos doesn't begin to describe the law school in the days immediately prior to the hearing. Reporters filled every open space; the telephones in the main office rang so often that the staff put them on mute; and emotions ran high, as everyone became consumed in the upheaval. My colleagues on the faculty pitched in to do what they could, taking telephone calls, fielding press inquiries, following up on leads, and trying to give direction to students whose concerns were quickly mounting. Some of the telephone calls and letters were from cranks; others, from people who wanted to offer information about Thomas' handling of sexual harassment claims within the EEOC, took too long to verify. We only had twenty-four hours before I would have to leave for Washington.

Two letters that proved invaluable emerged from the morass of information and paper. The first was from John Carr, a friend whom I met when I worked for Clarence Thomas. He'd been getting his law and business degree at the time and I kept in touch with him. He wrote to say that he recalled my telling him about the incidents with Thomas and was available to support my claim if he could. By midmorning Emma Jordan had pulled together several lawyers to help me, but we had no place to assemble. An overnight letter from Don Green, who had been a partner at the now defunct Wald, Harkrader firm and was now with Pepper, Hamilton and Scheetz, offered the firm's conference room as a meeting place for the legal team.

Ray arrived on schedule, and my nephew Eric picked him up at the airport. Poor Eric, then nineteen years old, seemed the one most baffled by the situation. He had always been very sensitive, and we had always been close, but I did not have time now to reassure him. The situation had us all baffled. Finally, it occurred to me that it might help if he could come along to Washington. He had to postpone a test to do so, but he got permission from his professor. Shirley Wiegand also asked if I wanted her to come along. At first I told her that I didn't think it would be necessary, but then I caught on to what she must have already realized: if things were as chaotic in Washington as they had been in Norman, I would absolutely need her help. She became the fourth in the party to travel to the hearing from Norman.

Meanwhile I contacted my sister JoAnn in Tulsa and my sister Joyce in California. JoAnn arranged for herself and my parents to travel to the hearing. My mother would turn eighty in a few days; my father in a few months. It would all have been easier to bear if I had had time to explain to them what had happened. But there was no time. Moreover, I didn't know much more than they did. No one had time for explanations; there was only time to organize ourselves. My brother Albert helped get my father to the barber and his suit to the cleaners. My brother Alfred picked up the dry-cleaned clothes and delivered them to my sister. Such was the level of our preparation for the hearing.

My sister Elreatha, also in Tulsa, decided to come as well. In California, Doris, Carlene, Joyce, and her daughter, Anita LaShelle, made plans for the trip. They would all arrive on Thursday evening. All the travel arrangements worked smoothly until JoAnn and my parents arrived at the airport in Tulsa to find that the charge privileges on my credit cards had been suspended. Even though I had not reached the credit limits, the number and amounts of charges for all the travel arrangements from around the country were such that the card companies were requiring a verification for any additional charges. Since they could not reach me, my parents' and sister's travel was temporarily stalled until other arrangements could be made.

With the help of campus security, Shirley, Ray, Eric, and I avoided the press on our way to the airport, but we boarded a plane filled with reporters making their way to Washington, D.C. On one leg of the trip, we sat in the rear of the plane and noticed that a man in our row was in handcuffs. I felt sorry for the poor fellow as the cameras panned to catch me and undoubtedly caught him too, handcuffs and all. Yet in a way I felt that we were all being taken into custody along with him. During the layover in St. Louis, airline security pulled a maneuver aimed at diverting the press in Washington to Dulles Airport instead of Washington National, where my flight would actually land. Some press people were fooled and so my arrival in Washington was perhaps the least publicized thing I had done in the last few days.

When we got to Washington that evening, airport security met us at the gate. We were tired, but all still fairly upbeat. Sonia Jarvis, my former roommate in Washington and friend since law school, and her friend Ray McFarland devised an ingenious plan to get me to the Capitol Hill Hotel without being followed by the press. It was worthy of a spy movie, requiring three vehicles and two drivers. One car followed closely the vehicle McFarland drove, in which I was a passenger. As we were about to enter the highway connecting the airport to Washington, the second driver faked a breakdown of his car, blocking the entrance ramp. This allowed McFarland and me to get a jump on the reporters and others who had been tailing the second driver. McFarland sped away, leaving his accomplice in a heated argument with the drivers behind him, and we had just enough time to switch to another car that was parked and waiting for us just inside the district. In a short time, we were at the door of the hotel. I checked in unobserved under the name J. C. West, conveniently borrowed from my friend Joy, who had made the hotel arrangements.

I awoke on Thursday morning feeling the hearing would begin in just over twenty-four hours with the public badly misinformed about sexual harassment. The steady campaign to discredit me was in full swing. Its obvious purpose was to persuade the public that my claim was baseless and that Thomas should be confirmed. The second purpose of the campaign was intimidation. The senators still hoped that the battle would not be fought in a hearing. Senator Biden had originally told me the subpoena would be delivered to me prior to my departure from Oklahoma. In fact, it was not served until Thursday, the day before my testimony, giving me ample time to retract my statement or otherwise capitulate—or perhaps to get into a fruitless and damaging war of words with the senators over the truth of the allegations before a public hearing could be held. With their press experience and contacts, the senators would undoubtedly have won such a battle.

I still do not know whether Senator Simpson's comment about the terrible treatment I could expect was primarily intended to keep me from testifying or merely to intensify anxiety during my testimony. But I do know that intimidating tactics are common in harassment suits. Defense counsel often issues warnings that range from manipulative ("You will ruin him and his family") to threatening ("You will be ruined"). In any case, when I did not withdraw prior to the hearing, the hostile senators attempted to establish as menacing a forum as possible, making good on Simpson's warnings of "real harassment." Behind the scenes, they maneuvered to make the hearing procedure as detrimental to my testimony as possible, well before my attorneys even arrived in Washington.

Sonia Jarvis picked me up at the hotel and took me to the law firm office to meet with my attorneys for the first time. All day various people came in and out of the conference room. I was uncomfortable with so many strangers involved, but with so little time to prepare, I could not carefully screen each individual. By midday several attorneys including Jarvis were present. Sue Ross and Emma Coleman Jordan, who live in Washington, were two of the first to arrive. John Frank and Janet Napolitano, who had taken the red-eye from Phoenix, arrived in midafternoon. Charles "Tree" Ogletree came in from Cambridge. He introduced Michelle Roberts, a trial attorney from Washington, to the group. Warner Gardner and Lloyd Cutler came at the invitation of John Frank. The numbers concerned me, but before I went over the statement I had prepared, each lawyer agreed that the discussion in that meeting was privileged—not to be shared with anyone.

The discussion was free-flowing and lively. Even in this group, no one had been involved in a procedure quite like this. Some attorneys thought the opening statement should be as detailed as possible; others disagreed. Lloyd Cutler in particular seemed uncomfortable with the idea that I should go into detail about the nature of the conduct I was complaining about. Cutler, a partner at one of the leading Washington law firms, Wilmer, Cutler and Pickering, had been counsel to President Jimmy Carter and had tried to save Robert Bork's nomination to the Supreme Court. After a break, he left the group. Though I never heard from him again, I assumed that he had made an assessment of the chances of my prevailing and had chosen not to be associated with my claim. At worst, I suspected that he would simply leave the team. But it was not crucial that he be there; though he had "insider" credentials in Washington, so did Gardner and, to a lesser extent, Frank.

In a clear breach of professional responsibility, however, Cutler went to the press and expressed concern about my testimony, revealing information that we had all agreed was privileged. He was cited as a source in a column by Lalley Weymouth that appeared in the *Wall Street Journal* after the hearing. The information Cutler had divulged was not only privileged but was largely erroneous. He told reporters that feminist scholar Catharine MacKinnon had been at the meeting. I had never met MacKinnon, and at no time was she at the meeting. In fact, we later learned that she'd been three thousand miles away in San Francisco. Despite their falsity, Cutler's disclosures would be used to discredit my claim—to suggest that others, like the absent MacKinnon, had put words into my mouth. My statement was based entirely on my own recollection. I made the decisions as to what to include in my testimony. Ironically, the one person who might have been described as a "handler" was the one who turned out to be the most untrustworthy. I learned that I was better off relying on my friends and other volunteers who were political amateurs than on Washington insiders skilled at trading information for political favors.

During the afternoon we decided that I needed more information to support my statements about how I spent my work time when employed by Clarence Thomas. I called Norman to ask Dean Swank to pick up the information. He was scheduled to arrive on Friday to serve as a character witness for me. When he and his assistant, Ovetta Vermillion, arrived at my home, they had to break into my house with a locksmith. They found the documents I needed amid the disarray I had left on Wednesday. Vermillion also found that a lighted lamp in my bedroom had been draped with a pillowcase. Under no circumstances would I have left a lamp in that condition. I concluded that someone must have broken into the house and attempted to set a fire. Any other time I might have panicked at the idea that my home was threatened while I was away. But at stake in Washington was something more important—my name, my integrity, and my right to be treated fairly. The situation at home was a disaster averted. Here, I did not know what disasters to expect, though I was certain they couldn't be far off. I simply focused on the next day's task.

Ellen Wells had been trying to contact me in Oklahoma, but was not able to reach me until I arrived in Washington. She, too, remembered my complaining about Thomas' behavior while I worked for him. And she was one witness who knew both me *and* Clarence Thomas. I was glad to see Ellen, not only because she could corroborate my testimony but also because she was a link to my former work that had survived the politics of the Thomas nomination.

Don Green appeared in the conference room from time to time. I had not seen him for ten years. He offered the room as a matter of professional courtesy as part of his responsibility to the confirmation process. I would remind commentators who criticized the offer as a show of partisan politics that even the criminally accused are entitled to adequate representation. For me personally, Green's offer was more than a courtesy. It was an offer of kindness, like so many during this time, that I will never forget and can never repay. At one point that Thursday, Green came in to advise me that the Senate had contacted him to ask why I had been "fired" from Wald. And though he told them that I had not been fired, they persisted with the accusation. Right after the hearing, John Burke, a former Wald partner, would swear that he had advised me to leave the firm—not the same as being fired, but enough to tarnish my professional reputation—though this wasn't true either.

During the day the press discovered our location. Then, as they had at my home in Norman, they staked out the building, as security would not allow them to enter. By that time two women had volunteered to handle press requests. Louise Hilsen and Wendy Sherman were veterans of Washington politics and press relations, Hilsen working for DeVillier Communications, Sherman formerly on Senator Barbara Mikulski's staff.

Though there was not complete disorder among my team, there was no clear order of command. Everyone did whatever was necessary to prepare me and the other witnesses for the following days and to provide the written material necessary for the hearing. Some talked to the witnesses, Hoerchner and Wells. Some focused on communicating with the Senate to get information about the process; others of us did things like copying and proofreading documents.

The day ended about 8:30, when I left to return to my hotel, escorted by Sonia and Anne Majorca, who had been on the Wald staff and was now working at Pepper, Hamilton. But the drama of the day continued when at least two vehicles followed as we drove away from the office building. Sonia evaded a van, but a motorcycle was harder to lose. She decided to pull into a police station on Capitol Hill, and as she did so the motorcycle driver sped away. But her day did not end when she left me. She still had to supervise the physical preparation of my statement, which Leslie McFarland, Ray's wife, would type.

By Thursday night a group of amateurs with very limited resources and not much time had accomplished a massive amount of work. The job they did would have been outstanding under any circumstances; under these circumstances it was nothing short of phenomenal. We were David against the Goliath of the White House, certain Republican senators, and, as I would later learn, the FBI. Yet when I went to bed that evening, I was content that we had acted with principle. And no matter the outcome of the hearing, my conscience was clear.

PART TWO

CHAPTER ELEVEN

On Friday, October 11, 1991, following three days of utter turmoil, I woke quite early. Kim Taylor, having flown in from California, had spent the night in the adjacent room. With little to do and uncertain about when I would appear for my testimony, I ironed her suit and helped her get ready for an appearance she made on my behalf on *CBS Morning News*. Hours later, after Kim left and I had dressed for the day, Sonia Jarvis and Charles Ogletree arrived at the room. We watched on the television set in the Capitol Hill Hotel as the hearing that would become known as the Hill-Thomas hearing opened.

In his opening statement Senator Biden decried the problem of sexual harassment and other forms of gender-related abuse or violence. "Sexual harassment is a serious matter," he began. Senator Biden insisted that "any person guilty of this offense is unsuited to serve not only the Nation's highest court, but any position of responsibility, of high responsibility in or out of government." Pausing, he further declared that "sexual harassment of working women is an issue of national concern." But a simple pronouncement could not make sexual harassment a national concern, much less the concern of some members of the Senate Judiciary Committee whose only objective right now was the confirmation of Clarence Thomas.

With that statement, however, Senator Biden set the stakes for the Republicans. He had declared that a harasser was unsuited for the Court.

Thomas' supporters were thus challenged to show that he was not a harasser. To do that, they would have to establish either that the acts I complained of were unoffensive or that I was simply fabricating the story. For the most part, the Republican senators chose the latter. While, on the evening before the hearing, Senator Biden had spoken about neutrality, Senator Thurmond apparently exclaimed, "Thomas is innocent, and we're going to prove it."

Biden was correct in his assessment of the severity of the widespread problem of sexual harassment in the workplace. Sexual harassment is a form of employment discrimination as defined in the EEOC guidelines and by case law. A party with a sexual harassment claim first files a complaint with the EEOC. That agency investigates the claim according to its own guidelines. Where warranted under the investigation, the EEOC can bring a suit against an employer or individual accused of sexual harassment. Alternatively, the agency can issue a right-to-sue letter which allows the individual to sue on her or his own behalf. For two decades prior to the hearing the problem of sexual harassment had been addressed under Title VII of the Civil Rights Act.

But as correct as Biden was in denouncing the problem, he was equally incorrect in assuming that the hearing about to convene was a proper forum for addressing it. From the sounding of the first gavel opening the hearing on October 11, the process was flawed. First, the committee had no experience in or rules for evaluating a claim of sexual harassment. Second, the committee had no rules for conducting the proceeding and chose instead to make the rules on an ad hoc basis, as the hearing evolved. Lack of experience and procedure detracted from the ability of the committee to reach a rational conclusion. Consequently, members of the committee resorted to one thing they did understand: partisan politics.

Though Senator Biden asserted that the committee had convened to hear evidence on charges of sexual harassment, he chose to deviate both from the EEOC guidelines governing investigations and findings of cause in such claims and from the procedures for hearing such claims developed in courts of law. In his opening statement Senator Biden declared first that standard rules of evidence would not apply to the hearing and second that Judge Thomas would at all times be given the benefit of the doubt. "The presumption [of truth] is with you, Judge Thomas." This presumption meant that if it were a case of my word against his, his would always be better. The EEOC guidelines presume nothing of the kind. In fact, those guidelines direct that the parties start as equally credible and that the balance is tipped by such things as contemporaneous declarations to other parties.

As Senator Biden put it, "this [was] an extraordinary hearing." Thus, he reasoned, the rules of law generally used for limiting questions, making speeches or statements, arguing with the witness, or even excluding irrelevant testimony would not apply. As the hearing proceeded without standard rules of evidence and guidelines for processing information, the relationship between such rules and guidelines and fairness became apparent more and more. The senators' tendency toward ad hoc rule making weighed in heavily against fairness. So apparent was this tendency that during the first day of testimony, the chair invited me to decide for the committee what rule of evidence should apply to a certain document. I knew then that the process had collapsed.

As the ranking Republican, Senator Thurmond also had his say in an opening statement. He, too, decried the problem of sexual harassment, but only briefly. The highlight of his statement was a chronicle of the nomination process that preceded this round of the confirmation process. His commitment to the nominee was clear in his praise for Thomas' integrity. Thurmond even asserted that not one of the witnesses had had anything bad to say about his character, though Thomas himself would later contradict Thurmond's assessment of the process by claiming that throughout his nomination claims of personal wrongdoing ranging from "drug abuse" to "anti-Semitism" to "wife-beating" had tainted the process. Yet to overpower the effect of my allegations, Thurmond recast Thomas as a person of unquestioned character, notwithstanding every other reservation voiced about his character. Thurmond followed his praise of Thomas with an attack on my statement, asserting that I had "chose[n] to publicize" my allegations the day before the vote, falsely indicating that I had voluntarily gone to the press with a claim and that the Senate had been unaware of it before the press stories appeared.

Each opening statement perfectly reflected what was about to take place. Biden spoke of fairness and objectivity and the desire to establish a proper procedure for getting to the truth. Thurmond's statement, on the other hand, laid out the objectives of the Republicans, which were to bolster the credibility of the nominee and to discredit my testimony. The Republicans charged ahead doing just that. Meanwhile, over the next few days, the committee's Democratic members bent over backward to show an impartiality that seemed at times honorable and at other times, if not cowardly, then certainly oblivious to the Republicans' tactics of misrepresentation.

While the Democrats set up a zone of neutrality between themselves and my statement, the Republicans fully embraced Thomas and all of his behavior in order to prove him not simply "innocent" but "the best man for the job." Once the cameras rolled, tempers started to flare and any sense of decorum was soon lost, as the senators either forgot the rules or deliberately avoided them. What followed was a chaos that pretended to order, a chaos disguised only by the politeness of the titles used to address the committee members, the stated rules of order, and the timekeeping.

The very first clash about process occurred when the Republican senators sought to introduce my statement of September 25 into the record during Judge Thomas' remarks on Friday morning, well before my actual appearance. Though contrary to Biden's early indications, Thomas was the first to speak. I agreed to that deviation from the process, but refused to allow the statement to be used prior to my appearance. Notwithstanding the leak, it was my statement, and I wanted it introduced when I was introduced. What soon surfaced was clear evidence of the senators' anger that "their" process was being disturbed by a woman who was of no political significance, alleging behavior that they claimed was so far outside their own experience as to be incomprehensible and perhaps irrelevant.

After listening to Thomas' "categorical denial" of all the behavior, an irate Senator Hatch denounced the decision to delay introduction of the statement and declared that no one was going to tell him what was to be admissible evidence in the hearing or when it would be admitted. He was prepared to decide on an ad hoc basis what was fair, and fairness to him meant the protection of the nominee's reputation from what he called "scurrilous allegations." Biden suggested that the committee recess to discuss procedure. Hatch objected, blaming unidentified parties within the committee for the inconvenience of the hearings to begin with.

"If somebody on this committee or their staff had had the honesty and the integrity before the vote to raise this issue and ask for an executive session and say this has to be brought—nobody did, and then somebody on this committee or their staff, and I am outraged by it, leaked that report, an FBI report that we all know should never be disclosed to the public, because of the materials that generally are in them," Hatch nearly ranted. The fastidious man in the dark suit with the buttoned-down collared shirt who appeared always in control now seemed anything but.

Hatch cleverly presented the sideshow of the leak perhaps in a hope that it would upstage the hearing or the claims I raised. Even more while decrying the leak and disclosure in the press, Senator Hatch himself engaged in leaking by referring to the contents of the statement and the FBI report. Without pointing to anything in particular, the senator talked about discrepancies between the two. Senator Hatch's strategy was ingenious. He could discredit me by pointing to inconsistencies that may have been nonexistent, negligible, or explicable, claiming he was held from proving his point by the confidentiality of the documents. Senator DeConcini, who also indicated his belief in Thomas' truthfulness, echoed Senator Hatch's undefined allegations of inconsistencies.

From my hotel room I watched the proceedings, astounded by the absurdity of it all, yet questioning whether I could begin to be objective. Hatch's tactics were clearly aimed at bullying the committee and the public into denouncing the claims I raised. Yet I was so shocked and overtaken by feelings of insecurity at the situation in which I found myself that I did not question the spectacle developing. Nor did Ogletree or Jarvis, who watched the opening with me. We just stared in disbelief—even Jarvis, who is never at a loss for words.

Over Senator Hatch's protest the committee convened to consider how to proceed with the hearing. During the recess Senator Biden's office contacted me. When the committee readjourned, Chair Biden announced that I had agreed to release my statement to the Senate at the time of my testimony. Though this had always been my understanding, Biden announced it as though it were a new development. Still, Senator Hatch remained unsatisfied, objecting that the FBI report should be open to discussion by the committee, and threatening to resign from the committee if it wasn't. "To be fair to the nominee," Hatch argued that the confidential document must be publicly discussed. Indeed, after the hearing adjourned, the FBI report fell into the hands of writer and conservative commentator David Brock. Brock quotes from its text in his book *The Real Anita Hill,* suggesting that he had access to those sealed documents.

Thus, even the first hour of the first day of the hearing revealed the truth in Biden's observation: this was to be an "extraordinary proceeding." Hatch declared aloud what Senator Thurmond had only implied. Order and impartiality were dispensable as the twofold Republican agenda became clear.

Having settled the quarrel about the rules, and then recovered from my family's disorderly entry, at 11:00 A.M. Senator Biden began his questioning of me. The thirty-minute quizzing period began with general inquiries about my background and professional life. Gradually, the questions became more specific and focused on Thomas' behavior at Education and EEOC.

"Let's go back to the first time that you alleged Judge Thomas indicated he had more than a professional interest in you," Senator Biden approached the subject of harassment in a matter-of-fact way. "Do you recall what the first time was and, with as much precision as you can, what he said to you?"

"It either happened at lunch or it happened in his office when he said to me, very casually, you ought to go out with me sometime . . . ," I recalled.

"Was that the extent of that incident?"

"That was the extent of that incident . . . I declined and, at that incident, I think he may have said something about, you know, he didn't understand why I didn't want to go out with him. . . ."

"Would you describe for the committee how you felt at that time when he asked you out? What was your reaction?" the senator questioned.

To describe what took place was difficult, but the emotional impact of having to recall my feelings about what had happened was monumental. I struggled to keep calm. "Well, my reaction at that time was a little surprised, because I had not indicated to him in any way that I knew of that I was interested in dating him. We had developed a good working relationship. It was cordial and it was very comfortable, so I was surprised that he was interested in something else."

The logistics of making arrangments to travel to Washington, informing and gathering my family, friends, and advisers together, had left me little time to prepare for my testimony. Yet as the questioning began I realized that no amount of preparation could have made it easy to address the kinds of questions that, ultimately, Biden asked. Senator Biden's tone became even more somber.

"Now I must ask you to describe once again, and more fully, the behavior that you have alleged [Thomas] engaged in while your boss which you say went beyond the professional conventions and were unwelcome to you. Now, I know these are difficult to discuss, but you must understand that we have to ask you about the . . ."

Perhaps to ease the impact of the intrusion into my memory, Biden asked the question differently. "Did all of the behavior that you have described to us in your written statement to the committee and your oral statement now and what you have said to the FBI, did all of that behavior take place at work?"

"Yes, it did . . . if you are including a luncheon during the workday to be at work, yes," I responded, thankful for the new approach.

But further probing was inevitable, and in short time the senator asked the question which had to be asked: "Can you tell me what incidents occurred, of the ones you described to us, occurred in his office?"

"Well, I recall specifically that the incident involving the Coke can occurred in his office at the EEOC."

"And what was that incident, again?" Biden asked.

"The incident with regard to the Coke can, that statement?" I said, perhaps hoping to avoid repeating what had so disgusted me at the time, having already described it once in the opening statement.

But Biden would not allow me to avoid the matter. He would not rely on the testimony I had given. "Once again for me, please," he half asked, half insisted.

Gradually, something moved from the pit of my stomach and expanded until it became a tightness in my chest. "The incident involved his getting up from a work table, going to his desk, looking at this can and saying, 'Who put pubic hair on my Coke?' "

At once, I was twenty-five years old again, standing in the middle of Thomas' office. By that time I had had several jobs and worked with many different people, but never before had anyone ever uttered such an absurdly vulgar and juvenile comment to me. Disgusted and shocked, I could only shake my head and leave the office. I heard him laughing as I closed the door.

The lapse was temporary. Biden's next question brought me back to the reality of my present situation. In its way it was equally shocking. "Was anyone else in his office at the time?" Biden asked.

"No."

"Are there any other incidents that occurred in his office?"

"I recall at least one instance in his office at the EEOC where he discussed some pornographic material and he brought up the substance or the content of pornographic material."

Chairman: "Again, it is difficult, but for the record, . . . what was the content of what he said?"

I probed my memory for the details the committee seemed to require.

"This was a reference to an individual who had a very large penis and he used the name that he had referred to in the pornographic material—."

Senator Biden: "Do you recall what it was?"

"Yes, I do. The name that was referred to was Long Dong Silver," I recalled.

But these details of what had happened would not satisfy the committee. Senator Biden wanted more. "Can you tell us how you felt at the time?"

I collected myself in order to respond. "I felt embarrassed. I had given him an explanation that I thought it was not good for me, as an employee working directly for him, to go out with him. I thought that he did not take seriously my decision to say 'no,' and that he did not respect my having said 'no' to him." I did not know any better words to explain to someone with power how it felt to be utterly powerless. Like my grandfather Henery Elliott, confronted by his white neighbor, my race (and for me my gender) gave me no right to say no to those whose gender and/or race gave them the right to decide for you. I was no better off than my grandmother Ida Elliott, who in the retelling of the story appears never to have been consulted in the matter.

"I—the conversations about sex, I was much more embarrassed and humiliated by. The two combined really made me feel sort of helpless in a job situation because I really wanted to do the work that I was doing, I enjoyed that work. But I felt that was being put in jeopardy by the other things that were going on in the office. I was really, really very troubled by it and distressed over it." I strained to define feelings that were so basic that defining words seemed unnecessary. Nevertheless, they were feelings so foreign to the committee members that full explanations were imperative if they were to understand.

"Can you tell the committee what was the most embarrassing of all the incidents that you have alleged?"

In the back of my mind I knew that by reciting the details of my experiences I was simply responding to those who claimed that I had overreacted to Thomas' remarks. Perhaps even Biden himself believed that the behavior which I complained about was inoffensive. Knowing why I was being asked to repeat details of the experience did not make it any easier. Yet I tried to keep the purpose in mind as I struggled to recite more of the behavior.

"I think the one that was the most embarrassing was this discussion of pornography involving women with large breasts and engaged in a variety of sex with different people or animals. That was the thing that embarrassed me the most and made me feel the most humiliated."

"If you can, in his words—not your—in his words, can you tell us what, on that occasion, he said to you?" the senator asked, seeking even more particulars.

Within the first hour of my appearance before the committee I was asked to repeat details of experiences which I had already forced myself to describe first to Metzenbaum and staff attorney Jim Brudney, then to the committee in my written statement of September 23, then to the FBI, and finally in my opening statement. Inherent in these demands for repetition was a fundamental hostility to the claim, as though each time what I had said before had been insufficient. "Tell us . . . once again . . . what was the most embarrassing . . . in order for us to determine." The hearing had only begun and I found myself wondering, "How many times . . . how much detail . . . how vulgar did the language have to be and . . . how uncomfortable do I have to feel in order for [them] to comprehend what happened to me?" By the end of the day, I would conclude that no amount of detail would satisfy the committee, though at no point during the day's questioning would I consider withdrawing.

"My time is up," Biden announced just before noon. "By the way, I might state for the record, once again we have agreed that we will go back and forth: half-hour conversation on each side. . . ." I had not been a part of this agreement that in essence the Democrats and Republicans would take turns with me.

"Let me yield to my friend from Pennsylvania, Senator Specter," Biden said, concluding his "turn," as Senator Specter prepared for his thirty-minute "conversation" with me.

Specter began by assuring me that he was simply trying "to find out what happened." But I was well aware of Specter's public statement that he had already concluded that he believed Thomas' denials. I thanked him when he asserted that he did not view the hearing "as an adversarial proceeding," still hoping that he would move beyond his initial reaction to the claim and see that his "duties [ran] . . . to the constitutional government and the Constitution." As an attorney he might have placed the significance of a Supreme Court appointment over the partisanship that had prevailed in the debate over whether or not to hold the hearing. Nevertheless, in short order, any hope that Senator Specter would transcend the political was dashed. He began his questioning with an unmistakably prosecutorial tone. He used a familiar cross-examination tactic—a tactic common in sexual harassment cases. He ridiculed my reaction to Thomas' behavior, suggesting that I was being oversensitive, even to the point of misrepresenting my testimony.

"Professor Hill, I can understand that it is uncomfortable, and I don't want to add to that." But his emulation of concern immediately turned to condescension. "You testified this morning, in response to Senator Biden, that the most embarrassing question involved—this is not too bad—women's large breasts. That is a word we use all the time. That was the most embarrassing aspect of what Judge Thomas had said to you."

"No. The most embarrassing aspect was his description of the acts of these individuals, these women, the acts that those particular people would engage in. It wasn't just the breasts; it was the continuation of his story about what happened in those films with the people with this characteristic, physical characteristic," I responded, trying to control my outrage. Senator Specter had taken this mortifying episode of my life in which my supervisor had described to me acts of bestiality and had deliberately reduced its offending elements to the use of the term "breasts," which, witheringly, he had dismissed as "not too bad." Despite the graphic details I had already described, Senator Specter ignored the numerous sexual references far more contemptible than anything merely anatomical and chose to focus on the innocuous-sounding word "breast," suggesting that I was overreacting. Of course, any woman who has ever been made to feel uncomfortable about the size of her breasts would know that even *this* term could be used to embarrass or demean.

By ignoring the far more contemptible and numerous explicit sexual references, the senator focused attention away from Thomas and his behavior and attempted to render a caricature of me and my standard of the offensiveness. A typical reaction to complaints of harassment, Senator Specter's scoffing portrayed me as the silly prude who can't handle normal adult conversation. But even if the senator had correctly reported my testimony, his portrayal of my experience as "not too bad" would nevertheless be inaccurate. Reference to breasts alone could certainly be demeaning. And a supervisor's constant references to women's breasts or breast size could be more damaging yet. Senator Specter's suggestion that a reference to a woman's breast was not a "bad" thing ignored the fact that the workplace is rarely a place where women go to discuss their own anatomy or the anatomy of other women, particularly when the discussion is of a sexual nature.

Though Senator Specter's announced purpose was "to find out what happened," his questions differed in tone and in substance from those of his Democratic colleagues. Almost immediately, Senator Specter seemed to be searching for inconsistencies between my statement and my testimony. I had found Senator Biden's questions difficult and embarrassing enough. And later in the day both Senators Howell Heflin and Patrick Leahy would ask similarly invasive questions about the substance of the claim and my motivation in my coming forward. But Specter's questions often required me to reconcile the details of my statement with comments made by others—comments about which I had no firsthand knowledge. Soon after his turn to question me arrived, Senator Specter began asking my reaction to various off-the-record statements made by Stanley Grayson, Carlton Stewart, Charles Kothe, John Doggett, and

Phyllis Berry, all of whom would later appear as witnesses for Judge Thomas and none of whom I'd spoken to in years. This line of questioning gave the Republicans two advantages: it put unsworn, speculative statements that portrayed me negatively into the record; and it required me to defend, without any notice, comments for which I had no framework or background.

"There is a question about Phyllis Berry who was quoted in the *New York Times* on October 7. 'In an interview Ms. Berry suggested that the allegations,' referring to your allegations, 'were the result of Ms. Hill's disappointment and frustration that Mr. Thomas did not show any sexual interest in her.' " The senator read Ms. Berry's remarks into the record as though her authority to comment had been established.

"You were asked about Ms. Berry at the interview on October 9 and reported to have said, 'Well, I don't know Phyllis Berry and she doesn't know me.' And there are quite a few people who have come forward to say that they saw you and Ms. Berry together and that you knew each other very well." Senator Specter once again took the comments I made out of the context in which I made them.

"I would disagree with that. Ms. Berry worked at the EEOC. She did attend some staff meetings at the EEOC. We were not close friends. We did not socialize together and she has no basis for making a comment about my social interests with regard to Clarence Thomas or anyone else." I attempted to explain, as I had in the press conference, that not only was Ms. Berry's statement wrong, incredibly wrong, she had had no basis for making such a statement. In fact, Ms. Berry undermined her authority to make such a statement about my personal interests in her own testimony. On Sunday, when called by the panel, she would testify that she had found me aloof and detached.

When asked about Ms. Berry's statement at the press conference on Monday, October 7, I had found myself wondering who she was, recalling her only vaguely and mostly just by name. Because I could not believe that her comment was being taken seriously, my response was rather casual. No one who knew me would have asserted that I had a sexual interest in Clarence Thomas, much less that I had been frustrated by a lack of attention on his part. Phyllis Berry and I were, at best, passing acquaintances. In fact, when pressed on the issue at the hearing, even Berry cited nothing that would lead her to reach such a conclusion. At the hearing Specter wanted me to respond to Ms. Berry's foolish comment, as well as to the suggestion by "quite a few people" that we "knew each other very well," and he gave no focus to Berry's admission that she had no basis for her statement about me to begin with. Senator Specter continued to rely on off-the-record comments as the source of his questions—an inherently flawed method for "find(ing) out what happened" in a formal proceeding where sworn testimony was available to the panel. It became apparent that I, like other harassment victims, would suffer from indictment by speculation and conjecture.

Later, Senator Specter asked my response to a comment appearing in *USA Today*. "Professor Hill, the *USA Today* reported on October 9th, 'Anita Hill was told by Senate staffers her signed affidavit alleging sexual harassment by Clarence Thomas would be the instrument that "quietly and behind the scenes" would force him to withdraw his name.' Was *USA Today* correct on that, attributing it to a man named Mr. Keith Henderson, a 10-year friend of Hill and former Senate Judiciary Committee staffer?"

"I do not recall. I guess—did I say that? I don't understand who said what in that quotation," I responded, genuinely confused by the question and the statement.

Specter's phrasing was confusing. I could not determine whether the senator was asking me to verify whether Henderson had made the statement to *USA Today*, whether I had made the statement to Henderson, or whether a Senate staffer had made such a statement to Henderson or to me. I had known Keith Henderson since my days in Washington, D.C., and despite our regular arguments about policies and politics, we were the best of friends. Keith, who is white and approximately my own age, had grown up in the South and was genuinely concerned about race relations and discrimination. But no matter how well intentioned he was, his solutions often seemed to rely on my willingness to adopt his thinking and approach to solving problems which I, not he, had experienced firsthand. I sometimes rejected his point of view on principle; other times out of my own sheer stubbornness.

After sending my statement to the Senate, I had spoken with Keith Henderson to determine whether he could discover whether the committee had received my statement. I knew that he had experience working on Capitol Hill, and I felt that I could trust him. My inquiry was not a request for substantive advice about sexual harassment or about the nomination itself. It was a request for information about the procedures for communicating with the committee. Never did I say to Henderson anything close to what the press account alleged. And a court of law would have regarded the newspaper statement as triple hearsay. It was what the newspaper *claimed* that Keith Henderson had *claimed* that a Senate staffer had said to me. Even if I had tried to make a comment testifying to what a staffer had told me, my own testimony would have been considered hearsay, since I would have been one party removed from the speaker, attempting to testify to what someone had said to me. And if a newspaper quotes me in an article or report, that quotation is, of course, hearsay, as are all newspaper quotes; they represent what the newspaper says someone else said.

Generally, the law assumes that hearsay is suspect. With certain exceptions, in a court of law hearsay is inadmissible. Rather than have one person testify about what someone else told them, the law prefers to have the party who supposedly made the statement testify. That party is then subject to cross-examination on that testimony. The problem with unreliability combined with the fact that no cross-examination is possible demonstrates why only excepted hearsay is admissible. By the time a comment attributed to one party gets repeated and interpreted again, it is likely to vary greatly from the original comment and may bear no resemblance at all to the original. The problem with the question about the *USA Today* quote, of which I was not offered a copy, was not only that it relied on triple hearsay but that it was confusing as well. The newspaper's subsequent retraction of the attribution of these comments to Keith Henderson underscores the need for such rules that limit the kind of evidence that can be admitted. In this situation, absent any rules of evidence, Senator Specter was allowed to introduce gross misinformation into a public forum without any accountability for the accuracy or truth of the information.

Nevertheless, rather than explain the question or the point that he was making, Specter pressed forward, reading the newspaper account once again and making certain that the information was in the record, despite the facts that it was hearsay, that I knew nothing about it, and that there was no basis on which to cross-examine the source of the information.

"Well, let me go on," he said. "Keith Henderson, a 10-year friend of Hill and former Senate Judiciary Committee staffer, says Hill was advised by Senate staffers that her charge would be kept secret and her name kept from public scrutiny." Senator Specter was once again able to introduce off-the-cuff comments into the record as though they had validity and relevance.

"They would," he continued, apparently referring again to Mr. Henderson's statement, "they would approach Judge Thomas with the information, and he would withdraw and not turn this into a big story, Henderson says."

Finally having completed his goal of creating a record with unsworn testimony, Senator Specter asked his question: "Did anybody ever tell you that, by providing the statement, that there would be a move to request Judge Thomas to withdraw his nomination?"

"I don't recall any story about pressing, using this to press anyone."

"Well, do you recall anything at all about anything related to that?" Senator Specter continued pressing for the answer he wanted.

"I think that I was told that my statement would be shown to Judge Thomas, and I agreed to that," I answered.

"But was there any suggestion, however slight, that the statement with these serious charges would result in a withdrawal so that it wouldn't have to be necessary for your identity to be known or for you to come forward under circumstances like these?"

By this time I was beginning to be worn down by Specter's methodology. Not only did his questions rely on unsubstantiated comments, but they kept changing in substance.

"There was—no, not that I recall. I don't recall anything being said about him being pressed to resign," I said, still attempting to respond to the first question.

"Well this would only have happened in the course of the past month or so, because all this started in just early September." At this point Specter moved from questioning to arguing by suggesting not only that the conversation with the staffer had occurred but that I should recall it.

"I understand," I responded. Had I been clearer of Specter's purpose, I would have advised him of the reason that I could not recall such a conversation. This was my weakness—I assumed a level of honesty in the questioning that did not exist.

"So that when you say you don't recall, I would ask you to search your memory on this point, and perhaps we might begin—and this is an important subject—about the initiation of this entire matter with respect to Senate staffers who talked to you. But that is going to be too long for the few minutes that I have left so I would ask you once again . . ."

"Well I can't really tell you any more than what I have said. I discussed what the alternatives were, what might happen with this affidavit that I submitted. We talked about the possibility of the Senate Committee coming back for more information. We talked about the possibility of the FBI, asking, going to the FBI and getting more information; some questions from individual Senators. I just, the statement that you are referring to, I really can't verify."

Unsatisfied with the answer, the Senator came back, "Well, when you talk about the Senate coming back for more information or the FBI coming back for more information or Senators coming back for more information that has nothing to do at all with Judge Thomas withdrawing, so that when you testified a few moments ago that there might possibly have been a conversation, in response to my question about a possible withdrawal, I would press you on that, Professor Hill, in this context: You have testified with some specificity about what happened

10 years ago. I would ask you to press your recollection as to what happened within the last month."

"And I have done that, Senator, and I don't recall that comment. . . . May I just add this one thing?"

"Sure." Senator Specter was by now exasperated.

"The nature of that kind of conversation that you're talking about is very different from the nature of the conversation that I recall. The conversations that I recall were much more vivid. They were more explicit. The conversations that I have had with the staff over the last few days in particular have become much more blurry, but these are vivid events that I recall from even eight years ago when they happened, and they are going to stand out much more in my mind than a telephone conversation. They were one-on-one, personal conversations, as a matter of fact, and that adds to why they are much more easily recalled. I am sure that there are some comments that I do not recall the exact nature of from that period, as well, but these that are here are ones that I do recall."

"Over the luncheon break, I would ask you to think further, if there is any way you can shed any further light on that question, because I think it is an important one." Of course the best way to shed light on the question would have been to call the staffers to testify as to who spoke to me. Specter never suggested that. Perhaps this would have been too invasive of the purview of the Senate. Perhaps Specter knew that no senator would have tolerated having a staff member questioned in the manner that he questioned me.

Specter's short-lived pretense of objectivity soon turned into an inquisitional performance that seemed to be directed as much to the television cameras as to me. When I allowed myself to think of it, the presence of the press was at once intrusive and reassuring. I did not relish saying the things I had to say on national television. Yet I hoped that the senators might temper their accusations and condemnations under the watchful eye of the media. I found no sympathy for my situation among the media. They were there for the story. Moreover, the hot glare of the lights and cameras and their sheer numbers left me cold inside.

Over the course of the morning as the questioning intensified, the room, SD–325, became unbearably warm from the lights as much as from the subject matter of the questions. I reached up to wipe oil from my nose. A hundred cameras flashed in response to that simple act—an act that was so natural to me that I had to think to realize what had prompted the photographers' sudden interest. No doubt they anticipated some drama—something momentous that might turn the entire proceeding. They wanted to capture the moment on film as it occurred but this was not such a moment. I was simply responding to a lifelong problem—skin which oiled up in the slightest bit of heat.

"Don't move," I told myself, freezing almost in midmotion. I resolved to become as motionless as possible. I had to be impervious to the lights and to the heat as well as the natural reactions of my body. Though I felt each one of the senators' attempts to humiliate me, I vowed not to so much as twitch. I ignored the numbness in my legs and even the pain from the tumors in my abdomen. From that moment on, I did not even take a drink of water in front of the camera. I ignored my dry throat. I sat throughout the "conversations" with the Republicans and Democrats with my hands in front of me and only occasionally would I even lean forward. Oddly enough, this exercise in self-control enabled me to focus on the questioning. Or perhaps it was some sort of divine intervention, some force from outside myself that took over when I needed it. And, of course, years of being impervious to and immobile in the face of hurt.

My family and friends gave me the only comfort of that day, though I grew more and more ambivalent about their presence in the room as the questioning became more invasive and the veiled accusations more apparent. I thought how hard this must be on them. They had to sit in silence throughout it. Behind me my father was seething with anger and frustration at his helplessness to do anything about what was happening to me—to his family. But I could not think of them any more than I could of my own personal discomfort.

It was 1:10 P.M. I had been testifying for two hours. When we broke for the first time, I was able to talk to my family. Everyone put a good face on during the break. It is our way. In the Senate office room that had become our ad hoc headquarters, we talked briefly about nothing in particular, all of us remarkably calm. Or perhaps we were just numb. There was no time to analyze what we felt before. Reverend William Harris, a pastor from the church that Emma Coleman Jordan attended, came and prayed with us while my legal advisers dashed about trying to get copies of the statements Specter was using in his questioning. All except for Warner Gardner, who, over a tuna sandwich, engaged me in a pleasant conversation, relating to the hearing only minimally. If he was attempting to divert my attention from the raptures of the proceedings, then it worked, at least for the moment.

But the processional of the twenty family, lawyers, and friends, led by two Secret Service escorts, wound its way back down the high-ceiling corridor of the Russell Building to the caucus room and the afternoon session. It was 2:15.

CHAPTER TWELVE

When the hearing readjourned that afternoon, Senator Heflin broached the subject of the *USA Today* report of the Henderson interview.

"Well, during any conversation with Keith Henderson, did you tell him that certain staffers had told you that if you went ahead and signed the affidavit, that might be a way to get [Judge Thomas] to withdraw?" Senator Heflin's tone was deliberate—confident. It was, in litigation terminology, an attempt to redirect—to clarify or reestablish the testimony I had given in the morning.

"No, I did not tell him that," I answered, grateful to be able to respond to a direct question about the newspaper article.

"Well, did you tell him that that was mentioned or that it would have been mentioned relative to this?" Senator Heflin asked.

"No, I didn't tell him that."

"Do you know whether or not Keith Henderson talked to certain Judiciary Committee staffers?"

"I don't know whether he did talk to Judiciary Committee staffers."

"Well, do you know whether or not there was a conversation between Keith Henderson and some staffer in which they were discussing the affidavit and saying that there were certain possibilities, which included the possibility that Clarence Thomas might withdraw his name?"

"That might have happened, but I haven't talked with Keith Hender-

son about that," I answered, hoping that this discussion would put an end
to the matter. I did not know what any Senate staff had said to Henderson, nor what he might have said to them. This much I did know: no
staffer ever promised me that Thomas would withdraw as a result of my
statement.

Later, Senator Specter would return to the same line of questioning.
In that exchange I allowed that Thomas' withdrawal might have been
discussed because of the procedure which would follow from my raising
the claim. This was a foolish concession, for I was uncertain whether that
particular possibility was raised, and any concession on my part would
only be used against me by the Republicans. At the time of my conversations with Senate staffers, no one had any idea of what was going to
happen. When I gave my statement to the Senate on September 23, I am
not certain that the staff even knew what process they would follow,
much less how Thomas would respond. Nevertheless, Specter continued
to press for a contradiction. "And now are you testifying that Mr. Brudney said that if you came forward and made representations as to what
you said happened between you and Judge Thomas that Judge Thomas
might withdraw his nomination?"

"I was attempting, in talking to the staff, to understand how the
information would be used, what I would have to do, what might be the
outcome of such a use. We talked about a number of possibilities, but
there was never any indication that, by simply making these allegations,
the nominee would withdraw from the process. No one ever said that,
and I did not say that anyone ever said that."

The tension between Senator Specter and me was measurable. The
process seemed to break down completely. Senator Specter would repeat
the same question until he got the answer he wanted—that a staffer
induced me to come forward with the story with a promise Thomas
would withdraw. Specter was only more provoked by admission that
Thomas' withdrawal might have been mentioned. In a court of law,
Specter's questioning would have been limited. A court might have
stopped him from repeating questions asked and answered previously or
even admonished him for arguing with or badgering the witness. But this

was not a court, as Biden had informed us from the start, and Biden was exercising little authority as chairman to limit the form of questions.

To the press and spectators, we must have sounded silly and ill tempered. More than one sigh erupted from the seats behind me as Specter returned to the questioning and I once more gave my explanation. Clearly, neither of us would budge from our position. Something in the back of my head said, "Just say what he wants you to say and get on with it." But I was much too stubborn to do that. And the more he pursued it, the more inclined I was to resist. Digging in was, perhaps, for me one way of hanging on to some amount of my dignity. By now I knew that his questions were both insincere and ill informed. Though I tried to answer him, I was equally determined that the senator not put words in my mouth. With every question he asked, it became clearer that despite any declaration to the contrary, he viewed me as an adversary. Rather than seeking to elicit information, his questioning sought to elicit a conclusion that he had reached before the hearing began. When he questioned me about comments I had made to a *Kansas City Star* reporter, his purpose of finding some inconsistency in my account became ever clearer.

"When you say that Judge Thomas would have made a better Supreme Court Justice, you are saying that, at one state of his career, he would have made an adequate Supreme Court Justice."

"Well, I am not sure that that's what I am saying at all. I am sure that what I was trying to give to that reporter was my assessment of him objectively without considering the personal information that I had." I had caught on to the fact that I could concede nothing in responding to Senator Specter.

"Isn't the long and short of it, Professor Hill, that when you spoke to the *Kansas City Star* reporter, that you were saying, at one point in his career he would have been okay for the Supreme Court?"

Explaining my feelings to this man was useless, for whatever I said he would doubt. Even inconsequential responses met with his skepticism. "No," I responded with no intention of saying any more. I had tired of his tactics. There was a pause of about twenty seconds. Perhaps the longest of the day. Neither of us spoke. The silence was palpable and intense. It seemed the room had grown accustomed to my explaining myself, but by now I was weary of it.

Finally, the senator broke the silence. "What were you saying as to Judge Thomas's qualifications for the Supreme Court when you spoke to the reporter in August?" For the first time in his questioning, Senator Specter asked me what I was saying instead of suggesting what I had said.

"One of the comments that the reporter made was that some have complained that he has a set ideology and that he won't be able to review cases on their own. My comment went to whether or not he did have that set ideology and it was that now he did, whereas a few years ago, I did not find that to be so."

Senator Specter's more open-ended question gave me a chance to explain myself. This form of question is asked in order to elicit information from witnesses believed to be trustworthy. In a nonadversarial, fact-finding hearing, the more open-ended questioning is appropriate because it allows for a greater exchange of information without assuming a conclusion. This was a small victory in what had become a battle of wills.

Senator Specter's questioning on the *USA Today* article was an attempt to indict Jim Brudney of Senator Metzenbaum's office. Senator Specter hoped to get me to say that Brudney had promised me that if I signed the affidavit, Judge Thomas would withdraw. This would lend support to the theory offered by Senator Hatch that my statement was a part of a Democratic conspiracy to derail the nomination. When the public demanded a hearing on my charges, Senator Hatch accused Senator Metzenbaum of leaking the FBI report to the press. Though Hatch offered no proof and Senator Metzenbaum had denied it, Senator Specter pursued Hatch's lead, operating on the preposterous theory that I had been duped into raising the claim by a promise from Jim Brudney.

Senator Specter's theory assumed not only a level of naiveté of which even I was incapable but also gross dishonesty on the part of Jim Brudney. There was no such promise, nor would I ever have believed Brudney to be in a position to keep such a promise. Specter sought the answers needed to support the theories the Republicans invented to explain my statement—theories spun out of pure conjecture and off-the-record comments from obscure and unrelated sources. Before and during the hearing the Republicans paraded before the press every possible explanation for my complaint other than the truth. The "spurned lover," the "oversensitive prude," and the "political conspiracy" theories were to prove favorites.

Though he never got the testimony he needed to support the conspiracy theory, Senator Specter soon found another use for his line of questioning on the *USA Today* article. These exchanges served as the basis for a charge on the following day that I had committed "flat-out perjury" in my testimony before the committee. The charge was baseless and, as I was not testifying when Specter made it, it was published by the press before I had any chance to respond. If I had won the battle of wills on the *USA Today* article, Senator Specter once again showed that the Republicans could prevail in the field of rhetoric. The headline would read, "Specter Accuses Hill of Flat Out Perjury," and no one would need to read the details to know that Specter was calling me a liar. Thus, Specter left the public to infer that, as a perjurer, I must have lied about everything I described. I doubt he much cared what the public believed about me as long as they believed that Thomas was worthy of the position on the Court.

Vermont Senator Patrick Leahy's thirty minutes of questioning focused on the FBI interrogation of my claim and the charges that the report was inconsistent with my opening statement. He wanted to know "what happened," but also why what happened was wrong—outside the realm of acceptable behavior for the workplace. Finally, he tackled the question "Why did you wait" to report the behavior? Once again I explained that I had always chosen the best way I knew to deal with the situation both while I worked for Thomas and later, when the Senate staffer approached me and asked about the behavior. Having dealt with the harassment, having dealt with the lack of process for investigation of the information, having dealt with the pre-hearing campaign, I was now having to deal with an irreparably flawed proceeding whose purpose was to investigate the claims. But even when the chairman announced that he planned to adhere to standard rules such as those regarding the relevancy of information, members would soon deviate from them.

As Senator Specter continued his questioning in the afternoon, he raised the affidavit of John Doggett, a law school friend of Clarence Thomas and a passing acquaintance of mine from Washington, D.C. At the beginning of the hearing Senator Biden had announced: "Certain subjects were simply irrelevant to the issue of harassment, namely, the private conduct, out of the workplace relationships, and intimate lives and practices of Judge Thomas, Professor Hill and any other witness that comes before us." The Republicans used this rule to protect Judge Thomas from the release of information about his habit of viewing pornographic material as well as his habit of describing what he had viewed in vivid detail to friends and colleagues. Nevertheless, the committee dispensed with the rule where it was convenient, allowing ready admission of manufactured information about my own personal social life.

Perhaps the best example of the breach of Biden's announced relevancy rule came in the affidavit and testimony of John Doggett. Nowhere was Senator Metzenbaum's warning about opening the proceeding to "all sorts of sworn statements" more warranted than during Doggett's testimony. Specter avoided the question of its admissibility as part of the hearing record in a way both sinister and unethical, as it had been distributed to the president, the press, and the public even before the entire committee was allowed to see it. Specter questioned me on the affidavit before I had ever seen it, though I would learn that within his statement, Doggett offered a theory about my mental state during the time I worked for Clarence Thomas. And despite Doggett's lack of professional credentials as a psychoanalyst, the senators not only publicized it but called me to account for it. Considering that he based his assessment on only two exchanges, the very idea is shocking. Biden's rules regarding competence and relevance of information had gone out the window.

Doggett's theory proposed that I had fantasized about a relationship with him. And when he heard about my charge against Judge Thomas, he deduced that it must have been born of the trouble he felt I'd had establishing relationships with men. Finally, Doggett concluded that what he had diagnosed as my mental instability caused me to send an affidavit to the Senate staff working on the confirmation hearing. Doggett's reasoning was flawed at every step. During his testimony he recited many details of his résumé, but nowhere was there a reference to expertise in conducting psychological evaluations. Moreover, he showed himself to lack any objectivity in evaluating the level of his own attractiveness, asserting that women generally found him "irresistible," a "fact" confirmed by his wife, who sat behind him at the hearing.

Though Senators Danforth and Specter were quick to use the Doggett statement and testimony as evidence that I suffered from erotomania, neither of them suggested that Doggett himself might be suffering from erotomonomania. One reporter described the disease as "a male delusion that attractive young women are harboring fantasies about them." Even without probing from the panel, applying the Republican standard of psychological evaluation, John Doggett showed himself to be a candidate for a diagnosis for this disorder. Had the senators been interested in a scientific pursuit, John Doggett would no doubt have made a good subject for their inquiry. Instead, Senator Specter took the offensive and went to the press to bolster Doggett's pitiful account and defend the committee's admission of it by describing it as "powerful" and "impressive."

In contradiction to the impression Doggett believes he left with me, my recollection is hazy at best. Nevertheless, the John Doggett whom I recall from my time in Washington was a man who often inflicted his attention on women even where it was not reciprocated. Following his testimony, several women callers to the Senate committee confirmed my recollection and challenged the notion that he was "irresistible." Many of the callers had apparently found Doggett and his advances repulsive. And one of the callers even sent in a sworn statement of an encounter in the workplace with Doggett during which he tried to kiss her against her will. Nevertheless, the evidentiary rules as enforced by Senator Biden allowed admission of John Doggett's testimony and excluded that of the women who called with a contradictory point of view. The idea of the admission of testimony like Doggett's in a proceeding as important as this is hard to believe. The reality of experiencing it, however, was completely appalling.

Nearly nine hours after Senator Biden swore me in, I concluded my testimony. The Republican senators had raised questions about the veracity of my statements, my professional competency, and my sanity. At 7:40 P.M. I was exhausted, my head ached, and the pain in my side from the tumors was excruciating after sitting in one position for hours. Underneath my suit, my body was drenched with perspiration from both the tension and the pain. Emotionally, I was numb but relieved.

As the procession filed out of the caucus room and down the hall to our "headquarters," I knew that I would need to return to testify, but I was glad that at least the first day was over. Someone found me a Tylenol, which I took in the bathroom off the conference room where my team and family had temporarily camped. It was one of the few moments I had had alone. I looked at the face in the mirror and marveled that it could still be mine. So much of what had happened that day suggested that I was living someone else's life. I splashed my face with cold water and prayed a short prayer. This time I was too tired to pray for understanding, and I just prayed for strength.

When I returned to my family and friends in our headquarters, the mood was decidedly hopeful, if less than upbeat. People had gathered over the course of the day to volunteer their assistance. Many had worked hard all day—gathering information and trying to get a sense of what would happen next. They, too, were relieved that the day was over. The combination of the emotional pitch and the work left everyone gathered there exhausted. Absent were the highly paid public relations handlers Senator Simpson suggested were supporting me. Absent also were the "special interest" groups many felt had encouraged me to come forward. Senator Simpson's suggestion that ours was a well-polished machine aimed at nailing Clarence Thomas advanced a gross inaccuracy. A simple snapshot of those present would have completely dispelled the notion. And perhaps it was owing to our amateurism that I do not recall a single photograph being taken of the gathering.

One insider's description of the Republican headquarters contrasts with what I witnessed in my own station. He described the atmosphere in the Republican camp as chaotic and resonant—very much like a "political rally." The observer, a veteran of highly contested legal claims, was uncomfortable with what he saw, finding it "not conducive to getting at the truth."

We ended the day with prayer. Though many who joined probably do not consider themselves religious, what happened had meaning for each of us. We all joined in a circle holding hands—family, friends, and strangers thankful for what we'd been able to do that day and praying for the strength to continue.

John Frank, an expert on the Supreme Court confirmation process, may have been the only member of the team to acknowledge the significance of what had occurred that day. When I arrived in our headquarters, he embraced me and wept. I wanted to weep as well, for I knew that I had lost something that nothing could ever replace. Just what it was I could not be sure, but inside I knew that I would never be the same. The challenge I had issued to myself at the beginning of my testimony—to tell what I knew as clearly as possible—was ringing in my ears. Despite the words of Senator Simon that I "had performed a great public service" by testifying, and Senator Herbert Kohl that "the pain [I had experienced would] vastly improve the way men and women respond to the problem throughout the country," I was not certain that I had accomplished my goal. I was certain only that I had survived the ordeal for now and was prepared to try again.

I said good-bye to my family at the Senate building, and Ray McFarland, my lone security adviser, drove me back to my hotel room. They were all unaware of my location, and because of the danger of being followed by the press, we continued to keep it that way. Between sessions they occupied themselves with a dinner at Gary Lee's house and some sight-seeing. On one trip to Georgetown my sisters bought me a gift of cookies and candy to help lift my spirits. They were well aware of my sweet tooth and knew just what might help to lift me out of the despair that we were all fighting. Except for two outings, one to dinner and one to church on Sunday morning, my father refused to leave his hotel room. Though I did not know it at the time, we shared the same sequestered experiences, each of us isolated in a rented room while events over which no one seemed to have control plunged ahead.

CHAPTER THIRTEEN

B ack in my hotel room that evening, I took a much welcomed shower. Alone with my thoughts momentarily, I struggled to sort out what had happened and what to do next. My head spun. I changed into the most comfortable thing I could find in my hurriedly packed suitcase—a sweater and jeans—and prepared to watch the hearing as the committee readjourned.

While I was waiting, I took out a handwritten letter that had somehow made its way from a woman in Washington to Michelle Roberts, an attorney on the team. This letter gave me a sense of the importance of the proceeding in which I had participated:

October 8, 1991

Dear Ms. Hill,

I am a black female attorney serving as an attorney adviser in a small federal agency. I know very well the inner workings of the legal profession and government.

I am writing because when I heard your story it made me weep. It brought back to me so vividly my past experiences with both racial and sexual harassment. It also reminded me of the experiences that my black female law school classmates as well as my white co-workers have related to me over the years.

(I just wanted you to know that you have my support and prayers.) I know the fear and the pain you had to bear when you experienced the harassment. I know you felt a profound disappointment when it was a black man in a high government position who victimized you. During the time we entered the legal profession, black women (Ivy League degree or no Ivy League degree) without "contacts" had little or no options. "Blackballing" is a very real threat in this profession.

I want you to know that you are brave. I want you to know that during this troublesome period, when in need, call upon the strength of all those black women that never had "opportunity." You will never be alone.

The writer and I shared more than just race and profession. We shared a common experience and understanding. As I took solace in finding a comrade, I was reminded of the differences between myself and my experiences and the panel I had appeared before that day. It was a gap that no amount of education or salary would ever erase. It was a gap that had little to do with party politics and everything to do with gender and racial politics. The real-world dynamics of harassment and racial community escaped those officials. Senator Hatch had suggested that as an attorney one should be able to tolerate harassment, and that a woman with an Ivy League degree would be well insulated from retaliation for complaining about harassment. But both the letter writer and I knew differently from our own experiences. None of the senators seemed to have a clue about how Clarence Thomas' race amplified my sense of victimization, making both the experience itself and the prospect of complaining about it more difficult. But in just a brief passage this woman had articulated what would have taken me volumes to explain. And when I read that letter, I knew that someone understood.

———

When my testimony ended, the Republican senators' campaign against me escalated, and the fact that the hearing was more about media control than Thomas' qualifications to serve on the Court came through clearly as the day came to an end. Judge Thomas' handlers had insisted not only that he be the first to testify on Friday morning but that he also be the last to testify on Friday evening as well. When Biden originally announced his plan to end the day with my testimony, Kenneth Duberstein threatened that Thomas would hold a press conference in front of the hearing room doors and claim that he had been denied the opportunity to defend himself. Biden therefore capitulated, never offering me the opportunity to respond in like manner. And so at 9:00 prime-time Friday night, Thomas took the stand as millions watched.

Initially questioned by Senator Heflin, Judge Thomas first informed the committee that he had not listened to my testimony. It was a clever move, for Senator Heflin admitted he didn't want to repeat the details to which I had testified, and without repeating the testimony, Heflin was hampered in questioning Thomas. And Thomas' claim that he had not seen it also insulated him from having to deny any of the particulars, positioning him perfectly to take the offensive. Which is exactly what he did. He delivered his most angry and intimidating remarks about the process, calling the hearing a "high-tech lynching," and accusing the Democratic senators on the committee, in a thinly cloaked fashion, of a peculiar form of racism aimed only at conservative blacks—a fusion of racial and ideological bias of which Thomas was now the target. The senators recoiled at the near accusation and were no doubt caught off guard by it. Unfortunately, none of the senators appeared sure enough in his own perspective on race to address such a charge. Everyone could agree that lynching was deplorable. And no one wanted to be accused of being involved in one, neither the senators nor the members of the public. All too ingeniously, Thomas made it clear that anyone who supported the charge of harassment would be figuratively engaging in the deplorable act of lynching. The truth of the claim of racism or the appropriateness of the lynching metaphor in the context of an accusation by a black woman against a well-placed black man didn't matter.

Thomas, through his "high-tech lynching" speech, drew a line in a sense, and listeners were given the choice of either siding with racism or siding with Judge Thomas.

Thomas further charged that my statement and testimony were the product of a conspiracy by "someone or some groups." Though he failed to assert who or how the conspiracy evolved, this statement, like so many of the Republican senators' statements, went unchallenged. Since the day the public became aware of the charge, the Republicans had been looking for some connection between me and a group opposed to Thomas. Of course, no such connection existed. Nevertheless, the committee members allowed Thomas to assert a conspiracy without requesting any evidence of one. Their knowledge of the roles that interest groups generally play in politics may have hampered them from challenging Thomas' assertion that interest groups were involved in this particular instance.

As I watched Thomas' testimony from my hotel room, I could not help but see the irony in his claim of racism. In the years that I had known him, he had always chosen, both publicly and privately, to belittle those who saw racism as an obstacle. In the case of his sister, he asserted that the real barriers to economic and political achievement were a lack of industry and initiative and a reliance on remedial programs. Yet, now having met an obstacle to his *own* dream, he blamed racism. I wondered if he might then change his mind about the impact racism had on other lives. To me Judge Thomas, as the nominee of a then very popular president, was unlike individuals who found themselves outside power trying to assert their rights against the powerful. He had aligned himself with power—the very power that had exploited racism for political purposes in the infamous Willie Horton ad. Thomas was no Thurgood Marshall, whose nomination to the Supreme Court had been challenged by segregationists exploiting racist ideas and claiming that, as a black man, Marshall was not smart enough to serve on the Court. Thomas was not being challenged by separatists because of the color of his skin. In fact, Thomas' challengers seemed to be painfully sympathetic to the racial implications of claims that he might be incompetent.

Thomas' current claim of victimhood was so stunningly out of character that it at first struck me as disingenuous. That his confirmation had suffered a brief suspension was the result of circumstances initially set in motion by Thomas himself. Later, however, I concluded that his remarks were less disingenuous than merely calculated, just as his earlier remarks belittling racism had been. The remarks he made in the hearing were calculated to defuse the Democrats before they'd had an opportunity to approach him about the harassment charges themselves. And they were calculated to win sympathy from a public that, through the passage of antilynching and civil rights laws, had decried the use of violence to curtail the social and political activities of blacks. What better weapon to use against liberals like Kennedy and Metzenbaum or a senator from Alabama like Heflin than the fear of being labeled a racist. A claim of racism coupled with a claim of ideological persecution captured the sympathies of not only those on the right but those in the middle as well.

Bewildered and angered by Thomas' remarks, I watched as the stunned Democratic members of the panel lost any moral authority they might have asserted in keeping the proceeding balanced. Two days later on Sunday afternoon, Senator Kennedy would attempt to respond to the allegations of racism. And as a proponent of civil rights legislation, he was in a prime position to take on the claim of racial bias. But however articulate and reasoned his speech, none of his Democratic colleagues seconded it. Thomas' claim of a high-tech lynching had given the Republicans something akin to a spiritual boost—a platform of righteousness. They had already indicated that they could indeed win a battle to control public information about the hearing. Judge Thomas' high-tech lynching claim gave them a moral justification for moving forward in their attacks against me. The Republicans could now claim that their aggressive pursuit of the Thomas nomination was motivated by their resistance to racism. Though Thomas supporters may once have claimed that racism no longer existed and used Thomas to support their assertion, they now could claim to deplore racism and use Thomas' treatment as an example of why it still had to be fought.

And though I know the power that the label of racism had over the

Democratic senators, I would not understand until days later the extent to which I, too, had been labeled a racist or an accomplice of racism.

Had the questioning of Judge Thomas been similarly argumentative, the proceeding would have had the appearance of fairness. But Judge Thomas' questioning that evening by Senator Hatch and other senators was deferential, even conciliatory. "Judge Thomas, I have sat here and I have listened all day long, and Anita Hill was very impressive," Senator Hatch said. "She is an impressive law professor. She is a Yale Law graduate. And, when she met with the FBI, she said that you told her about your sexual experiences and preferences. And I hate to go into this but I want to go into it because I have to, and I know that is something that you wish you had never heard at any time or place. But I think it is important that we go into it, and let me just do it this way."

Hatch prepared Thomas for his questioning by apologetically explaining the necessity for his action. "She said to the FBI that you told her about your sexual experiences and preferences, that you asked her what she liked or if she had ever done the same thing, that you discussed oral sex between men and women, that you discussed viewing films of people having sex with each other and with animals, and that you told her that she should see such films, and that you would like to discuss specific sex acts and the frequency of sex. What about that?"

"Senator, I would not want to, except being required to here, to dignify those allegations with a response. As I have said before, I categorically deny them. To me, I have been pilloried with scurrilous allegations of this nature. I have denied them earlier and I deny them tonight." This Clarence Thomas was almost deferential. Yet only minutes later he would go on the attack—an attack that would clear the way for his confirmation.

Not only did the questioning of Thomas beg an answer which allowed him to exonerate himself but the language used to describe the nature of the conduct which I testified to was much less sexually graphic than when I was questioned.

"Did you ever have lunch with Professor Hill at which you talked about sex or pressured her to go out with you?"

"Absolutely not." Oddly, the senator did not ask if Thomas had asked me out—only if he had "pressured" me to go out. Thomas might have answered in a way that was truthful to him, not seeing the numerous requests as pressure.

"Did you ever tell Professor Hill that she should see pornographic films?" The senator meticulously went down his list of questions, mentioning the gist of the charges but relieving Thomas of the responsibility of responding to any of the details.

"Absolutely not." The questions begged the answer and Thomas knew that he must take the hard-line approach. Any deviation might result in the public concluding that while he had not sexually harassed me he had acted improperly toward me. He could not risk that reaction.

Senator Hatch prompted Judge Thomas, "Did you ever talk about pornography with Professor Hill?" Judge Thomas responded accordingly, "I did not discuss any pornographic material or pornographic preferences or pornographic films with Professor Hill."

Though there is no clear evidence that Hatch and Thomas practiced the questions, their interaction worked so well as to appear choreographed. Each knew his role—step by step. Senator Hatch knew the right question; Thomas knew the proper response—aimed at clearing the nomination. The "conversation" between the fastidious Orrin Hatch and the president's "most qualified" nominee, Thomas, played smoothly. They were so unlike the awkward "conversations" that I had with the members of the committee earlier in the day. Even the questions from the Democrats on the committee sometimes suggested untruthfulness or skepticism. Then it occurred to me that as the president's nominee Thomas had prepared for weeks for their "conversations." Moreover, he had practiced with them in the days before the leak of my statement. He spoke their language. In this sense, Biden was right: "the presumption was with" him. He came to the committee as an invited guest. I, on the other hand, was an intruder whom the public had forced upon the committee.

Perhaps the Democrats were deferential to Thomas because of his position on the bench. Nevertheless, in a hearing where both parties are assumed to be on equal footing, no discrepancies based on title should exist. Yet the tenor and approach to Judge Thomas were different. The willingness to ask him difficult or embarrassing questions was missing.

"Well, if [Hill's allegations] did not occur, I think you are in a position, with certainly your ability to testify, in effect, to try to eliminate it from people's minds."

"Senator, I didn't create it in people's minds. This matter was investigated by the Federal Bureau of Investigation in a confidential way. It was then leaked last weekend to the media. I did not do that. And how many members of this Committee would like to have the same scurrilous, uncorroborated allegations made about him and then leaked to national newspapers and then be drawn and dragged before a national forum of this nature to discuss those allegations that should have been resolved in a confidential way?"

"Well, I certainly appreciate your attitude towards leaks. I happen to serve on the Senate Ethics Committee and it has been a sieve," Senator Heflin said, establishing their common concern.

"But it didn't leak on me. This leaked on me . . . You have robbed me of something that can never be restored." Thomas portrayed himself as a victim. He would have nothing of the camaraderie offered by Heflin.

"I know exactly how you feel," Senator DeConcini reassured Thomas.

By Friday night rumors were confirmed that another woman named Angela Wright had come forward with similar information about Clarence Thomas. Though no one on the team knew her, we all waited anxiously to hear what she had to say. This and the day's events floated through my consciousness as I fell asleep that night.

On Saturday, October 12, the lines of communication between our team and the committee leadership seemed to break down just as the coordination between Judge Thomas and the Republicans on the committee, reportedly, was coalescing. I sat in my hotel room all day, alternately watching the hearings and sports. Shirley Wiegand kept me company, watching television with me. Shirley is decidedly not a sports fan, but she, too, was weary of the rapidly deteriorating process and needed relief from the performance by the committee. For me, watching sports was a welcome alternative to the hearing. In sports there are rules and officials who enforce those rules and the penalties for violations. For Shirley, it was a true act of friendship. Throughout the day she brought me food that she encouraged me to eat, and kept me informed about the conversations she overheard on the street. Though we both brought our work to Washington from Oklahoma, I was too distracted to do mine. And just as I was about to turn completely into myself, she gave up doing her reading and focused on diverting me from the sense of gloom that nearly overtook me.

Shirley Wiegand was my lifeline to reality—the person who kept me believing that the entire world had not gone mad, though it certainly seemed that way. An accomplished attorney before she entered law teaching, she stood away from the strategy and pace of negotiating my "case" with the committee. Instead she was stuck with the uninteresting job of hand-holding. Some in the press would even misrepresent that true friendship, to exploit the salacious and unfounded suggestion that our relationship was sexual in nature. But none of it, not the politics, not the media attention, meant anything to her. Shirley simply acted out of concern for me. Everyone should have a friend like her.

Saturday morning, Senator Hatch pulled one of the most dramatic and bizarre stunts of the entire proceeding. During the Friday session I had testified that Thomas had referred to a pornographic film character, Long Dong Silver, in his discussion of pornography. I had also testified that Thomas had made a remark about pubic hair on his Coke can. Hatch received information from a local law firm that the book *The Exorcist* contained a reference to pubic hair in a drink and that a reported court decision referred to "Long Dong Silver." Based on the purportedly unsolicited information arriving mysteriously in his office, Senator Hatch asserted that I had fabricated my testimony based on the court case and the book. Hatch waved the book about during the proceeding as though it were the smoking gun found at a murder scene. It did not matter that I had read neither the case nor the book, or that the passage in the book differed critically from what I explained Thomas had said to me. What had come to matter was the theater of it all—and its impact on the public mind. And, despite his initial rule excluding irrelevant information, Chairman Biden entered the misinformation into the proceeding record.

The campaign continued with the Republicans taking the position that they had "to win at any cost." Senator Danforth would admit later that he pursued this strategy with no regard to fairness for me. To suggest that he had no regard to fairness for me also indicates a lack of regard for fairness to the confirmation process itself, as a fair process generally requires fairness to all sides involved. And despite the successful smoke screens established by some members of the Senate, there was something that informed an increasingly impatient public that the senators had co-opted the process. I would not learn this until returning home when I'd begin to hear from people who wrote or called after watching the hearing on television. For now I was isolated in my hotel room with the sense that public sentiment was the same as the senators kept telling the public it should be.

A key part of the strategy to discredit me was to obtain statements from former students at Oral Roberts University. Senator Danforth seemed to be looking for statements from anyone who would attest to anything negative about my professional competence, my personality, or my sexuality. The senator received just the kind of information he wanted. (The positive, supportive comments he received in interviews with fellow teachers, he ignored.) These requests from members of the Senate gave students the opportunity to promote whatever comments or allegations they wanted to make. Senator Danforth did not care whether the allegations were steeped in racism or sexism so long as they reflected negatively on me as a person, generally, or on my credibility, particularly. Since the students would be accountable to no one for the comments they made, it gave those who may have harbored a grudge a perfect opportunity to act upon it.

The tone set by the senators in their own unsubstantiated remarks encouraged them to do so. The law school environment fosters intense competition under the best of circumstances. Disappointment about a single grade, the most obvious competitive standard, often grows into a grudge. The environment at Oral Roberts University was particularly tense because of the uncertain future accreditation status of the law school and its ultimate transferral to Regent University. Students felt uncertain about where they would complete their education and whether doing so, under the conditions of the institution, would enable them to sit for the bar and to obtain employment. Students had no control over the accreditation of the law school or its transfer. Good grades, the mark of advantage over which they had some control, were seen as a way to maintain a competitive edge. And for some students, under these circumstances, grades took on exaggerated meaning. Under the guise of background information, any student who bore animosity toward me or the institution for something as unrelated as a disappointing grade might come forward. Given the lateness of the inquiries—coming on the weekend of the second round of the confirmation hearing—and the lack of will on the part of the Democrats to pursue my claim, they were virtually assured that their charges would not be investigated.

Thomas' supporters sought out students who would provide statements asserting that I was a radical feminist, a lesbian, a sexual aggressor, or an incompetent teacher. Senator Danforth's campaign included calling several of my former students ten to twelve times over the course of two days. Yet even with the breadth of his inquiry and persistence of his search, Senator Danforth was able to obtain only one affidavit, the contents of which were denied by the "witnesses" listed in the document. This affidavit was dubbed the "pube affidavit" because it contained descriptions of alleged sexual remarks, advances, and bizarre activity—including putting pubic hair in student papers I returned—that the former student attributed to me. The alleged remarks, according to the document, were made in the presence of the students named in the affidavit. But when the Senate contacted those named students, they denied witnessing any such activity. Still, despite the fact that no one questioned how the young man had concluded that the "short curly hair" he says he and others found in their work was pubic hair, Danforth moved forward with them.

Moreover, Danforth disregarded the likelihood that a young black woman at a Christian university could engage openly in such activity without some institutional sanctioning or even castigation from the dean of the school. Yet neither Dean Kothe nor his successor, John Sanford, endorsed the affidavit. And despite the fact that Kothe testified as a witness for Thomas, he did so without impugning my character. John Sanford, who at the time of the hearing was at Regent University, an institution associated with the Reverend Pat Robertson's ministry, gave a favorable assessment of my character, as did other former Oral Roberts faculty then at Regent. The Republicans on the committee ignored their statements as failing to fit in with their political objective, even though the statements came at considerable risk, given that Robertson openly supported Judge Thomas' nomination. The word of the former student who submitted the affidavit was worth more to Danforth in a political sense even if not in a logical or moral sense. Senator Danforth used the document in an effort to bargain with the Democrats over control of the hearing, and the Democrats—unwilling to place any value in the word of a black woman or to pursue the statements of the white male colleagues who supported her—allowed it.

Even after Thomas' confirmation when it was clear that Danforth had "won," he was not satisfied. Danforth attempted to get the press to publish the more inflammatory contents of the affidavit. To complete the political task, it was not enough that Thomas was confirmed. From beginning to end, Danforth knew that my life—not just my allegations—had to be destroyed.

When I worked for Clarence Thomas, he entrusted me with keeping him informed about media reports that reflected on the agency. Each morning I read five newspapers from across the country—scouring them for stories about the EEOC or the Office for Civil Rights at the Education Department. I was particularly watchful for negative stories. Despite some emotional attachment to the agencies, I did not personalize the negative stories. I enjoyed comparing stories from different newspapers about the same event. Reading them and responding when necessary were part of my job.

As I sat in my room over the weekend of October 12, I was reminded of that part of my job. I attempted to keep up with what was occurring outside my room by reading two newspapers, *The New York Times* and *The Washington Post*. I was so emotionally involved that reading the reporting was difficult—reading the opinion pieces, whether favorable or not, was almost impossible. The reporting of the entire episode had been disappointing from the beginning. It covered the allegation of harassment as a political scandal and my claim as a maneuver in a political cause. Lost was the report of the experience of an everyday person as a victim of harassment in 1982 or caught in the politics of the 1991 hearing.

Some individuals with political and legal experience worked behind the scenes talking to the senators about fairness in the process. Both Marcia Greenberger of the National Women's Law Center and Judith Lichtman of the NOW–Women's Legal Defense Fund went to Capitol Hill daily during the hearings to help keep the Senate focused on the harassment issue. Marcia Greenberger would say later that she was never treated so well as she was by the staff of the Senate cafeteria once they discovered what she and Lichtman were trying to accomplish. But I was not in contact with either of them or their organizations, and their story, which seemed more likely to be reported, was not my story.

Though I am grateful for the work of both women and today count them both as personal friends, I confess that for me the complaint was personal and I did not want to lose that focus. I did not want to be involved in the politics of representing all women, nor did I have the energy to focus on the claim as a statement about the concerns of other workingwomen. At that point of the hearing, my interest was in surviving the immediate crises of an individual citizen who had gotten caught up in the game of Washington politics at its worst. Because it was poised to report the politics fed to it by the Republicans, the press failed in its coverage of the personal aspect of the story and only rarely made mention of the broader implications of harassment.

On Saturday night a group of Thomas' witnesses had portrayed themselves as average everyday working women in contrast with me—whom they portrayed as an elitist, intellectual university professor out of touch with the concerns of most women. Some members of the press seemed to buy their portrait, ignoring my background and accepting without question their qualifications for speaking on behalf of working-class women. Following their lead, many of the news stories that focused on harassment tended to present the issue as a class problem. A *New York Times* reporter suggested that most working-class women and black women, in particular, were unconcerned about sexual harassment in the workplace.

The very thing which made them valuable in Washington, their own insularity and tendency to see everything in decidedly political terms, skewed the perspective of the members of the Washington press corps. Yet the reporting over the weekend missed the point of view of the target of harassment as well as the private citizen battling the resources of powerful Washington politicians. Few were reporting on the lack of all the protections of a normal legal process or the Republicans' subversion of the confirmation process. The Republican senators and their own point of view induced them to see and portray the hearing as a story about my participation in the "derailment of a Supreme Court nomination." The press seemed to identify too readily with the politicians, and as one commentator put it, "reporters had once again bought the Republican sales pitch."

The many complexities escaped the reporters and editorial writers covering the hearings. When I did read the editorials in *The Washington Post,* I was greatly disturbed. They seemed to convey an unwarranted animus toward me and the fact that the committee was hearing the claims that I raised. I later learned that Juan Williams, a journalist responsible for profiles of Thomas in the *Atlantic Monthly* and *The Washington Post,* wrote one of the editorials despite a clear conflict of interest. The editorial was entitled, "Open Season on Clarence Thomas" and described the charges as "a speck of mud [flung] at Clarence Thomas in an alleged sexual conversation between two adults." The opinion piece as-

serted that my claim arose as a result of Senate staff members' search for
dirt on Thomas. Williams dismissed my charges as much for what he saw
as their insignificance as for my lack of credibility.

Interestingly, at the time, Williams was under investigation himself for
allegedly sexually harassing one of his colleagues on the paper. And other
women had lodged informal complaints about Williams' behavior as
well, alleging a pattern of unwelcomed comments and behavior which
they found too intimate but which Williams defended as merely "socially
awkward." After some at the newspaper protested this lack of objectivity,
the *Post* management disclosed the apparent conflict of interest and relieved him of his editorial duties on the matter, though it also ordered a
reporter who wanted to do a story on the matter not to write it. By this
time, however, Senator Hatch had already cited the article during the
proceedings to support his conspiracy theory and Rush Limbaugh had
read the column on his syndicated radio program.

Around the country, as the hearings were airing, editorials voicing
opinions appeared even in small-town papers. And the *Post* was not alone
in its irresponsible editorial decisions. An absurdly extreme example of
messy journalism appeared in a student paper at the University of Utah.
In articles purporting to present both sides, one columnist described me
as "dirty, depraved, schizophrenic, and grossly sexual, a sheer idiot or a
sore liar." He described my charges as "sexual hallucination" and the
testimony "the mere rendition of a mind obsessed with bestial bondage
and influenced by definitions from the Sodom and Gomorrah *Anatomical
Review.*" The "other side" posed the question of whether the behavior
actually constituted sexual harassment and explained the definition of the
behavior according to state and federal law. The piece also questioned
my motives and my judgment in not coming forward previously. Clearly,
a lack of balance existed. One columnist attempted to inform the public
about the problem and give them a method for analyzing the issue. The
other columnist followed the lead of the senators, invoking lewd and
preposterous name-calling. The same paper suggested that the media,
provoked by "female leaders, especially in Congress, and various

women's groups," were engaging in tabloid journalism by simply reporting on my claim. This newspaper's best defense is that it is a student
paper, a defense the *Post* could not argue.

Though it is difficult to say whether the attitude displayed behind the
scenes by the *Post* and in public by other papers may not have influenced
the reporting of the story, it does speak to the lack of sensitivity in and
ignorance about handling claims of sexual harassment in one of the
country's most sophisticated and influential newspapers.

Television commentators voiced open hostility to my claim on
"news" shows as well. Fred Barnes declared that I "was spinning a mon-
strous lie" and Morton Kondracke compared me to Tawana Brawley,
while John McLaughlin, himself accused of sexual harassment, compared
me to the journalist Janet Cooke. These two comparisons were to
women who were found to have fabricated stories (one about her alleged
sexual assault, the other about a child drug addict who didn't exist but
whom she portrayed as real) who were also black. Ironically, neither of
these commentators compared me to Oliver North to make their point
about truthfulness. If they wanted to pose that I was being untruthful on
the stand, North would have served as a better comparison, since North
admitted that he lied in his testimony before a congressional committee.
The choice of two black women as comparisons had inescapable gender
and racial implications. Unfortunately, this was as close as some commentators came to seeing the human element of my story. To prove that
I could not be trusted to tell the truth, they recalled stories that they saw
as examples of other untrustworthy black women. Either out of laziness,
insensitivity, or malice, rather than write a story about me, they retold
the stories of others.

Whether fueled by the press coverage or inciting it, Senator Danforth
and Senator Simpson next began enlisting students at the University of
Oklahoma to carry out their campaign against me. Chris Wilson, a law
student with whom I had never had interaction, stated that his goal in the
days following the hearing was "to go about the business of making
[Anita Hill's] life a living hell." During the hearing, he was busy as well.

He sought other law students who would participate in a letter-writing campaign aimed at painting me as a political partisan and radical feminist. His failure to find law students willing to engage in the task did not dissuade him. He went to an undergraduate fraternity, which sent pre-drafted letters to senators. They targeted the senior senator from Oklahoma, David Boren. Only one student who allowed his name to be used would assert anything about my politics. Yet neither he nor the student who was responsible for enlisting the fraternity participation in the campaign had ever been in one of my classes, and neither had I discussed politics with either of them. To the students involved, many of whom were eighteen or nineteen, the effort to discredit me must have seemed like sport. The letter-writing campaign might have seemed to them like a fraternity prank that they had all probably participated in at some point. It was, I am convinced, little more than a game to them—a game in which they had nothing to lose, but from which they could gain the political favor of a powerful Washington elite. The real pity is that these students were encouraged to participate in the sport by adult men who had been elected and sworn to protect the rights of the citizens of the country. It is a sad commentary and no coincidence that the students enlisted for this crusade, from both Oral Roberts and Oklahoma Universities, were all white males.

Senator Simpson used the letters solicited from the fraternity members to stage his dramatic claim. "I have all kinds of incriminating stuff coming over the transom. I've got letters hanging out of my pocket," he said, flapping his jacket. "I've got faxes, I've got statements from her former law professors, statements from people that know her, statements from Tulsa, Oklahoma, saying, 'Watch out for this woman.' But nobody's got the guts to say that, because it gets tangled up in this sexual harassment crap. I believe that sexual harassment is a terrible thing . . . [but] I don't need any test, don't need anybody to give me the saliva test on whether one believes more or less about sexual harassment . . . So if we had one hundred and four days to go into Ms. Hill and find out about her character, her background, her proclivities, and all the rest, I'd feel a lot better about this system."

To say that Senator Simpson was doing his typical grandstanding with the solicited canned information is to miss the point. Simpson was restating claims he had raised about my character and raising new ones as well as denigrating the whole concept of sexual harassment. When asked by the press to support this allegation, Senator Simpson declined. But the purpose of his jacket-flapping display was not to prove any of the contents of the documents which he purported to have, so much as to put the idea in the mind of the public that it could not trust me to be truthful. Moreover, no one with an honest understanding of the seriousness of sexual harassing behavior could have called it "sexual harassment crap," as Simpson did then, or distinguished its pain from that of "real harassment," as he had done earlier. And in advising that the committee should have one hundred and four days to look into my background, as it had to review Thomas', Simpson must have forgotten that I was not being considered for the Supreme Court. I was not being scrutinized for a position of public trust. I was simply giving evidence as a witness. No one else acting in that role had ever been scrutinized or had to be qualified in such a manner. In one statement, no part of which was made in my presence or objected to by the chairman of the committee, Senator Simpson questioned my background, character, and "proclivities." Journalist William Safire later gave definition to the term "proclivities," lest there be any doubt that Simpson was questioning my sexual orientation and following up on earlier efforts to get Oral Roberts law students to state that I was a lesbian.

On Sunday Senator Simpson suggested that there should be an investigation of me—to discover my "proclivities." As if to follow that lead and notwithstanding the lack of relevance to the issue of harassment, Lynn Duke, one of the reporters at The Washington Post, telephoned Keith Henderson seeking verification that I was a lesbian who had had an affair with my roommate in Washington. Henderson took her to task for resorting to the same myths that the senators had to explain the claim.

The senators' actions were explainable: their political agenda was more important than painting a clear picture of the nature of the problem. However, the *Post,* whose objective was to inform the public, in stooping to the same tactics, was irresponsible. Even if the claims about my sexual orientation had been true, in pursuing the information the newspaper seemed only interested in satisfying the public about intensely private matters, unrelated to the claim. The investigation resembled so closely voyeuristic tabloid journalism as to be indistinguishable. Unfortunately, Duke was not the only reporter to pursue this approach to the story.

By Saturday afternoon, after the "high-tech lynching" claim, it appeared as though none of the members of the committee were my allies. And with the media blitz organized and executed by the Republicans, even time was against me. In pensive moments I listened to what was going on before me and wondered how it might have turned out differently. How might I have avoided being sucked into the nastiness that I was witnessing? Had I refused to participate when called or lied when questioned, might the whole matter have ended in September? At one point I closed myself into the bedroom of the hotel suite and started to cry. Almost instantly, however, I reminded myself that it would do no good for me to fall apart at this point. I pulled myself together and returned to the living room area where Shirley Wiegand was preparing for the following week's classes. When called, I did what most citizens confronted with such a situation would do. Having made the decision to disclose what I knew, I had to complete it no matter how badly the process was failing. I just prayed to live through the next few days.

Though the team had been apprehensively hopeful, after my testimony on Friday, less than twenty-four hours later we felt we had been crushed. Thomas had concluded his second day of testimony. The Republicans had stepped up their crusade to shatter any chance that the substance of my complaint be heard by bombarding the media and committee with false information and taking control of the process. We were clearly outnumbered, outfinanced, and, in terms of media and political sophistication, outfinessed. On Saturday, October 12, my time for reflection was scarce, and it was certain that no official was going to rein in a process that had become devoid of balance and even lacking in civility or decency. With little time to second-guess or ponder the past decisions, I had to act to protect myself from the attack being waged.

Despite my own isolation, the lawyers and other volunteers were working to establish some way of responding to the attack. Clearly, to go on simply denying the negative assertions of the senators was to give them a credibility they did not deserve and to allow their allegations to set the terms of the discussion. As much as my attorneys, Emma Coleman Jordan, Sue Ross, and Charles Ogletree, had tried to protect my testimony in case I was called again, and as eloquently as they had spoken on my behalf, I could no longer remain outside of the fray of the events. We needed some positive act in order to reverse the downward turn of the process, and the circumstances demanded that I be the one to take it. With some hesitance in his voice, Ogletree reminded me that I had told the committee that I would be willing to take a polygraph examination. "Would you still be willing to do so?" he questioned. At that moment I was thinking like a client and not like a lawyer. Had I been a lawyer advising a client in a legal proceeding, I would have discouraged her from doing so, because of the risk of manipulation of the results. "Sure," the client in me who wanted some exoneration responded readily.

Charles Ogletree arranged for the examination. He was thinking like the seasoned criminal lawyer he is, and thus was the one who had qualms about the decision to go forward with the polygraph examination. And as he would report to me afterward, he hardly slept on the Saturday night before the examination.

CHAPTER FOURTEEN

On Sunday morning I dressed to go to an undisclosed location; to take an unfamiliar examination; to be administered by someone whom I did not know. I had taken many exams in my life—to enter college, law school, professional life. I had always prepared for the examination for weeks before taking them, but over the past few days I began to believe that life turns on the unanticipated—those things that we do not even contemplate and therefore cannot plan. That the credibility, reputation, and future that I had so thoughtfully planned for might turn on an examination which I had only the night before decided to take seemed ironic but fitting in light of the occurrences of the previous days.

I received three telephone calls before I left the hotel to take the examination. One was from Sonia Jarvis, who called to give me a scripture for my reading Sunday morning. The Reverend Beecher Hicks called to share a scripture with me as well and to pray with me. He and Reverend Harris, who had come by the caucus room to minister to my family, had graciously arranged to have cars to take my family to his church, the Metropolitan Baptist Church, a predominantly African American church in Washington, D.C. I was later relieved that my family not only enjoyed the sermon but was warmly received by the congregation.

After Thomas' "high-tech lynching" comment and the charges of conspiracy, I worried that the manipulation of racial sentiments in the black community might be turned against my family. They were easily identifiable after their appearance on television on Friday and owing to a strong family resemblance. On Saturday, as they shopped in Georgetown, strangers asked their identity. The press had been following them, and my brother Ray says that he saw the same Secret Service man throughout the weekend at various spots throughout the city. But after their visit to the Metropolitan, where they were welcomed, my immediate concerns about their well-being were relieved.

The third call came from a group of friends, Ronald Allen and Gary Phillips, two law school classmates, and Keith Henderson. Ronald Allen had been involved in the hearings as a legal adviser to Judge Hoerchner. The three were down the hallway in the hotel where I was staying and wanted a chance to visit with me. They were visibly distressed, looking as though they hadn't slept much the night before. They had been behind the scenes in the caucus room and knew that the proceedings had taken a pro-Thomas direction. Moreover, they felt that the core legal team had not chosen a successful strategy. I had been close with Gary and Keith when I lived in Washington and had shared some of the information just prior to the press story. The experience they were now having, both up front and behind the scenes, deeply pained them. They suggested that I take a more proactive posture, bypassing the committee, if necessary, in order to be heard by the public. Realizing that they were in agony on my behalf, it was difficult to dismiss them. In retrospect, given the extent to which things had collapsed, they were right to question the "strategy" of our team. Though they deserved some assurance, I could not give them any. The media attention and the Republicans' campaign were such that the fewer people aware of the polygraph examination, the better.

Gary and Keith, particularly as Washington residents with contacts with the federal government, recognized the antics of the Republicans as politics in the purest and ugliest form and believed that the only way to combat them was to counter their political maneuvering. Aware that the Republicans were attempting to gather negative and harmful information about my witnesses and other supporters, they were fearful, with good reason, that any show of support for me could result in professional retaliation. I knew that no ordinary citizen could match the resources of the senators. Moreover, I viewed the experience as a choice about how I was going to live my entire life, not just these few days in Washington. When the episode was over, Senators Simpson, Hatch, Specter, and Danforth, I had no doubt, would continue to act in the same fashion; this was the way of life they had chosen—and it was politics as usual for them. But it was not what I had chosen. I had left it eight years prior and wanted no part of it, particularly now. Moreover, no matter how smart, resourceful, and committed our team was, we were not equipped to play their game.

I reminded Ronald, Gary, and Keith that I had started out saying that I did not want the matter to be tried in the press and that I intended to maintain that posture throughout the proceeding, no matter how tough it became. Though they were not satisfied with my responses, they did not push. Keith, perhaps better than the other two, knew firsthand that once I had made up my mind on a matter of principle, I would not budge. More important, I am certain that they did not want to cause me any discomfort. Disappointed, they left the room just minutes before I left, to take the examination, accompanied by Shirley Wiegand, Charles Ogletree, and Ray McFarland.

Despite the task that I was about to undertake, I was grateful to be out of the hotel room. The day was a typically overcast cloudy autumn day, but being outside offered me a glimpse of life that I missed in the grim reality of watching the hearing from my hotel room. Ray McFarland delivered us to the appointed place, the law office of Arnold and Porter in northwest Washington, D.C. One of the partners there, Charles Ruff, a well-known Washington, D.C., attorney and former president of the Washington, D.C., Bar Association, arranged the polygraph examination. Because it was Sunday morning, Ruff met us in the lobby to give us access to the conference room and office in the secured building. The stillness of the building with its huge empty corridors gave the process an even greater sense of mystery. Ruff spoke only briefly with Ogletree, Wiegand, and me, before he took me to a small conference room where the polygraph equipment was set up. We were all anxious to get the examination under way. It did not seem the time for small talk.

Through the corridors of expensive modern furnishings and tasteful artwork selected to inform visitors of the law firm's good judgment and prestige, Ruff led me to the conference room. There I met Paul Minor, the polygraph expert. After introductions, Mr. Minor explained to me his background and experience with the examination. Mr. Minor, too, was a man of few words, except to recite his credentials. He'd begun with the army and then with the FBI as polygraph program coordinator, revamping the agency's use of the examination in investigations. Throughout his career the FBI had ranked his work as "exceptional." Letters from William Webster himself attested to the agency's confidence in him. Finally, he started his own private investigation firm. All told, Minor had about twenty years of training and experience using the polygraph. Clearly, he had explained the process many times before. But his stern face and tone indicated that he was not particularly interested in responding to questions about his expertise. All of which indicated a hostility—at the least a criticism—as though he were on the verge of chastising me. "So what," I sighed to myself with a sense of resignation. After all, his demeanor was no worse than what I had experienced from the Senate Judiciary Committee members just two days prior. I had come to expect no better. At least no one could accuse Minor of being biased in my favor. It occurred to me that whether I reported the results of the examination or not, the information would surely get out. The press, I was certain, would somehow learn of the examination and the matter would be disclosed whatever the result.

The conference room itself had a strangely calming effect. It was small, with no windows, and neutral-colored, textured walls on which hung few embellishments of any sort. The drone of the fluorescent lights and the walls themselves muted any outside noises, a welcomed break from my hotel room, where the unavoidable television set served as a constant reminder of the hearing. From Friday to Sunday morning my scenery had not changed, as I had holed up in the room listening to the testimony of Thomas and his witnesses well into the night.

Paul Minor's explanation of how the examination process worked made me realize its importance. As he ran through the questions he would ask, ensuring that I understood them, I thought of all the different ways I'd been asked the same questions over the past week. At one point he asked me if I had ever done anything to encourage Clarence Thomas' behavior or to give the impression that his conduct was invited. It was like FBI investigator Luton's question about whether I dressed provocatively at work. And not unlike so many other questions which amounted to a familiar accusation, "You must have done something to deserve this." But here, rather than anger, the question stirred self-doubt. Minor, Luton, and now even I couldn't help but reflect society's training to question the behavior of the accuser, rather than the behavior of the accused.

"Sometimes," I tried to explain, returning to the period ten years prior, "when these things happen, you wonder whether you have done or said something that might be misinterpreted. But I had done nothing purposely to give Thomas the impression that I was interested in him other than as his assistant." Once more I searched my mind for something that Thomas might have misconstrued and found nothing.

The pre-test interview completed, Minor began the test. Through a system of wires and suction cups and Velcro as I recall, he hooked me to the polygraph machine—which began to measure my blood pressure, heart rate, and respiration. I sat facing the wall and with my back to Mr. Minor and his polygraph machine. Over the drone of the lights, I could hear the graphs of my responses to his questions being drawn onto white paper as it fed through the machine.

Paul Minor: "Have you deliberately lied to me about Clarence Thomas?"

Anita Hill: "No." The machine scratched out a graph of my response.

Paul Minor: "Are you fabricating the allegation that Clarence Thomas discussed pornographic material with you?"

Anita Hill: "No." Again, the machine scratched out my response.

Paul Minor: "Are you lying to me about the various topics that Clarence Thomas mentioned to you regarding specific sexual acts?"

Anita Hill: "No."

Paul Minor: "Are you lying to me about Clarence Thomas making references to you about the size of his penis?"

Anita Hill: "No."

Interspersed among these relevant questions were control questions. Over and again for thirty minutes we each took our turn, Minor, then me, then the machine—my credibility, perhaps even my sanity, were measured. "Let's take a break," he said halfway through, but shortly thereafter we began the routine again. At the end, he excused me while he read the graph to detect deception in my responses to the questions.

I rejoined Shirley, Tree, and Ray, who had been waiting in one of the offices on that floor and we vainly attempted conversation. After a while, Mr. Minor called Charles Ogletree in to discuss the examination results. He had found no indication of deception. When I saw the look of relief on Tree's face as Minor reported the results, I got my first glimpse of the anxiety he'd gone through in asking me to undergo the polygraph examination. Despite any confidence he had in me, he, too, must have known that the examination could not remain secret. We were both overjoyed that it was over and pleased at the outcome. Minor and Ogletree planned a press conference to announce the results of the examination.

Within minutes of completing the polygraph examination, I was back in the car. For a brief period I enjoyed the free feeling one feels out of doors before we retraced our route and returned to my hotel room—the sanctuary that was quickly becoming a prison. I rushed straight to the television, concerned that I may have missed something of importance. Because the scheduling of testimony had been haphazard, I was uncertain what I had missed. Fortunately, the committee conducted little business in the morning, so that we returned in time to see the end of the testimony of the panel of my friends, the corroborating witnesses.

For about an hour they had been testifying that I had told them of Thomas' behavior well before the confirmation process began. The hostility to them had soon become apparent. "I want to know," demanded Senator Charles Grassley, Republican from Iowa, "do you want to see Judge Thomas on the Supreme Court? And I would start with you, Judge Hoerchner."

"Senator, I am only here to tell the truth about what I was told back in the early 1980s. You have heard the truth today, and it is up to you to decide what to do with it," the judge responded.

Senator Grassley continued his search for political animus. "Ellen Wells?"

"I echo what the judge says. I am here to give you this information that I know to be the truth, and for me to sit here and to say what my personal opinions may be about Judge Thomas's qualifications for the Supreme Court, I think would not be appropriate, it would not answer to what I am here for," Ellen Wells offered.

"Professor Paul?" the senator asked, moving on to the third panelist, law professor Joel Paul.

"Senator, as a legal scholar and an attorney, I have been asked the question many times prior to these allegations, whether or not Judge Thomas should be confirmed. I did not take a position then, I am not taking a position now. I am simply here to tell the truth about what I was told by Professor Hill four years ago, that she was sexually harassed by her supervisor at the EEOC," Paul explained.

This response seemed to provoke the senator more than any. "I am kind of puzzled. If you have reason to believe that Judge Thomas is a sexual harasser or guilty of sexual harassment, why wouldn't you sign a letter against the nomination?"

"First of all, Senator, I was asked to sign a letter prior to these allegations. Second of all, Senator, I believe that Professor Hill told me the truth in 1987, but I believe that you, Senator, and the other members of this committee sitting here trying to determine the facts should wait to hear all the evidence, before making a determination. As I said in response to Senator Simpson's question, if Judge Thomas, in fact, committed the acts alleged, then I don't think he should be confirmed. If he did not commit the acts alleged, I have no position." Paul's response was noncommittal and lawyerlike—not one upon which he could be indicted. Perhaps this is what angered Senator Grassley all the more.

"It seems to me like people in your position ought to have a personal view of whether or not Judge Thomas ought to be on the Supreme Court and that you would welcome an opportunity to express it, and that you would think that, for a non-lawyer like me, it would be important for me to know it to determine whether or not you have got any bias."

The senator's lecture to Joel Paul and the rest of the panel assumed that they would allow any questions they had about Thomas' qualifications for the Supreme Court to control their recollection about what they had been told. This was a decidedly Washington insider perspective—politics controls over any moral or ethical sense of right or wrong.

Clearly, both Senators Grassley and Simpson were trying to put the panel members in a no-win position. It was impossible to explain to professional politicians that one may have a political difference with someone and not act on it. And lawyers, in particular, often have substantive differences, yet choose not to act on them to oppose a court appointment. Moreover, I know of no lawyer who would risk disbarment by fabricating a story to prevent a presidential appointment. If any of the witnesses said that they were against the nomination, then the senators would claim it was that bias that led to their testimony. If they said that they favored the nomination, the senators could use that to undermine the seriousness of Thomas' behavior. The witnesses were right to keep their opinions out of it.

Grassley and the others had the benefit of many legal scholars, who in the first round of the hearing had talked about Thomas' qualifications to be on the Court. In the end, Professor Paul got the better of the exchange with Grassley and provided perhaps some comic relief at the senator's expense. In response to Grassley's remark about the importance of forming an opinion about Judge Thomas' qualifications, Professor Paul shot back in a professorial form designed to put an end to questioning. "Senator, I didn't have the opportunity during the original round of hearings to review the record, but if you would like me to review the record, I will be happy to come back and present you with my opinion."

Immediately following Professor Paul's retort, Senator Leahy reminded Grassley that only members of the Senate had taken an oath requiring them to vote on the nomination of Judge Thomas. Referring to himself and his Senate colleagues, Senator Leahy asserted, "We are the only ones who must state an opinion."

Finally, the questions turned to the substantive issues of the hearing. Both Susan Hoerchner and Ellen Wells testified that they had discussed the behavior I described in my testimony with me when it occurred in 1982. Neither had a political or personal axe to grind with Clarence Thomas or any of the senators. And both had undertaken to testify at considerable risk. Hoerchner held a job that was a highly public, appointed position. Wells lived and worked in Washington in jobs that constantly interfaced with the federal government.

Having failed at efforts to attack their credibility, instead of accepting the testimony as credible, members of the committee now sought to shame them for not originally encouraging me to file a complaint. Senator Simpson, in his questioning of Judge Hoerchner, expressed disbelief that Hoerchner, acting as "a counsel or friend," hadn't advised me to "do something" about the harassment I experienced. Senator Grassley echoed Simpson's assessment and offered his own that it confirmed nothing about "any sexual harassment by Judge Thomas of Professor Hill." Ironically, individuals who had taken great risk to offer testimony were now being admonished for irresponsibility in not giving counsel to pursue the claim earlier and dismissed with the conclusion that what they had to say, truthful or not, did not matter anyway.

From my perspective those who testified to corroborate my account were wonderful friends. They came forward and held firm in the face of unwarranted hostility from the Republicans. Thomas' supporters developed huge dossiers on the political and social activities through their investigators. And each of the witnesses risked the further wrath of the Republicans even in the aftermath of the hearings, a wrath manifested in challenges to the employment of at least two of the witnesses, Susan Hoerchner and Joel Paul. Moreover, they risked the response of an angry public. They, too, received threatening letters and phone calls in response to their participation in the hearing. One vile individual actually mailed fecal matter to Judge Hoerchner at her office.

But far more important to the process than their loyalty as friends was the integrity of these members of the panel. And it was that, as much as anything, which brought them forward, each separately and against the odds, to testify. Judge Hoerchner was the only member of the panel who, prior to the leak, had been aware of the statement I sent to the Senate. John Carr, with whom I hadn't spoken in years, wrote a letter reminding me that I had told him about Thomas. It arrived in Oklahoma the day following my press conference. And after attempts to reach me in Oklahoma failed, Ellen Wells came to the offices of Pepper, Hamilton and Scheetz the day before the hearing to confirm her recollection of the harassment. My last prior contact from Ellen had been a Christmas card she mailed the year before. Joel Paul contacted the Senate directly, through his own attorney, and spoke with the press even before any member of my team had spoken with him. He and I had not been in contact in years. None of the witnesses knew each other, having met for the first time in the Senate building during the hearing. The very idea that these four people, living in three different cities and coming from four different walks of life, could have conspired to come together in that setting is preposterous.

When I heard them testify, I consoled myself in the realization that no matter what the senators on the committee concluded, those who knew me during the time knew that I was telling the truth. Late in the hearing, on Sunday afternoon, when many members of my team balanced precariously on the edge of bitterness, Senator Kennedy summed up the import of their testimony eloquently:

> [Some people] just don't want to believe you and they don't want to
> believe Professor Hill. That is the fact of the matter, and you may be

detecting some of that in the course of the hearing and the questions this afternoon. But I hope . . . that after this panel we're not going to hear any more comments, unworthy, unsubstantiated comments, unjustified comments about Professor Hill and perjury, as we heard in this room yesterday. I hope we're not going to hear any more comments about Professor Hill being a tool of the various advocacy groups after we've heard Ellen Wells and John Carr and Joel Paul, all who have volunteered to come forward after they heard about this in the newspapers, comments about individual groups and staffers trying to persuade her. I hope we're not going to hear a lot more comments about fantasy stories picked out of books and law cases after we've heard from this distinguished panel or how there have been attempts in the eleventh hour to derail this nomination. I hope we can clear this room of the dirt and innuendo that has been suggested [about] Professor Hill, as well, about over the transom information, about faxes, about proclivities. We heard a good deal about character assassination yesterday. And I hope we're going to be sensitive to the attempts at character assassination on Professor Hill. They're unworthy. They're unworthy. And, quite frankly, I hope we're not going to hear a lot more about racism as we consider this nominee. The fact is that these points of sexual harassment are made by an Afro-American against an Afro-American. The issue isn't discrimination and racism, it's about sexual harassment. And I hope we can keep our eye on that particular issue.

That speech helped me to realize that I had not failed and neither had my witnesses. Nevertheless, the speech, as heartfelt and well delivered as it was, would neither lift the Republicans from the mire in which they willingly wallowed nor rally the Democrats to the higher cause of redeeming the nomination process. The fact was that the public had heard the cries of racism, perjury, conspiracy, and untruthfulness. And however unfounded, those cries hit their mark. Even had all dirt been cleared from the hearing room at that moment, it could not have been swept away from the public's mind. Kennedy's involvement in the recent rape trial of his nephew, William Kennedy Smith, made him vulnerable, and the Republican senators could and would in the end dismiss his admonitions. With no Democrat on the hearing panel to take up the cause, Senator Kennedy's speech was too little, too late.

CHAPTER FIFTEEN

To know that Wells, Hoerchner, Paul, and Carr were willing to stake their reputations to testify was one of the most moving events of the hearing. But even before I knew of the investigations that were being conducted into their lives, I had decided that I could not ask any more of my friends to face the treatment that the Republicans had dealt out. Though several people had volunteered to come forward and vouch for my character, I felt it would have been a senselessly brutal act to send them into the hearing. Tactically, some felt this was a mistake. But I do not believe that another panel would have convinced the committee, and by late Sunday afternoon, the time allowed for the hearing was drawing to an end.

The only witness whose testimony could have been crucial whom the committee hadn't called was Angela Wright. Hearing from her would be far more significant than bringing on another panel of character witnesses for me. After all, this proceeding was about the question of Thomas' behavior and character, not mine.

All weekend long we had waited to hear from Angela Wright, a woman at the EEOC whose experience with Thomas had been similar to mine. Even as late as Sunday afternoon, the committee's chairman was uncertain about the remaining course of the proceeding. But what happened in fact differed from what Biden had previously outlined. Angela Wright never appeared. She had been subjected to attacks about her credibility even though she had not been called. Judge Thomas himself had said that she was a "worthless" employee whom he had to fire. Various panel members described her as disgruntled and her testimony as unreliable. We heard a variety of stories about why she did not testify. The one offered the most was that Wright had gotten cold feet and was afraid of being exposed by the Republicans. Later we learned that the stories we heard had been untrue. It was Chairman Biden himself who withdrew Wright's subpoena.

What appears to have happened was that the committee simply refused to call her. The chairman claimed that they had run out of time, even as panels of women testifying for Thomas continied to appear. Again the committee's action raises the question of relevance. Like the testimony of John Doggett and many of the quotes from newspapers, the comments from women claiming that Thomas had behaved inoffensively toward them were simply irrelevant to the question of whether he had behaved offensively toward me. Since I had not claimed that Thomas treated all of the women on his staff in a sexual manner, in a legal proceeding on sexual harassment their testimony would not have been admitted. I can think of no legal proceeding or quasi-legal proceeding where persons who are not victims of an alleged offender are called to testify that they were nonvictims of the offense.

Angela Wright's testimony, on the other hand, was relevant for several reasons. In the face of my testimony, Thomas had claimed that he never treated anyone on his staff in the manner described by me. Angela Wright's testimony would be enough to rebut that claim, as would the testimony of Sukari Hardnett, a woman who served as Thomas' special assistant in the mid-1980s and gave the committee a statement asserting that she, too, had witnessed similar behavior by Thomas. But Angela Wright's testimony was relevant on its own without my testimony. According to Angela Wright, Thomas had commented often on the anatomy and appearance of women in the office, making many derogatory remarks about women's figures. He had asked her the size of her breasts and commented that certain parts of her appearance "turned him on." Wright would also testify that Thomas showed up, uninvited, at her apartment one evening. And though according to Wright, Thomas' suggestions had not "bothered" her, Wright's corroborating witness, Rose Jourdain, would describe how Wright had come into her office crying in response to remarks by Thomas. Regardless of whether Wright was describing Thomas' behavior as sexual harassment, it was relevant to the confirmation hearing because it reflected on the judgment and professional character of the nominee.

Similarly, Sukari Hardnett asserted that Thomas attempted to date her and that when she refused, his attitude toward her became less friendly. According to Hardnett, he then attempted to enlist her help in getting friends of hers to date him. In addition to rebutting Thomas' claim that he treated female staff members as professionals and took no personal interest in them, Hardnett's observations, like Wright's, reflect on Thomas' carriage and demeanor in the workplace.

Hardnett's and Wright's testimonies would have been relevant as support to my claim, in establishing a pattern of sexual advances and comments in the workplace and directed toward his assistants. In considering the conduct, much can be made of the similarities between Hardnett, Wright, and me. We were all roughly the same age at the time of the incidents—all younger than Thomas. We were all single women and thus could be easily viewed as vulnerable. We are all from southern or rural backgrounds with relatively few connections to power in Washington. And we are all black.

In the end, the Senate seemed hostile to hearing from any of us. Neither Wright nor Hardnett was called, and I was allowed to testify only after public pressure mandated it. Later I learned that a fourth woman, Kaye Savage, had also tried to contact the Senate, to testify to Judge Thomas' fascination with pornography. At the time I lived in Washington, Kaye, who worked in the Reagan White House as a political appointee, was a mutual friend of mine and Thomas'. The committee dismissed her without even taking her statement. And in addition to rejecting the information offered by these witnesses, the committee refused to hear from experts in the field of sexual harassment. Dr. Louise Fitzgerald, a noted psychologist and academician who has worked for years studying sexual harassment, was ready and available to provide the committee, formally or informally, with information about sexual harassment. Dr. Fitzgerald did provide the committee with a fact sheet on the issue. But the committee would later cite lack of time as a basis for not calling her.

By late afternoon the morning clouds had turned to drizzle. After hearing from the panel of corroborating witnesses, the committee took a brief recess. Back at the hotel, having returned from church, my family waited, unaware of my activity that morning. Emma Jordan hurriedly gathered them for an announcement about the polygraph examination and the press conference, while outside the Senate building, Paul Minor and Charles Ogletree held a press conference to announce the results of the polygraph examination. After explaining his credentials and administration of the test, Minor announced that "there was no indication of deception to any relevant questions." Scientific evidence now refuted the conjecture of the Republican senators that I was lying. There was elation and even weeping among some individuals of the crowd. Just as intense was the reaction from the Republicans. Senator Hatch assailed Ogletree and the examination as "exactly what a two-bit lawyer would do." Senator Danforth's response was more calculated. He shifted from accusing me of lying to a theory that he and a Connecticut psychiatrist, Dr. Jeffrey Satinover, had been exploring since the prior evening.

Two days before, Senator Specter had offered John Doggett's assessment of my psychological state to explain that I simply imagined Thomas' interest in me. When their reference to Doggett's pseudo-psychology failed, the Republicans attempted to use real psychiatry to condemn my claim. True to form, rather than rely on real evidence of disorder, the Republicans built a case on off-the-record comments and sheer conjecture. In addition to Satinover, Senator Danforth consulted a psychiatrist, Dr. Park Dietz, and learned of a condition called De Clarembaults's syndrome, commonly called erotomania. The syndrome, characterized by obsessive romantic interest in a person, is named after a

French psychiatrist, Dr. Gaeton de Clarembaults, who identified the disorder in a patient in 1921. A person suffering from the disorder imagines a romantic relationship with a targeted individual though no romantic interaction has taken place. A sufferer will obsess over the target, sending cards or letters that express romantic interest, and may even attempt to confront the target directly. One extreme example of the syndrome involved John Hinckley, Jr., who attempted to assassinate President Reagan to gain the attention of the target of his romantic interest, actress Jodie Foster. Incidentally, Dr. Dietz testified about the syndrome at the Hinckley hearing.

In offering this syndrome as an explanation for my testimony against Judge Thomas, Senator Danforth neglected three crucial factors. First, the situation to which I testified at the hearing did not fit the scenario of someone suffering from De Clarembaults's syndrome. I never had a romantic interest in or involvement with Thomas, nor did I believe that Thomas had a romantic interest in me. To the contrary, at all times, I knew that his actions were motivated by control and intimidation. He was attempting to flex his political muscle as well, believing that, as a presidential appointee, he was entitled to certain liberties with people less powerful. Though I testified to what I thought were his motives at the time of the hearing, the senators were guided by the belief that a claim of sexual harassment is genuine interest somehow perverted. Certainly, if I had harbored an obsessive romantic interest in Clarence Thomas, someone in the workplace would have known about it and would have testified to that during the hearing. But only two people claimed that I felt a romantic attachment to Clarence Thomas, Phyllis Myers Berry and Virginia Thomas. In her testimony, Ms. Berry admitted that she had no facts on which to base her theory. Virginia Thomas and I have never met. And one can imagine that she is guided by her own romantic interest in her husband when she assumes that other women find him attractive as well.

In addition to ignoring the fact that the behavior I engaged in did not begin to approximate the symptoms, Danforth ignored the relative obscurity of the disease and that sufferers of the disorder are far more likely to be male than female. The likelihood that I would suffer this dysfunction is extremely rare. When compared to the likelihood that I, as one American woman in three, would experience sexual harassment, Danforth's reliance on this explanation for my testimony seems not only result-oriented but sinister. An impartial fact finder would have regarded the disorder only as a last resort, given the lack of factual support, and would have at least entertained the notion that my testimony was true before pursuing the idea that I suffered so rare a psychological disorder. Senator Danforth was being nothing less than illogical in believing the least likely explanation rather than a more likely one, and his actions represent irresponsible and dangerous misuse of psychiatry—a misuse calculated to appeal to stereotypes rather than to clear reasoning or science.

Years after the hearing I would telephone Dr. Dietz. Relying on his sense of professional integrity and willingness after the fact to put politics aside, I questioned him about his role in the hearing. He seemed willing to talk to me, giving me the best time to contact him and returning a telephone call twice until we finally connected. He reported to me that he first got involved through a telephone call from a political lobbyist for conservative causes who had liked an antipornography position he had taken prior to 1991. Senator Danforth ultimately flew him to Washington to consult with the Republicans.

During our conversation Dr. Dietz defended his role in supplying the information about De Clarembaults's syndrome while arguing that he "wanted to keep psychiatry out of it."

"Dr. Dietz," I inquired, hoping for redemption for the profession, "have you ever studied individuals who were sexually harassed?"

"In my practice, I have had occasion to see patients who have been victims of harassment," he was quick to respond.

"You must then be familiar with the symptoms of those suffering from sexual harassment—based on your work with your patients," I offered. He allowed that he had counseled a number of sexual harassment victims.

"Did any one of the Republicans ever ask you about the symptoms of actual sexual harassment victims?" I asked. He paused, explaining that he was asked about his work on erotomania. "Did anyone ever ask you how to distinguish between someone suffering from delusion and an actual victim of sexual harassment?" I pressed.

He paused again. "No, no one ever asked."

Late Sunday evening it became clear that neither Wright nor Hardnett or the witnesses who could support their claims would be called to testify. As I listened to the testimony of John Doggett, followed by the panels of women who testified that Thomas behaved properly toward them, the whole affair moved beyond the realm of the unreal into the surreal, from an intensely painful experience to a spectacle as ludicrous as it was bizarre.

The media's lack of sensitivity about harassment, the brevity of coverage allotted, along with the media manipulation by White House staff members and consultants, may explain the faulty coverage. And these factors may shed light on why, throughout the process, an independent press went along with the Republican perspective. But I can make this observation only with the benefit of hindsight. At the time of the hearing, I read, watched, and listened, searching for something in the stories and commentaries that showed that they indeed reflected my experience. Finding very little, my feeling of isolation grew all the more intense. Fortunately, in the days and years to follow, the press would look more closely at the issue of sexual harassment and begin the work of a more complete appraisal of the hearing itself. Unfortunately, however, much of the damage to the issue of harassment, my reputation, and the idea of citizen involvement in the nomination process had already been done. And as absurd as some commentary and reporting was, I felt the sting deeply. By Sunday night I had had more than enough. I would not subject my friends to any part of the committee's character assaults, nor would I myself. Neither the press nor the committee seemed interested in getting to the truth of the matter.

CHAPTER SIXTEEN

When I was a child, I eagerly accepted invitations from relatives and family friends to go home with them. Unlike JoAnn, who was more of a homebody, I followed aunts and uncles and neighbors whenever allowed. Because I was so willing, I got a number of invitations. "Why don't you let us take Faye home with us?" Mrs. Reagor would suggest. After some consideration and stern admonitions to "be good" and "mind" Mrs. Reagor or whoever was taking me, my mother would pack a few of my clothes, and off I would go, anxious for the new experience. But a few days into these short visits, I would always grow impatient. My family had no telephone, and soon I longed to hear my mother's and father's voices, as well as the playful teasing of my brothers and sisters. My visits would end with me as eager to return home as I had been to leave.

As I sat in my room at the Capitol Hill Hotel on the morning of Monday, October 14, 1991, I felt the longing simply to go home, as if leaving Washington and going to Oklahoma would put an end to the entire matter. "We're leaving this morning. Make sure everyone is ready to leave by ten," I told JoAnn that morning from my room at the hotel. "But what about the rest of the hearing?" she asked, surprised by my announcement. I explained to her that there would be no additional panel; I would not testify again and the hearing would adjourn.

JoAnn, the sister closest to me in age and experience, was my family contact throughout the hearing. When we were growing up, though nearly four years my senior, JoAnn had had to accompany me at bedtime. When I wanted to visit a burial ground which was located on our farm, my mother instructed the reluctant JoAnn to join me. When I, at eight, was ready to have my ears pierced by our Aunt Sadie, as my sisters Joyce and Carlene had done, my mother and I coaxed the reluctant older sister into doing the same.

Throughout this entire ordeal JoAnn, whose reputation in our family is of one quick to anger, had been a paragon of patience and calm. She did not know where I was but I spoke with her every day of the hearing trying as best I could to keep her informed of the events as they unfolded. And she tried to comfort me, though she, too, must have been angered and confused by it all. Finally it happened. All that I had for days dammed up burst forth like a geyser. Through tears I confessed to her, "I just want to go home."

The testimony that I had given on Friday provided enough for those interested in hearing the truth to make an informed decision. I struggled to find a reason for a second appearance—something that could be accomplished. Few of the senators had any positive goal for the process. The Democrats were impatient from the beginning, and the Republicans seemed only interested in finishing my destruction. Even as I was preparing to go home, Senator Danforth was trying to publish allegations by Oral Roberts University students. Though I knew nothing of his plans, I decided to go home without testifying again.

Beginning the job of gathering the family together and getting them home, JoAnn first went to my parents. "Is Faye leaving today?" Daddy asked. "I'm not leaving here without Faye," he declared. She assured him that we would all be leaving. So instead of bracing for another day of testimony, they prepared to travel back to their respective homes (except for my sister Elreatha, who stayed in Washington to spend time with her son, Gary Lee). My parents and JoAnn would head back to Tulsa; my sisters Doris, Joyce, and Carlene and my niece LaShelle to California;

and Ray, Eric, Shirley, and I to Norman, Oklahoma. After making arrangements for the care of her toddler, Matthew, Louise Hilsen also traveled with us to Oklahoma to handle the press inquiries.

Our entourage of eleven boarded the airplane together. I sat beside my anxious father, who was on the second airplane flight in his life, and my equally anxious mother, who complained that the portions of airplane food were too large. Connecting to our various destinations in Dallas, we entered the Dallas–Fort Worth International Airport to the glare of television cameras and the inevitable crowd they seemed to generate. Arrangements had been made for courtesy carts to escort us to our connecting flights, but the hostility of the crowd was evident even before we could be driven away. As we moved through the gauntlet which had formed, we could not avoid the jeers and catcalls. "Shame," one woman hissed. "Wench," someone else shouted at me. I could detect only one person who offered support and encouragement. She was at the edge of the crowd as we made our way through it. I focused my attention on her—the rest melded into a blur of hostility.

As we prepared to board our connection for Oklahoma, we realized that my father was not with us. He had left to go to the men's room and had not returned. "Go see if you can find him," I told Eric. "We're getting ready to board." Panicking at the thought of his eighty-year-old grandfather lost in the airport, my nephew went to find him. He returned with my father in tow just in time for my parents and JoAnn to board the airplane to Tulsa. Our flight to Oklahoma City left a few minutes later.

As I sat on the plane for the short flight from Dallas to Oklahoma City, I tried to anticipate the reception we would receive in that airport. But my apprehension proved unnecessary, as the crowd gathered in the Oklahoma City airport was welcoming. Just as someone had organized the hostile crowd in Dallas, friends had organized this gathering at the airport to make sure that my return there was welcoming. I was just as surprised to get this reception as I had been to receive the jeering in Dallas, not yet grasping the full impact of the situation. I had been in a hotel room shielded from much of the public sentiment for nearly three days. But I began to realize that my life was going to be an unsettling series of ups and downs for the foreseeable future.

Nevertheless, I was glad to be home. In less than an hour after I arrived in Oklahoma City, I would give my first comments since testifying. I was happy to be on campus in the student union—a familiar setting. Just prior to my entering the room, I spoke with Charles Ogletree. "You should know that they have people in the crowd who are going to try to discredit your statement," he warned. I was still unaware of who or what all was behind it. My only response was to stay with the comments I had prepared.

The crowd gathered in the ballroom was much larger and friendlier than I had expected. I looked and saw Frank Elkouri, a retired member of the law school faculty. His face and the face of his wife, Edna, caught my immediate attention. I had known them since I came to Norman in 1986. Their worried though somehow hopeful and smiling presence among the crowd reassured me. I did not know that Frank's stomach had been wrenched with pain because of my ordeal. Another colleague, Peter Kutner, had taken to driving his car aimlessly for hours the day following my testimony. Others were just angry. The faces in the crowd came into focus as I recovered from the sheer surprise of it all. In the union were people with whom I had worked or served on committees or seen on campus and in the community. All helped to assure me that I had returned home. My brother Ray introduced me over the noise of the crowd. As I approached the microphone, I smiled for the first time in what seemed a long time.

My message was brief. I wanted to reiterate my purpose in going to Washington and the sincerity of my claim. But mostly, I wanted to thank them for their support. In my hotel room Senator Simpson's Sunday afternoon theatrics about letters from Oklahoma had shaken my confidence. The people present in the room did not share whatever negative sentiment had been conveyed to him—with one notable exception. As Ogletree had warned, a placard held high in the crowd declared that my statement was "not sworn testimony." Interestingly, though clearly unintentionally, the sign was an implicit endorsement of the statements I'd made in the hearings, which were sworn testimony. The young man holding the sign had apparently anticipated that I would say something about Thomas. Perhaps he even thought that I might attempt to give the further testimony which I agreed to forgo. Oddly, the same misdirected message appeared over and again indicating that, however ill thought out, it *was* planned. The message on the sign was not as important as the indication that it gave of some organized effort to attack my statements. This kind of organized effort would mean difficulty for me beyond the problems I faced in Washington.

My welcome back to Norman, and to Oklahoma, was largely positive. Yet early on, individuals began a campaign to drive me out of Oklahoma and, in particular, out of my position on the faculty of the university. That lone placard gave scant notice of the insidious things to come.

CHAPTER SEVENTEEN

In Washington, Senators Hatch, Specter, Danforth, and Simpson kept up their attack. Danforth released a statement by John Burke, a partner at the Wald firm, challenging my claim that I had left the firm voluntarily. Burke recalled that I had worked extensively with him and other lawyers in the tax, general business, and real estate sections of the firm. Burke further alleged that he advised me that I should look for other employment. Of course, those statements were completely false. I never worked with him and never received any kind of evaluation from him.

Danforth released the statement despite the fact that Donald Green, the partner "responsible for associate [attorneys] evaluations" as well as the firm records, disagreed with it. Green first submitted an affidavit to the committee, responding immediately to the Burke statement. And he followed up with a letter which provided more complete information based on the firm's written records, informing Senator Biden: "There was no indication that Professor Hill ever worked on a legal matter with Mr. Burke or under his direct or indirect supervision. Professor Hill did perform a brief assignment for another partner more senior to Mr. Burke in [Burke's] field of law. Professor Hill's work was favorably reviewed by that partner. There was another first-year African-American woman associate who did work with Mr. Burke during the time described in his affidavit, who was given an unsatisfactory evaluation and who was asked to seek other employment."

Nevertheless, when Senator Danforth circulated Burke's statement, he did not include Donald Green's response. Again, the truth of the allegations did not matter. At the same time and for months thereafter, Danforth attempted to circulate slanderous allegations made by Oral Roberts students. Allegations were submitted to the press to destroy my personal and professional reputation in order to cast doubt on me. This attack was not about the truth—it was about destroying me.

Before I returned to Oklahoma, some well-wishers had sent flowers to the law school. Some of my colleagues had taken the plants to my home. After the press conference I went home with a bouquet of balloons to a walkway lined with flowers. In contrast to the scene outside, inside, the bomb threats and hate mail began to arrive. My telephone rang constantly, and since I had no way of knowing in advance whether the caller would be friendly, I answered—but always with trepidation. When I grew tired of the threats and condemnation, I let the answering machine take over the job of receiving them. Eventually, an additional telephone line gave me the security of knowing that I would not miss calls from friends and family.

My neighbors Dewey and Katherine Selmon and Wilma and John McFarland brought over casseroles; friends called to offer their assistance and comfort; my mother came to stay with me and help me deal with the stress and turmoil; and on the weekends JoAnn would come with her two younger children to assist and to divert my attention from the fracas. Jonna and Jerry, my niece and nephew, were always a distraction.

One evening, as we were sitting down to dinner, David Swank came by the house. He asked to speak to me alone. "Campus police have received a call—a bomb threat," he warned. "They are taking it seriously. Just to be on the safe side," he advised, "you may want to go to a hotel for the night." I went to my mother and sister and suggested that they spend the night in a local hotel. When I told them why, they insisted, "We'll stay here with you." Though I would have felt better had they left, I knew that I could not begin to run from the threats. This was one more test of my will but not one that I would choose for either of them or the children. True to their nature, they stood with me. Each of us prayed for safety that night. Thankfully, there was no bomb. I could never have forgiven myself if anything had happened to my family that night.

One of the first salvos in Oklahoma came on the day I returned. The same woman who, in September, had claimed I collided with her car now telephoned a local television station to complain that I had been involved in a hit-and-run accident with her. She left the impression that I had crashed into her vehicle and fled the scene in a speedy getaway. She neglected to tell the reporter that I had given her my insurance information or that she had failed to follow up with my agent by setting an appointment for a damage assessment. According to the police, there was no basis for her claim. Louise Hilsen's presence on that day was invaluable. She and Shirley Wiegand took the inquiries from the television station, answered what they could, and referred them to my insurance agent. The story did not run. But knowing that this woman had motives other than the truth, I took my car to the insurance claims adjuster, whose inspection indicated that no such collision had occurred. Nevertheless, in the weeks to come, the *Washington Times* newspaper would carry an editorial chiding me for irresponsibility in the situation. Clearly, every aspect of my life was going to be manipulated to serve political and economic gain.

Physically exhausted and nerves frayed from lack of sleep, I returned to work on Tuesday, October 15, 1991. Reporters filled the halls seemingly occupying every vacant space. In an effort to stem the requests, I agreed to a few interviews that, with a few exceptions, the *Los Angeles Times'* Roberto Suro interview being one, seemed particulary off the point. The pressure was bent on discovering a political plot. One reporter from *The Washington Post* was determined to discover when I had developed my sense of "racial awareness"—when, in Senator Heflin's words, I developed my "militant attitude about civil rights"—as if that held the key to understanding my role in their imagined scheme. Mostly, the interviewers asked the same question, albeit sometimes phrased differently: Why didn't you simply remain quiet? In the more trying times, I asked myself the same question.

My students could not wait for the press to leave the school, and they expected me to be in class once the hearing had concluded. The time I spent preparing and teaching my classes allowed me to escape the events that had led to national and international attention. But unfortunately, in the classroom, the press presence and the hearing itself led to friction. My relationship with my first-year contract class was disrupted. And despite my best efforts through the fall and spring semesters, the relationship remained strained. The students in the upper divisions who were taking my commerical law class made the most of a difficult time for us all. More mature than the first-year students, they pulled together despite the disruption. They continued to study and work hard on their assignments and were focused even when I was distracted. As a teacher, one hopes to be an inspiration to students. During the fall of 1991 the group of second- and third-year students in my commercial law course were *my* inspiration.

Some students even volunteered to be my unofficial security guards. This effort was organized by Butch Carol, a bodybuilder, who enlisted others from his weight-lifting group "to help out." Friends remarked about how impressive my security looked. And, as photographs of me surrounded by tough-looking, muscular men appeared around the country, some in the press reported that they were professionals. We all chuckled over that; Butch and his recruits were some of the shyest and gentlest people at the school.

Pain from my tumors increased with the stress of the other discomforts in my life. Yet I was in no physical or emotional condition to face the surgery necessary to relieve it. I postponed the operation which had been scheduled for the Thanksgiving holiday period. I could not face the physical trauma, or the prospect that the growths might be malignant. Once classes were completed, just before Christmas, I would. For the time being, however, the upheaval in my life which had begun immediately after the press leak continued at the same pace.

The week of my return, Eric had minor surgery, the first in his life.

Complications from the procedure landed him bleeding and in intense pain in the Norman Regional Hospital emergency room in the middle of the night. I could only pace the floor in the waiting room in response.

Prior to my testimony, University Media Services had coaxed me into appearing in a promotional video for the university. On Friday a member of the press informed me that the university's president, Richard Van Horn, had withdrawn the video that was to be aired during the upcoming football game. Later the video would run without my brief and rather innocuous appearance. When I learned that the clip had been pulled, I was hurt. This editing was a shunning—a clear effort at disassociation by an institution of which, prior to my testimony, I had been such an integral part that I was asked to appear in the piece. And as I was working in the provost's office on the same floor of the same building as the president's office, the fact that I learned of the president's decision from the press rather than from the university added insult to the injury. It was a thoughtless slight. Perhaps not a deliberate one, but one that nevertheless added to the burden imposed by every other. The university office of media services sent the following explanation to the dean's assistant:

> *We have replaced the footage and voice of Professor Hill with new information strictly as an attempt to make sure our institutional message on undergraduate education is clearly understood and not over-shadowed by the visibility of Professor Hill as a result of her media exposure nationwide. In other words, Professor Hill's appearance on the tape would have changed the focus of the spot and diffused the institutional message. . . . Professor Hill is one our best and brighest and articulate faculty members, and we may use her in a spot later this year.*

I supposed that some explanation for removing me from a university promotional tape was better than none. I assumed that I had been solicited to do the spot for the reasons spelled out in the last sentence of the explanation. Yet I knew that the university acted not simply because of the fact of media exposure, but because of content of the exposure. Explanation aside, there as no excuse for the failure of the public affairs office to communicate the decision to me directly. This simple act was the harbinger of a general distancing from me by some in the administration—of making me precisely the outsider the senators had portrayed.

I had been home for less than a week when a crank from Seaside, California, reported that I had sworn to him in August that Thomas had not harassed me. Norman Spaulding's slanderous report appeared in a newspaper which he published and edited. Of all the allegations that were to appear about me, this story was the most preposterous. I have never been to Seaside and never gave an interview to anyone named Norman Spaulding. Had it not been so blatantly false and exploitative, it might have been almost funny. Spaulding claimed that I appeared in the Seaside City Council meeting on August 1 or 15 wearing a hot-pink suit and two-inch hot-pink heels. Though no record of any introduction appears on the audiotape of the meetings and everyone on the council denied it took place, Spaulding alleged that I was introduced to the City Council. Following the meeting, he claimed, he interviewed me for thirty minutes and gave me tips on how to fabricate a better sexual harassment claim. But however laughable it all was, Paul Harvey reported it on his nationally syndicated radio program, and the *Washington Times* ran a story on it in the newspaper's A section. Norman Spaulding had no doubt achieved his goal, with the participation of the national media, and no one seemed concerned about the cost to me.

Almost immediately upon my return home, the *Daily Oklahoman,* Oklahoma City's only daily newspaper, began running editorials on the hearing. They generally proclaimed that Clarence Thomas should be confirmed and that his opposition had invented the testimony. Editorializing was not limited to the editorial pages, as the news reports portrayed me as a party to a conspiracy against Thomas. The newspaper has made clear its position on the issue. But what the *Oklahoman* has never made clear to its readers is that the editorial page is controlled by an individual who helped to launch Clarence Thomas' career as a judge.

Patrick McGuigan, before taking the position at the *Oklahoman,* was a

Washington, D.C., operative during the Reagan and Bush administrations. McGuigan liked Thomas because of their shared anti-affirmative action sentiments. Influential with the Bush administration, McGuigan reportedly called in a favor in getting Thomas appointed to the District of Columbia Circuit Court, putting Thomas in a position to move on to the Supreme Court upon the retirement of Justice Marshall. This clear apparent conflict of interest has not caused the newspaper to relieve McGuigan of his responsibilities on this issue. Yet McGuigan has made it clear that he will not be persuaded against his promotion of Clarence Thomas by the truth of my testimony or anyone else's. His recurring diatribes are repulsive, but are a reality with which I have learned to live—like the obscene letters and telephone calls I continue to receive.

Little of what happened to me during the week after my testimony made sense. Now there was no time to ponder my new circumstance as people stopped on the street to stare at me or pointed and whispered "Look, it's her," no more than four feet away from me. Some thoughtless cad posted my telephone number on an electronic bulletin board, effectively multiplying the prank calls. Total strangers who wrote or called or accosted me to condemn me to hell for real or imagined views which they attributed to me were now an integral part of what had once been a very private existence.

But accepting the hard fact that I had become a symbol of an issue and had thus lost something of my right to privacy was not enough. I had to accept being treated by people as less than human. I had become the female counterpart of Ralph Ellison's "Invisible Man." I was obvious, but my humanity was not—like a figure in a wax museum to be admired, poked, glazed at, and photographed. Or insulted. Once a young couple in front of me at a counter began to speak about me in intentionally audible whispered tones. "Yes, that is her," he said. "Well, I just know she lied," she responded. "Look at her. I can't believe she has the nerve to be seen in public," she said. Finally, exasperated, I remarked that it was rude of them to "whisper" right in front of me. In a bizarre response, he referred to his friend: "We were just talking about the time she was raped." I retreated, realizing that anyone with so little sensitivity as to personalize rape and speak of it so glibly would have no qualms about offending me or anyone else.

Another time while I was shopping for paper towels, a woman came up to me and said, "You're Anita Hill, aren't you?" When I answered yes, she said, "I want to give you a big hug." In the next motion, without any further warning, she embraced me. I was so taken aback by the idea of a stranger hugging me in the middle of Target that I left the cart there and headed for the parking lot. What I had not yet grasped was the way that my testimony had touched so many women emotionally that they wanted to respond by touching me physically.

I was not used to such displays from strangers. I was hardly used to it from friends. Perhaps, if all of the reactions had been the same, I might have adjusted to it, but they varied jarringly from experience to experience. Some frightened me. Some shocked me. Some angered me. Some even amused me. Many made me want to withdraw; others made me want to strike back. But I was determined that none of them keep me from continuing with my life, and I adjusted by learning not to react to become the inanimate that others ascribed to me, not because I had changed, but, in Ellison's words, "because of a peculiar disposition of the eyes of those with whom I came in contact."

PART THREE

CHAPTER EIGHTEEN

On the morning of October 15, 1991, the news from Washington was that Clarence Thomas had enough votes to be confirmed as an associate justice of the Supreme Court. His seat on the Court was assured despite West Virginia Senator Robert Byrd's impassioned plea on the Senate floor against the nomination and announcement of withdrawal of the support from four senators who had initially been counted as yes votes. The remaining yes pledges, including those of Democrats Alan Dixon of Illinois, Chuck Robb of Virginia, Richard Shelby of Alabama, and David Boren of Oklahoma, still outnumbered the nos.

Busy at school, I tried not to think too much of the count and assumed the nomination's success. But the press members who returned with me to Norman after the hearing were a constant reminder. "Do you have a comment?" they asked, as if talking to a politician who was about to watch a vote on a piece of legislation she had sponsored, rather than the individual whose story was being judged. So skewed was their perspective that I had nothing I wished to share with them. I asked Ovetta Vermillion, who had the uneviable task of fielding their requests throughout the day, to tell them that no comment would be forthcoming.

The more persistent were not satisfied and followed me as I left the law school for home once again, camping across the street in a neighbor's yard. Once inside my house, I would pull the shades and try to block out what was happening across the street. I would not allow the invasiveness of television cameras into my home. But no curtains could close out the clamor that the scene in my neighbor's yard represented. For it was everywhere, inside my head and out. No matter how hard I tried "not to think about it," my power of concentration met its match, and, like millions of others around the country, my mind focused on the vote. The major television networks carried the vote live and my colleagues in the law school watched the televised proceedings from the atrium on the second floor. My mother, Eric, and I sat in my den in front of the television, watching for the inevitable—at worst, my final humiliation; at best, no more than I had expected all along.

The tension and nervousness of the senators showed through the veneer of the count's formality. The networks carried the vote almost as if it were a sporting event. For added drama, one broadcaster carried a live videotape of Clarence Thomas' mother watching the proceeding from her home in Pin Point, Georgia. When it was completed, Clarence Thomas succeeded Thurgood Marshall as associate justice of the Supreme Court, by a 52–48 vote, the narrowest margin of any Supreme Court nominee in history. The four-vote margin was much slimmer than what had been projected early on, though to the three of us it seemed like a resounding victory.

Out of kindness or perhaps their own hurt, Eric and my mother sat speechless, staring at the proceedings. Not wanting to say anything that might intensify or invalidate my reaction, they awaited my response. "Well, that's that," I remarked, the first to break the silence. Though the words lacked profundity or insight into my feelings, they served the purpose of allowing us all to exhale simultaneously. Ironically, my usually circumspect mother was the first to voice her emotion. "The dirty rascals," she declared of the Senate. A pained and angry Eric remained silent. I tried to maintain my dignity, resisting any sort of outburst that would only make matters more painful than the whole episode had already been. "It's okay," my mother said, trying to console me. "You did the right thing." She was her usual self—short of words and to the point.

I realized that both Eric and I were products of a guarded way of dealing with life's disappointments that had been passed from her to us, just as it had probably been passed from her parents to her.

Immediately after the vote, President Bush pronounced Thomas a "wonderful inspiration" and congratulated him for a job "well done." Meanwhile, Thomas' mother, Leola Williams, admonished me to pray about what I had done. She could never know how much I had prayed all along and would continue to pray. Oddly, I connected with her. Like my own parents, she, too, had become a part of the media spectacle.

A cadre of reporters, the persistent ones who followed me home, now gathered at my front door. I answered the doorbell knowing that ignoring them would only lead to baseless speculation or worse intrusions by the less responsible members of the group. "How do you feel about the vote?" a reporter asked. The question was inane, and I could not even begin to articulate an answer. How I "felt about the vote" got jumbled together with a myriad of feelings I had about the leak, the hearing, the process, and the people on my step. I could assign any one of many emotions to the vote—disappointment, hurt, outrage, hope, embarrassment, disillusionment. A clever sound bite would have been in order, but I had no handler or spinmeister to prepare me. The way of modern journalism, reducing persons to icons, appeared at that moment to have lost its skill for dealing with mere human beings. My mother and Eric were not public relations experts, and there was no one else there or behind the scenes who was. I managed a brief statement composed as I stood there in front of them. I was "disappointed but not surprised" at the vote. Having one week earlier shared a wholly humiliating experience on national television out of responsibility to the judiciary confirmation process, I now wanted to keep private any humiliation and resentment out of responsibility to myself and my family.

The group of reporters jotted down the few words that came from my mouth. The experience had made us more "aware of the problem of sexual harassment" and better "informed about the confirmation process." Finally, I responded, "What I hope is that none of this will deter others from coming forward. This is an important issue and the dialogue will not stop here." I had no inkling of the magnitude with which that prediction would be fulfilled.

Stepping back inside from the doorstep with two of the people I hold dearest in life beside me, I felt far removed from the hearing, the demonstrations which followed, and the Senate vote. That was all I wanted—to find the peace in my life that had vanished with the leak of my statement. And for a short while I believed that once I went inside and was alone with my family, it would all be over. The following morning, October 16, 1991, Erma Hill would be eighty years old. I wanted to believe that, come morning, that would be all that mattered.

Having achieved their goal, the persistent ones left, only to be followed within half an hour by another slightly less aggressive group who'd respected my desire to make no comment. Now they felt obligated to pursue a statement. It did not matter what I said; I was simply footage to be wired back to the studio. Had I not been tired and somewhat disgusted by it all, I might have seen the humor in the competitive frenzy of the press corps. But by that time, I saw little humor in any of it. "I already said everything that I have to say," I told them. "Well, just repeat what you told the last group," they instructed, trying to ensure that they had something to return to their employers. In the end, I gave the statement again. These, after all, had been the polite ones—the ones willing to respect my privacy at the risk of missing some scoop of news. Over the past week, I had learned that politeness only went so far in the "news" business, and in the coming months that lesson would be reinforced. I would also learn that just as I had been powerless in becoming a part of a news story, I would be equally powerless as I attempted to retreat from it.

The impact of the emotions that had erupted during the hearings was greatly and lastingly felt. The feelings involved were strong enough to pull together a community which had as its core women who had experienced sexual harassment but never before complained or who had complained only to find that asserting their rights resulted in greater distress. The community was held together by outrage and a deeply felt cause but had no clear outlet for either. What we now needed was policy, procedures, and accountability to deal with harassment. That was forthcoming as well. Rather than mushroom out of the hearing as the outpouring of stories had, the establishment of law and practices would evolve in a heuristic, trial-and-error manner over the next few years. But in time the strength of the community, developed during the hearing, would generate political and legal change.

At the same time that the feelings engendered by the hearing caused the emergence of one community, they threatened to splinter another. The African American community had been torn by the Thomas nomination itself, and the final round of the hearing with its allegations of racism splintered the community even further. I felt caught in the middle of the group that, though splintered over the nomination, was willing to cast me out for what was not so much an offense to Clarence Thomas as it was a breach of an unspoken pledge of solidarity to the African American community. By divulging information that was derogatory to a prominent African American, in the eyes of many I had done injury to the entire community far greater than Thomas could ever have done.

I was psychologically torn between two communities, both of which I belonged to by birth, chance, and choice. And while many members of one community embraced me, many members of the other shunned me. What we needed, in both cases, was leadership to help us to focus on the greater community goals. But for the time being none was forthcoming and I felt as though I were adrift.

Even religion turned against me, or I should say was turned against me. Thomas' mother had been gentle in her admonition, but others purporting to speak for the church or God or both advised me to confess my sins, or worse, condemned me to "burn in hell" for my sin of testifying. Before long a few voices, speaking on behalf of a church or religion, would attempt to console me for the experience I had endured, but not before I had grown to distrust the church, if not religion itself.

At the same time, the state and university communities in which I lived and worked became the object of the political forces of the issues raised in the hearing. The very places to which I had returned to escape the racial and gender politics of Washington, D.C., became the outlet of it all. Oklahoma, the place that my grandparents had seen as a place of refuge, once again proved to be as harsh as the place from which they and later I had fled.

CHAPTER NINETEEN

The immediacy of the response to the hearing speaks to its instinctive nature. It was as though the hearing touched a nerve that sent sharp pains to the stomachs of women throughout the world. That pain urged them to respond. There was no strategic plan—no complex analysis of the issue. Something from within impelled women to participate. Immediately following the hearing, demonstrations against the Senate's action and against sexual harassment began to take place. Mostly women demonstrated against confirmation of Thomas in Washington, D.C., on the steps of the Senate buildings. In cities around the world the message of outrage was almost universal. Mostly women protested the hearing; they protested the vote to confirm Thomas; they protested the existence of sexual harassment and the insensitivity to it demonstrated by their elected representatives. In Norman and in Stillwater, Oklahoma, sites of the college campuses for the state's largest universities, women whose activities had been long abated seized the moment of awareness—or perhaps the moment seized them. On the campus of Oklahoma University a student who had been in Washington during the vote organized demonstrations, meetings, and seminars on and about sexual harassment and women's social progress. Robin Drisco, a member of the staff of the local women's center, established a local chapter of the National Organization for Women. Throughout the country other women were doing the same. Women who thought that women's legal rights were protected against abuse realized that the law alone was not enough—that they, too, were vulnerable. They knew that the public had to be made aware of lingering sexism and that women had to be involved in making them aware.

The energy created by the furor over the hearing continued at a high pitch for months. Though I was aware of it, it was mostly as though it was happening in some other world. During the demonstrations, I was teaching my classes. During the rallies, I was responding to the backlog of telephone calls. During the seminars, I was answering questions for the investigation of the leak of my statement. It did not occur to me that all of the activity was about me, because it was not. The activity was about every woman who hurt because of the hearing. The hearing exposed a vacuum of understanding so massive and powerful that it would have sucked all of me into it had I not tried so hard to hang on to what was left of my life. Thus while others were organizing, rallying, and protesting against the hearing, I was trying to keep the experience at bay and to regain my health.

Despite the fact that I had papers to grade and an upcoming surgery, I was thrilled to finish my last class for 1991. I limped into December on what little reserve energy remained after the hearing and subsequent coverage. By December 18, 1991, surgery provided a strange kind of relief. Forced bedrest was the only thing that would have stopped what had become endless and tiresome activity. That morning I was apprehensive—trying to prepare myself in case the worst occurred. The doctor had all but ruled out the possibility of a cancerous growth, but some possibility remained. JoAnn, Mama, and I joked nervously in the moments before the anesthesiologist administered the sedative. Shortly afterward, in the surgery room everything went white as I counted backward from one hundred. I was out at eighty-eight.

As is normal following surgery, I woke up to ice-cold hands and feet. "Would you get my socks out of the suitcase?" I asked JoAnn. Her face and my mother's were the first thing I saw when I woke. Someone flashed a Polaroid photograph in front of me. "Look what they found," someone said. Dr. Melanie Gibbs, my surgeon and gynecologist, had photographed the tumors and cysts they removed from my body. To my doctor's surprise, there were about eighteen in total. The largest pale pinkish glob was no less than six inches in diameter. Two others were roughly the same size. The smallest was a bluish gray glob about half an inch in diameter. Thankfully, none of them were malignant. She had performed a myomectomy, removing only the growths and leaving intact the uterus.

Gradually, other faces appeared as my family and friends crowded into the small hospital room. "She looks so little," said Eric, looking away. He was unaccustomed to a helpless "Auntie Faye." My mother asked how I felt. My mind suggested that I was happy to see them, but all my body wanted was sleep. Somewhere in the recesses of what thoughts I could muster through the haze of the anesthetic, I wanted to lapse into a state of physical semiconsciousness and wake up days later, fully rested and refreshed. But of course, I woke the next day feeling sore, stiff, and hollow inside. Ray appeared that day at my hospital bedside to serve as my chief nurse. Despite the pain and mild depression I felt between naps, his face was a welcomed sight.

"Mary Brown" was the name that appeared on my chart. It was the unimaginative choice I had chosen to register under in an effort to avoid pity for me, intrusion, or speculation about my condition. So, on the morning of December 20, when the press descended on the hospital, after some initial concern, I was certain that it was not for me. It turned out that Governor David Walters' son, Shawn, had been brought to the hospital after an attempted suicide. From my window I could see the entrance to the hospital, where the press milled about relentlessly. My nurses complained that they couldn't even enter the building without encountering cameras and reporters. From my vantage point, watching the mayhem, I could empathize, in a small way, with the intrusion the Walters family must be experiencing as Shawn Walters clung to his life before dying a few days later. The press was there throughout. Shawn's tragic death was the culmination of all the pressures placed on the twenty-one-year-old, not the least of which was the continual press attention to his personal difficulties. The value of privacy is grossly underestimated until it's been stolen from you.

I went home on Saturday, December 21—at the height of the holiday season. The reds and greens of the holiday meant little to me, the gray, damp December weather itself a better match for my disposition. On Christmas Day my mother, Ray, and I said grace over a quiet Christmas dinner. Though I admittedly had much to be thankful for, I felt little cheer and a small portion of the gratitude I had felt at Thanksgiving. For the first time in memory, my mother and father were apart at Christmas. JoAnn had picked my father up at the farm, and he had had Christmas dinner with her family in Tulsa. The week following Christmas passed and my mood changed only a little, though I attempted to be cheerful and gracious for my mother's benefit and those who came to visit me.

Because my mother does not drive and the doctor had advised me not to, we were housebound, a condition which I do not tolerate gladly. The expenses for my family's trip to Washington were mounting and with the recuperation came the time to consider the experience of the hearing. Back to me came the feeling that I had had as a child—the year of my father's injury and my aunt's death, the year we waited to learn whether my brother John would be sent to fight in Southeast Asia.

I was hurting, both emotionally and physically, and I was angry. "Why did they do this to me?" I asked myself. I was sure that nobody had an answer, least of all my friends and family. I prayed, mostly out of hope, but partly out of spite, that I would survive. Mostly, I wanted my life back for my sake, but, in addition, I was determined that my detractors would not have the satisfaction of stealing it.

On New Year's Day Mama found a long-forgotten bag of black-eyed peas in the cupboard, and the two of us brought in the year in a traditional way. "Do you think they're still good?" I questioned skeptically, recalling that Eric had sold them to me many years ago as part of a church fund-raising project. "We'll soon find out," was my mother's response. In Owasso, JoAnn prepared the "good luck" peas for my father when he arrived on the farm with his delivery. Her husband, Jerry, made the corn bread to go with them. Again my parents were apart, but in spirit the family was together.

Gradually, my family, friends, and the hundreds of holiday cards and greetings I got from people around the country lifted me from the dark gray corner of my mind. Someone sent me a tape of Truman Capote reading "A Christmas Memory," in which a young boy and his cousin make fruitcakes for everyone they know, as well as Eleanor Roosevelt. It amused and touched me. Then someone else sent me fruitcakes as a gift, and despite my apprehension in face of the death threats, I ate some. Soon the stiffness and soreness lifted and my mobility returned.

An ever-attentive nurse, my mother did not share my belief in the possibility of an expedited recovery. Dr. Gibbs had said that I could return to work six weeks after the surgery. Until then, she instructed me to be mobile but cautious. While Mama erred on the side of caution, I erred on the side of mobility. At my urging, a few days after New Year's, my mother and I took a walk in the neighborhood. I overdid it, all the time hoping to hide my grimaces. I was successful in the deception, and the walk convinced her that I was well enough to be left alone. She returned home, and within three days I boarded an airplane for San Antonio, Texas, for the annual meeting of the Association of American Law Schools.

The trip did wonders for my spirits but, in fact, set back my recovery. Still, all things considered, it was a worthwhile junket. The collegiality which I always experienced at this meeting had special meaning coming within months of the hearing. The minority law teachers' section, of which I was a member, and also the women's section, of which I was not a member, honored me with two presentations. The warmth and the camaraderie expressed at those functions belied the stereotypical image of law professors. The issue and the event touched the human side of all of us, and these individuals seemed happy to have that side exposed.

Best of all, much of the legal team was reunited. Emma Coleman Jordan had organized a reception for the team, which grew to include a hundred or so of the law professors present at the meeting. Professor Jordan, there with her husband, Don, and two children, Kristen and

Allison, was about to take over the position of president of the association. This responsibility followed a year as president-elect which included her participation in the hearing. In addition to her official responsibilities, she pulled together a gathering of friends and supporters with seeming ease, just as she had pulled together the legal team.

The outgoing president, Guido Calabresi, then the dean of the Yale Law School, was present at the reception as well. Dean Calabresi had testified in support of Thomas' nomination in the first round of the hearing at the urging of Senator Danforth, another Yale Law School graduate. In short, Calabresi sought to convince the Judiciary Committee that Thomas had the capacity to grow into the role of associate justice. His was certainly no ringing endorsement of the nomination, but coming from a dean of a prestigious law school it was important.

I had known Dean Calabresi since he taught me torts in my first year of law school. As a professor he was a favorite among first-year law students, perhaps because he was more spontaneous in the classroom than his colleagues. Yale being the kind of school that it is and my being in the same profession as Calabresi meant that we saw each other from time to time professionally. I was fond of him, and when we saw each other, he seemed to be sincerely interested in my welfare. In the nearly twelve years since I graduated from law school, I had not returned, however, to New Haven. What, exactly, he thought of the Thomas nomination at the time of his testimony or even on that evening, I do not know. (Rumor has it that he called Danforth during the hearing and tried to dissuade him from smearing me.) That evening he seemed genuinely disturbed by the debacle which had unfolded in October 1991. And he delivered an invitation, partly at the encouragement of the students, for me to speak at Yale.

Like Professor Jordan, many of the members of my legal team were law professors. Professors Susan Deller Ross, Kim Taylor, Charles Ogletree, Shirley Wiegand, Kimberle Crenshaw, and Tania Banks had all been present in Washington and were now reunited in San Antonio. The occasion took on a lighthearted tone, though I suspect that what we were all feeling as much as anything was relief that the grueling process was over. I was also proud and grateful that they had helped me through it.

Classes began on January 13, 1992, and back in the classroom and into a routine, my emotional and physical recovery inched forward. As the spring of 1992 approached, I realized that I was destined to relive the uncertainty and turmoil of the summer and fall of 1991 all over again. After some consideration, I decided to decline all of the invitations to appear on talk shows. The usual format they followed did not lend itself to helpful discussion about the issue. My presence would have only made matters more volatile. Moreover, I was sure that the focus would be the politics of the nomination or the personalities of Judge Thomas and me. I wanted to talk about harassment. Of all the hosts, Phil Donahue and his producer seemed the most sensitive and open to a change in format. Whether out of self-consciousness or mistrust, I declined their invitation as well. Directly following the hearing, neither I nor the public was ready to discuss the issue rationally. Still, if only partly to refute the idea that I had become a recluse, in January I granted an interview to Ed Bradley of *60 Minutes*. I had long admired his work, and he struck me as a sincere individual, less affected and more animated than most of his professional counterparts.

I did not relish being in front of the television camera and felt too self-conscious to enjoy the experience. Yet I was beginning to appreciate the value of a visual image. I had learned a lesson from the print media. No matter how provocative or inflammatory the question asked, what appeared in print was only the exasperated response, with the hostile question omitted or toned down to a gentler version. For example, before the hearing a reporter called me and told me that the Republicans were trying to say that I was pursuing Thomas by frequently talking to him and persistently telephoning him. "That's garbage," I responded. That statement was later characterized as a denial that I had called Thomas' office. It was pitted against the telephone log which showed that I had called the office eleven times in ten years. Of course, the logs did not show that I had actually talked to Thomas that number of times and revealed nothing about the business nature of the calls, and neither did the news stories. Yet my statement about the inferences being drawn from the logs was used to show my untruthfulness. So despite my discomfort with the television camera, I concluded that the format of even a taped and edited interview reduced the opportunity for a manipulation of the question and response.

The interview itself was less than satisfactory from my perspective and likely from that of the *60 Minutes* crew as well. Ed Bradley was relaxed and comfortable. His producers were courteous and professional. But it was only January, and I was still badly wounded and mistrustful of the press. I could not bring myself to discuss the pain from the hearing that had not ended in October but continued with attacks from local Republicans. The Senate investigation of the leak was still pending and I did not want to jeopardize it or myself. The positive impact of the letters and support I received and the sense of urgency that the stories of harassment generated in me were my only focus. I could not help feeling that, if people glimpsed the urgency that I felt from reading these letters, they, too, would see the need for remedy in these matters. In January 1992 I tried to show the public this in the interview, but was either unable to convey the message effectively or was addressing a television audience that was not ready for it.

Though the hearing was over, my contact with the Senate was not. On October 24, 1991, the Senate had passed Resolution 202, which called for the appointment of a "special independent counsel to investigate . . . recent unauthorized disclosures of nonpublic confidential information from Senate documents in connection with the . . . nomination of Clarence Thomas." Less than two weeks after the vote to confirm Clarence Thomas, the Senate had taken swift and clear action to investigate "the leak" of my statement to the Senate. The pity was that they had not acted promptly in investigating my statement. When the investigation was announced, I got the clear impression that the establishment of the special counsel was as much to investigate me as it was to investigate the leak. Peter Fleming's appointment and the institution of the investigation only confirmed my feelings.

Through a contact from David Swank, Andrew Coats, an Oklahoma City attorney, volunteered to represent me in the investigation. Coats' dual experience in criminal law and politics made him ideal for the job. From October, when the investigation was announced, until Fleming's final report was issued in May, I felt as though I were under the continual scrutiny of the Senate. Resolution 202 called for the use of the FBI in Fleming's investigation. The unprecedented way in which the White House used the agency during the hearing persuaded me that the Senate might misuse it again.

I met with Peter Fleming and his assistants twice in the winter and spring of 1992, first on February 11 and later on April 23. Held in Mr. Coats' office, each meeting lasted approximately five hours. Fleming questioned me about where I had been and to whom I had spoken from July through October 6. He was particularly interested in telephone conversations. He asked me for the "records of all transmissions" of telecopy machines in the "University of Oklahoma Law School, or in the University Provost's office"; "records of the Federal Express overnight service utilized by the University of Oklahoma Law School to the remainder of the country for the entire month of September and the first week of October"; and my home and office telephone records, as well as the "telephone records for every telephone at the University of Oklahoma Law School" for that time period.

I submitted all of my personal records to him, and Dean Swank and Provost Richard Gibson submitted their department's records. He asked for specifics about calls to my parents and my sisters and colleagues with whom I had been in contact. I answered his questions thoroughly. Fleming questioned me about my statement, how it had been notarized, to whom I had given it. I answered and submitted the logs of the person who notarized my statement. Fleming questioned me about anyone whom I might have talked to about the statement and about people I never even knew—individuals associated with interest groups in Washington. He interviewed my friends, colleagues, and members of the legal team—"every person [I] called during this period who would have been in a position to speak with the press."

I had nothing to conceal and wanted to know the source of the leak. But I was certain that I was being forced to revisit this painful episode to satisfy the Republicans in the Senate who were offended on behalf of President Bush and Judge Thomas. They were still bent on some retribution for their embarrassment in having the claims reach the public. As I relived the experience, I was keenly aware of the fact that the special investigator neither questioned Judge Thomas nor requested his or Senator Danforth's records. No one seemed concerned with my hurt or embarrassment.

The Fleming investigation included inquiries into Timothy Phelps' and Nina Totenberg's activities. As the two reporters who first aired the story about my interview with the FBI and statement to the Senate, both likely knew the source of the leak. Totenberg had a copy of my statement. How it came to her is still a mystery. Their cooperation was limited; both rejected requests for interviews. Fleming countered by issuing subpoenas to Phelps and Totenberg demanding that they appear and bring with them documents relating to the investigation. Again, Phelps and Totenberg resisted but were later deposed. Citing the First Amendment's protection of the press, they continued to withhold the names of their sources and the records of their telephone calls.

Fleming asked me to write a letter to the Senate Rules Committee supporting his request "to compel answers from Tim Phelps and Nina Totenberg." Though I had a personal interest in finding out who had leaked my statement, I refused to be used by the Senate in their fight with the press. I found it ironic that the same body which had treated me so ungraciously would seek my assistance in this matter. I was only as important to them as I was useful. Finally, the chess match concluded when the Senate declined to seek further information from the two reporters.

As a lawyer I have a healthy respect for the First Amendment's free press protections. Yet I was bothered by the fact that the reporters, the ones closest to the source of the leak, were protected from the government's intrusion and I was not. As a private citizen I have some constitutional protection of my privacy but none which the Senate felt compelled to recognize. Despite the fact that Peter Fleming had even asked for the details of telephone conversations I had with my sister JoAnn, most indications were that Fleming was trying to be reasonable in his inquiry. Despite Fleming's best intentions, the process designed to be a violation of my privacy proved to be just that. Yet I did not have the status and connections to shield myself from any inquiry no matter how far-fetched it seemed. I did not have the time or resources to fight the Senate and the FBI. Moreover, by the time of the investigation, I had depleted any energy with which I could wage such a fight.

After months of the investigation, I saw it as yet another examination of me, rather than a means of improving the confirmation process. And though Fleming seemed to view his role as that of neutral fact finder, his questions about contacts with interest groups made clear that he was pursuing the Republicans' conspiracy theory. I was willing to cooperate with an investigation, but what was developing was an effort to discover whether I was deliberately or negligently responsible for the public awareness of my statement.

In his letter to Andy Coats dated March 31, after reviewing all of the information gathered to date, Fleming expressed regret that the investigation called for a second interview. Through no fault or even intent of Peter Fleming, the investigation became a replay of the hearings. Once again, I was questioned extensively about private confidential matters while Thomas was given deference. And the press, which could not and should not be castigated by the government, failed to respond to legitimate concerns that the public has about confidentiality of government documents.

A three-hundred-page document that failed to identify the source of the "unauthorized disclosure of" my statement was the end product of Fleming's investigation. On May 5, 1992, an assistant sent me a copy of Fleming's report. The letter accompanying the report was brief to the point of perfunctory.

Dear Professor Hill:

I enclose a final copy of our report.

Sincerely,
Mark H. O'Donaghue

By the time I received it, I had stopped wondering about what conclusions Fleming might reach. Yet, despite my temporary indifference and my misgivings about the investigation, I was stung by the fact that nowhere in the letter was there any acknowledgment of my cooperation in the investigation—there was certainly no "thank you."

Like so many things that occurred in my life during this time, I viewed the conclusion of the investigation with mixed feelings. I found one thing in the contents of the report about which I could be positive. It made clear that I had in no way deliberately acted to set in motion the public hearing of the matter. This message no doubt escaped the diehard conspiracy proponents but it was a consolation for me. And by May of 1992 I needed affirmation.

The attacks on my personal and professional integrity continued. Threats of violence, now routine, were no less frightening and only slightly less disconcerting. Rumors spread that there was a reward being offered by a "conservative women's organization" to anyone who could find "dirt on Anita Hill." David Brock's virulent "hit piece" had appeared in the *American Spectator Magazine* supplying Thomas' supporters with new perversions for their attack on me.

Official involvement in the episode, which peaked with the televised hearing of October 1991 and the vote to confirm Clarence Thomas to the Supreme Court, ended with the special investigator's submission in May. But this was the only sense in which it was finished. Within various communities in the population, the matter was far from completed— mere mention of the proceedings evoked highly pitched and emotional debates. Those debates grew into rare frank conversations about gender, race, sex, and finally, sexual harassment.

Though the impact of the hearing of 1991 on my own life is of course profound, that is not what made this event significant. What made the hearing significant is the reverberations felt in a number of communities: the African American community, the community of all women, the academic community including my university and law school community, and finally my community of relatives and friends—all communities in which I have some involvement. I measure the importance of the hearings on how it changed—if in some cases only in terms of the dialogue—these communities and my relationship to them.

CHAPTER TWENTY

Notwithstanding its familiarity, the drive to the law school from my home, even with its four stop signs, is too brief and distracting to provide much time for reflection. In the aftermath of the raucous days surrounding the hearing, the halls of the school portray the kind of calm that exists only after a period of chaos. But underneath that surface the chaos continued. My requisite cup of coffee in hand, I pause at my office door for inspiration from the quote I have displayed there for years. "You gain strength, courage and confidence by every experience in which you really stop to look fear in the face. . . . You must do the thing that you cannot do."

I clipped these words of Eleanor Roosevelt together with her photo from a 1987 calendar which depicted the words of a different "peacemaker" each month of that year. Roosevelt's words speak directly to the law school experience, an experience which tries most students and some faculty. Originally, I chose this quote to allay the fears of my first-year law students. But for years these words had accurately applied to my own challenges as well, and never more so than in 1991. Each day as I entered my office, they provided me with a bit of determination to face my own fears. For just as the actions of the Judiciary Committee had issued a challenge to other women, it challenged me as well. And inside my office, just beyond the quotation, new demands awaited my response.

I open the door to my office and am reminded of the comments from students about the calming effect of its blue walls. The colors and textures of the room, the Wedgwood blue of the walls, the textbooks impressively bound in a fabric intent upon resembling leather, the soft tans and browns in the painting of an African woman and her child, even the wood of the oak desk, have a calming, familiar effect. They contrast the piles of mostly unopened mail that amassed daily. The letters I received had become priceless to me. As I struggled to understand my situation, each offered the promise of new insight. Each day I set about to read at least a few, treating each like the precious item any one might be. By this time the trays of letters and cards arriving daily totaled about six hundred. They were coming with increased frequency. It was October 24. I woke that morning to the news that Clarence Thomas had been sworn in as an associate justice of the Supreme Court. But the event had little real consequence in my life. For a moment the thought of it stung me lightly but when I arrived in my office to the mail, the faxes, the telegrams, and the ringing telephone, it did not matter.

Careful not to spill my coffee, I sit at my desk and clear off a small space. On this day, I discover a missive that fulfilled the promise.

Dear Professor Hill,

Don't believe the things they say to you about bringing shame on a black man. They said those same things to me when I divorced my husband. Some men bring shame to themselves by the way that they behave. You did the right thing. Hold your head up.

I was at once consoled and dismayed by this letter. Though happy for the affirmation that I had done the right thing, the accuracy of her observation about the reaction from the black community saddened me. I was just beginning to feel the toll that that reaction would take on me.

Growing up in Oklahoma, I was always keenly aware of my race and the social and psychological implications of being black in a state whose history and politics were often aligned with those of the Jim Crow

South. The penalty for failure to understand racial dynamics was severe even if only rarely dealt. The stories of racially motivated beatings and lynchings and restrictive laws in the state, though old, had lost little of their power to remind us that we were an identifiable minority with a history. My father told of the threats against eligible blacks of mixed Native American descent who sought to register on the tribal roles or to vote in the general elections. My uncle told of his fear when his car broke down at night on the outskirts of a "sundown" town. My mother told of the fifteen-hour bus ride to a relative's funeral in Arkansas and being restricted from using the rest room facilities at various stations along the way. Ten of my siblings graduated from segregated schools. So even in the unlikely event that the color of my and my family members' skin had somehow become insignificant, the stories about race and the racial dynamics I experienced reminded me who I am and what that meant to others. More than the racism, it was the culture of the black rural community from which I derived my identity. The programs at the local black high school, the tiny wood-frame churches sprinkled throughout the countryside, the food, the music, the language, were all uniquely black and often uniquely rural. I knew who I was. I had always identified with the black community.

Yet in 1991 that community, the source of my social and psychological identity from childhood, became the source of my greatest discomfort. Voices in the community rose to condemn me for committing a community sin—bearing witness against a black man made all the worse because my protest involved matters of sexuality. For the first time in my life, I began to question my place in the black community and its place in my life. Nevertheless, in this letter I saw not simply the community's condemnation but an affirmation of my continued membership in it. A USA Today poll of African Americans showed that 63 percent thought that Thomas should be confirmed, though only 47 percent said that they believed Judge Thomas was telling the truth. Though only 20 percent believed my accusations, 43 percent said that the racism in the process was directed at Thomas. At the conclusion of the hearing, President Bush appealed to the Senate based on that very sentiment in the African

American community. On the day of the confirmation vote, Bush described Thomas a "wonderful inspiration" who had the "overwhelming support of the American people."

There were other voices in the African American community. In November a group of African American women had taken out an ad in *The New York Times* and various papers around the country condemning the actions of the Senate Judiciary Committee in not fully investigating my claim and in the way it conducted the hearing after the leak of my statement. Shortly after the hearing, Jewel Jackson McCabe, founder of the Coalition of 100 Black Women, a national civic and social organization made up of local chapters, invited me to New York to receive an award from the organization. Some of the local chapters agreed; others did not, reflecting the mixed feelings of the larger African American community. Nevertheless, I knew that only through black women as individuals and as groups would I regain my place in the community. Some black men had spoken out on my behalf. During the hearing, Roger Wilkins and an ad hoc group, Concerned Black Men, attempted to engage the press in a more realistic discussion about the issues raised. After the hearing, the Reverend Jesse Jackson became a supporter, but these voices were drowned out as the politicians played on those who expressed hostility to me and my claim. Nevertheless, I knew there were African American women who fully appreciated my dilemma and embraced my right to speak as their own.

As I explored my feelings toward the community of my birth and choice, my first concern was for the two African American women who followed me at Thomas' office, Sukari Hardnett and Angela Wright, both of whom told of similar behavior. I felt a sense of guilt and indebtedness to them both. Perhaps if I had brought a claim against Thomas, Wright and Hardnett may not have had to endure Thomas' behavior. I even recalled other incidents long forgotten. Once when a black female law student, who was married at the time, had sought my advice about a clerkship with Thomas, my own self-doubt kept me from vetoing the idea. I counseled her, never mentioning Thomas' behavior toward me but suggesting that she proceed cautiously before pursuing the matter—

making sure she knew what she wanted. "Perhaps as a married man, he has matured," I thought to myself. "Perhaps he will treat her differently because she is married," I rationalized at the time, recalling that I, like Hardnett and Wright, had been single and Thomas was recently divorced.

Despite the similarities in experiences, both Wright and Hardnett deny that what happened to them was sexual harassment. Though outwardly different, our reactions represent similar ways of dealing with the dilemma raised when black women are harassed by black men. In my own way, I may have denied the behavior, or its effects, by attempting to maintain some semblance of a cordial relationship with him to give the appearance that I had moved beyond the hurt and pain. My reaction was not atypical. After the hearing one writer, a black woman, described her experience with a black man for whom she had once worked. During an interview in his home the man, a minister, husband, and father, propositioned her and bragged about his sexual experiences with "ninety-some women." When she tried to leave his home, he blocked her way until he heard his son's car in the driveway. After some prodding she told her boss at the newspaper, but assured him that she "would separate [her] feelings about the man from [her] assignment and do a good story, because a good story was there and that was [her] job." When she reported the story to her friends, they refused to believe her, and eleven years later she still refused to reveal the name of her harasser publicly. We prove we are conditioned "to handle" such behavior in order to prove that we belong to the race and to establish our womanhood. This conditioning teaches us to deny both the nature of the behavior and the harm we feel from it.

The dynamics of race, gender, and community expectations made it harder for me to sort out my responsibilities to other women who had worked with Thomas. Both Wright and Hardnett were older and better politically or socially connected than I, if not by much. Though each maintains that she was not intimidated by Thomas' behavior, Wright's friend recalled that at the time it brought Wright to tears and sent her away from him trembling, fearful, and angry. We all grew up in a society that tolerated harassment and in a pocket of that society, the black community, where our racial allegiance was measured by our own tolerance of it.

In our community rules against protesting harassment, domestic violence, and even rape are reinforced by the stories about violence toward and lynching of black men. The experience may hurt the individual, but disclosure, we are told, hurts everyone. "You must protest if a white person calls you a 'nigger' but you must not complain if a black man calls you a 'whore,' " is the message we hear, despite the similarly degrading impact. The dilemma to which we are subjected results in a form of self-denial that contributes further to the degradation.

I recognize that Wright's and Hardnett's and my own responses can only be understood within a cultural framework. Yet I am also aware that contextualization of experience can be misused. For example, during the hearings Orlando Patterson, a sociologist from Harvard University, declared that raw sexual language was part of the courting ritual of black American males whose origins are in the rural South—a dialogue misunderstood by the kind of puritanical, white middle-class mores I had adopted in my protests. Patterson concluded that I was rejecting my own cultural standard in favor of "white" standards and associations, a taboo in any community with strong ethnic identification, and one engendering particularly strong disfavor in the African American community where "trying to act white" is viewed as a mortal sin.

Not only does Patterson's analysis cast racial blame on the complaining victim of sexual harassment, but as Kimberle Crenshaw pointed out, Patterson's "courting ritual" explanation gives license to all men, black and white, to use obscenities in social interaction with black women. By placing the theory and language in the context of "courting," as opposed to a form of maintaining a gender hierarchy, Patterson suggests an interaction, process, or dialogue that black women not only tolerate but enjoy and invite. Thus, black women who are being true to our culture know, understand, and appreciate it. Black women like me who object are being "uppity" and are not "black enough." The theory is strikingly similar to those espoused to perpetuate slavery and segregation in America. Some justified slavery and the legalized subordination that followed the Civil War as the natural order of the culture of the agrarian South. Those same apologists claimed that the systems were enjoyed by both blacks and whites. As such, blacks "liked" being slaves, could function no other way, and often used slavery and segregation to their benefit. Those who objected were being "uppity" and denying their culture and proper place.

Patterson's argument plays on historic political discord in the black community as well. Within the black community the volatile issues surrounding class distinctions evoke some of the same internal conflict raised in discussions of the oppression of black women. Both raise the question of who is best qualified to represent the race. The class conflict reaches back as far as the divisions between W. E. B. Du Bois and Booker T. Washington. The former argued for equality in all aspects of the society, while Washington asserted that blacks should pursue skills and crafts and forgo, at least for the time being, social equality. The class division is evident today among those who theorize that social programs such as affirmative action strengthen only the middle-class blacks, who have in turn abandoned the "community," at the expense of poor and working-class blacks.

By declaring the theory to apply to southern and rural blacks, Patterson is suggesting that the black northerner or intellectual might differ in his courting. Moreover, Patterson is operating in a cultural climate where rural and southern equates with poor and uneducated in the minds of many. The woman who objects to this form of pursuit is attempting to be not only "white" but "bourgeois." Patterson thus says that the sexual or social pursuit of rural black women, in particular, involves a level of communication which upper-class or urban black women might reject but which the former have no right to resist.

On Monday, October 7, following my first press conference, I received a telephone call from a man who introduced himself as an officer of the Chicago chapter of the NAACP. His purpose in contacting me was to explain that my complaint was absurd because, he asserted, "Thomas was simply doing what black men do." The unfortunate response to the caller's "that's just the way black men are" theory is that "black women know how to handle themselves." Both trap men and women into a crude way of interacting.

Both Wright and Hardnett appear to be strong women who handle themselves well in many situations. I was only too grateful that they did come forward once the press carried my statement. But who could blame any of us for not wanting to become embroiled in the clash that had erupted? We were trained to simply keep our own counsel or at best tell only a few friends. They were advised as well not to encourage confrontation. "Handling" the situation means telling the person who engages in such behavior to stop doing it, finding ways to avoid contact with the person, and ignoring the hurt, fear, embarrassment, and emotional injury the behavior causes—for the good of the race, we are told. But those feelings exist no matter what your race. We must deny our gender in order to maintain our racial identity.

The invocation of cultural excuses for gender subordination and abuse is not only a distortion of community mores, it is a manipulative excuse for illegal behavior. Patterson's theory represents the unscientific way in which the larger community often deals with ethnic culture—substituting myth for fact, mimicking for analysis, but in essence only validating prejudice. Thus, rank gender subordination, a subtext in our community, continues because of the fear of racism. Unfortunately, that subtext is becoming more and more the main theme as portrayed in popular culture as violence against black women by black men increases, as it does in society in general.

A community standard which requires that women "toughen up to" gender abuse for the sake of the community creates a complex set of dilemmas. Particularly where toughness requires her to participate in her own denigration, she loses her individual dignity. A requirement that she show her toughness by not protesting such behavior places her at odds with other more broadly accepted definitions of feminine traits and makes her responsible for ending the behavior. In sum, it encourages a dangerous and vicious cycle of abuse.

As I sat about piecing together the role of social and cultural perception in the events of 1991, I knew that I must look beyond the simple facts and the pat explanations to the broader issues and deeply held presumptions. I even looked to history for a present-day explanation, believing that any society is a total of our experience past and present. In our slave history black women in America experienced the economic exploitation of their sexuality. Even before the law prohibited importing slaves into the country, slave owners saw procreation as a way of increasing the number of new slaves in their holdings. Thus, slave owners used slave women as labor and as a means of continuing the institution of slavery by reproduction. Slave women were forced to reproduce in whatever way the owner deemed necessary. Owners encouraged the raping of slave women to enlarge the slave population. Owners and overseers who participated in this abuse had to justify it to a society which held itself out as maintaining "high moral standards." They did so in the same manner in which they justified slave ownership. Black people, in general, had been cast as wild and animalistic, subhuman, and thus the enslavement of them was justified as being for the good of both blacks and whites.

Black women's sexuality, similarly, was cast as wanton, perverse, and animalistic. As a group they were presumed to be unchaste and eagerly available. Thus, their sexual violation was not an offense. Black women who might have the temerity to complain were accused of being delusional or imagining that they had something to complain about. As the justification goes, the men were participating in activity which the women invited by their nature. Since they presumed that black women welcomed all sexual activity, their violations could not be viewed as rape. The justification often went further, painting black women as sexual aggressors. Thus, those who engaged in sexual activity with black women became the victims. This unenlightened image of black women's sexuality continued after the end of slavery. And society continued to exploit the image for purposes of titillation as well as justification for abuse of black people in the same way that it exploited other myths of intellectual and moral inferiority it invented to excuse slavery.

Judge Thomas tapped into society's shame about the myths of black sexuality when, in his "high-tech lynching" speech, he claimed that the sexual harassment charges pandered to sexual stereotypes of black men.

His friend Harry Singleton asserted that he and Thomas had discussed how they had to be above reproach in the Reagan administration, given the sexual "stereotypes all black men deal with." Neither Thomas nor the senators nor the press recognized how the attacks of the Republican senators pandered to the stereotypes about black women's sexuality. Falsely casting me as an erotomaniac whose desire for an object prevented me from discerning reality from fantasy fit neatly within the myth of black women's sexuality. Thus, despite the lack of any supporting evidence, the theory became believable. False claims about sexually provocative comments, behavior, and demeanor aimed at young white males at Oral Roberts University fit within the myth of black women as sexual aggressors who victimize white men. Despite their contextual absurdity, these claims became believable to many. Comparisons between me and the young Tawana Brawley, who exaggerated, perhaps even fabricated, claims of depraved abuse and violence, went unchallenged, despite their dissimilarities, because they fit within the stereotypes of black women's sexuality. Orlando Patterson's observation is as false and just as dangerous because it relies on and supports these myths.

Thomas' selection and my shunning had its intended effect. Discussion in the white community turned away from the myths of black male sexuality and regrettably focused on the myths of black female sexuality. In 1925, in her prize-winning essay *On Being Young—a Woman—and Colored,* Marita O. Bonner asked, "Why do they see a colored woman only as a gross collection of desires, all uncontrolled reaching out for their Apollos and Quasimodos with avid indiscrimination?" But for the timing, Miss Bonner might well have been asking the question about the Senate Judiciary Committee members and Senator Danforth who sought to portray me as an erotomaniac. She could well have been referring to David Brock, whose fraudulent portrayal of me, presumptuously entitled *The Real Anita Hill,* hinged on sexual mythology about black women and society's willingness to believe it. Because Brock supported his case with fabricated and misquoted sources, I was at first amazed that the press gave him such broad license to define me. (He admits to never having talked to anyone who was at any time close to me. On the other hand, the information which he reports on Clarence Thomas comes from many of Thomas' political allies—in some cases the same people who provided information critical of me.)

When I realized the insidious resonance of these myths, the fact that reviewers failed to question Brock's lack of balance is no longer surprising. In today's society, with its demand for quick answers, David Brock's writings and others of its ilk often pass for analysis. Today's investigative journalism too often relies on salacious rumors to define a character. Yet despite the refutation of most of his material, many will believe David Brock because they are more comfortable rejecting my testimony than that of Judge Thomas. For to reject Judge Thomas' testimony, one must conclude that a perjurer is sitting on the nation's highest court. Moreover, those who have invested in his career, many of them highly placed and powerful, such as Senators Danforth and Specter, have placed their own judgment on the line in supporting him. To capitulate now would mean to admit a gross error and might even call for recompense.

David Brock is a product of the times in which we now live. As a white male he is given permission to define me, a black woman, on whatever terms he chooses, without establishing any credentials to do so. He is presumed to be free of bias, no matter how obviously biased his work may be. Many accept his claim to sources without reference to who they are or what their bias may be. Responsible journalists failed to see that there is a special danger in this approach, where it targets individuals who have been historically portrayed negatively without support. All too often all women and all men and women of color must then rebut the assumption created by misinformed definitions of us despite glaring logical inconsistencies. None of the critics questioned why a woman, as ambitious and politically and sexually aggressive as the woman portrayed by Brock, would ever go to Oklahoma to teach at an unaccredited, conservative, Christian law school. No one ever asked why that same aggressive, ambitious character would wait ten years to "get Clarence Thomas."

Brock was very adept at getting many of his reviewers to view me through the same warped prism from which he views me. They, like

Thomas' political supporters, do not relish facing the hard question of what acceptance that Thomas was untruthful means. Would journalists have an obligation to demand his removal from the Court? Would journalists have then to consider that their own role in covering the hearing may have contributed to the likelihood of the confirmation? Unwillingness to address these questions provides incentive to believe both Clarence Thomas' and David Brock's dishonesty. That same history and culture make it easier to believe mine.

All of Brock's false claims, accusations, and theories fall into a void about black women, another void about women who raise harassment claims, and still another, even larger void of misogyny. Brock's claims made about a black woman and supported by an expert of black social behavior in the context of claims of sexual impropriety presented a perverse and incredibly burdensome obstacle for me to overcome. In the context of the hearing, false rumors about my behavior and wishes flourished. One source falsely asserted that I did not want Angela Wright to testify because I feared that her more "openly sexual" demeanor might negatively reflect on my testimony and my more reserved demeanor. One colleague from Oral Roberts University, who ascribed overtly sexual intentions to my behavior, suggested that my reserved demeanor was intended to be a sexual come-on.

Angela Wright's reaction of denying that Thomas' comments bothered her and even my reaction of trying to maintain a cordial relationship are ways of coping with years of these combined stereotypical definitions of our sexuality. At one point in preparing for her testimony, Wright was told to borrow a skirt because the pantsuit she was wearing was not demure enough. Perhaps Thomas relied on our vulnerability to these stereotypes when he targeted Wright, Hardnett, and me—three young, single, workplace subordinates—for this kind of attention. Certainly, consciously or not, the Republican senators and some analysts relied upon them when they attacked our charges about the behavior.

Ironically, the community gives women and girls a guide for "handling" sexual harassment. We are urged by our culture to put harassers in their place or ignore the harassment. No matter how inadequate that guide is, it was at least available. The community chose Thomas as the black male to represent the race. Consequently, I had to be rejected. And there was no guide for handling the community shunning I received for my testimony. No one offered me a map to help me find my way back into the community.

The accusation that African American women bring down men is one that typically cuts deep to the quick of those accused of such behavior. It was a clever and calculated use of the politics of the African American community and our sensitivity to racism. The idea that I was a woman used by liberal whites and in particular feminists to bring down Clarence Thomas certainly had that very visceral effect upon community members.

The extreme to which this may be carried was tragically demonstrated in the Mike Tyson rape trial. Desiree Washington, the eighteen-year-old black beauty pageant contestant who accused Tyson of raping her in his hotel room, hit the barrier of community politics late in 1991 when she made her claim. Despite the fact that she, too, is African American, the community, led by a group of ministers, threw its support to him. In his defense, even while the facts of the incident were being discovered, they asserted that Mr. Tyson was a victim of his own success. Accordingly, in combination with racism the Indiana district attorney prosecuted him for rape because of his achievements and popularity combined with his race. To believe this, Ms. Washington must be cast as a liar or a pawn in the scheme to bring down Mike Tyson. Thus, the community declared that the potential for racial bias in the prosecution was more important than the possibility of sexual assault. More important, it played into the hands of the stereotypical portrait of African American women as untrustworthy attestants to sexual misconduct no matter who is the accused. Unfortunately, the support Ms. Washington received from feminists hurt her in the eyes of the community, fueling the community distrust of her claim. She was seen as a pawn of the criminal justice system as well as the tool of white women. Since white women are the very individuals whose claims of rape, though often manipulated, lead to the lynching of black men, Ms. Washington by proxy became a party to Tyson's "lynching."

The picture of a lynching is as repugnant to the black community as any, and false rape charges have too often been the tool for advocating lynchings. Through rape some members of the white community manipulated racist fears of black sexuality. George Bush himself selected convicted rapist Willie Horton as a symbol of his tough stance on crime. And certainly, Mr. Tyson deserved the benefit of the doubt of his innocence, as does anyone accused of a criminal offense. Nevertheless, in denouncing Ms. Washington's claim as part of a conspiracy, the community played on another set of racist notions—those about the sexuality of African American women.

Race has been a determinant in the conviction rates for all crimes. Part of the present and the history against which the African American community reacts is that blacks are more likely to be convicted of rape than are whites and that for years in the South the rape of a white woman by a black man carried with it the death penalty. What the community does not react to is the fact that historically there was no criminal penalty in the South for the rape of a black woman by any man, black or white. Moreover, studies of rape today show that the likelihood of conviction in a rape trial depends more on the race of the alleged victim of the rape than on the race of the accused. The conviction is less likely to occur if the accuser is black regardless of whether the accused is black or white. Thus, there is evidence that society has bought into the stereotype of the dishonest and untrustworthy black woman more readily than it has the stereotype of the oversexed black man.

I accept that both may have been at work in Mike Tyson's conviction. The Tyson defense team played a dangerous card portraying him as a sexual aggressor whose behavior, no matter how bad, was part of a common knowledge Ms. Washington shared. Notwithstanding this obnoxious and offensive portrayal of Mike Tyson, many among the community leadership chose his perspective over hers. It was a predictable choice given the racial reality as they saw it—the reality of blackness as male and moreover as the successful male athlete role model, no matter how he treats African American women.

The same approach would be echoed by Ben Chavis in his reaction to his dismissal by the board of the NAACP. Chavis was accused of settling a sex discrimination suit that had shades of harassment with $300,000 of badly needed NAACP funds. In response, many said a woman caused his demise, and shamed the African American community for political reasons. Nevertheless, whether or not Chavis ever harassed his accuser, it was Chavis who used the money of the nation's leading civil rights organization to settle his personal claim, and ultimately it was Chavis whose behavior brought him down. In the same way it was Clarence Thomas' own behavior which led to his public scrutiny and embarrassment.

Thomas and Chavis as a pair of black men publicly accused of sex harassment certainly represent two sides of the political coin. Chavis, whose career had been in civil rights from the 1960s era of the movement, was everything Thomas had denounced politically. Yet their responses to the accusations of sexual misconduct are strikingly similar. Chavis claimed that the accusations and his resulting dismissal as director of the NAACP were motivated by those who objected to his change in the political direction of the organization. He challenged his dismissal, which was little more than suspension with pay until the matter was adjudicated in court, and sought a federal court order for his reinstatement. Chavis claimed that he had been "lynched," even "crucified." He railed against those whom he did not name who would seek to let outsiders dictate whom the organization would and would not communicate with.

Thomas, the other side of the political coin, has aligned himself with what is now called the Black Conservative and New Right Conservative movements. He openly denounced those who remained in the civil rights movement in the 1980s and 1990s as individuals who do nothing but "bitch and moan" about the inequalities in the world. When confronted with the accusations of sexual harassment, Thomas, like Chavis later, categorically denied any impropriety in his behavior. Thomas defiantly declared the proceeding a "high-tech lynching," refusing to take on the role of society's bogeyman, the sexually aggressive black male. Many commented that Thomas' use of the lynching metaphor to refer to accusations brought by a black woman was ahistorical. Yet the historical image of the lynched is so powerful that it defied the ill-fitting analogy. And one need only look to recent history to discover another irony in Thomas' defiance.

Thomas, who refused to be cast as the ominous carnal villain, was, after all, nominated by George Bush, who had taken that role to its lowest and most manipulative depths in the form of the Willie Horton political ad which used the image of the villainous black man as rapist to attack Bush's political opponent, Michael Dukakis. When it came to exploitation of racial fears, George Bush proved that he could indeed work both sides of the street. In the first instance he could exploit the racist fears held by society and in the later he could exploit the fear in society of being labeled racist. Both efforts represented brilliant and cynical rhetorical strategies and both worked.

Moreover, Thomas declared that the accusations were constructed by persons or groups who wanted to punish him for having the temerity to pursue his political agenda. In doing so he countered the response that the brutal lynchings of black men to which he referred do not stem from charges by black women. He pointed the finger at "someone who had put [me] up to this," perhaps "the feminists." Commentators Drs. Nathan and Julia Hare contributed to the perspective when they asserted, with no foundation at all, that I was an instrument of white feminists—outsiders who were trying to destroy the black community.

The willingness of African American intellectuals to embrace this theory and point the finger at feminists as malevolent outsiders ignores a community history as well as a modern reality. It turns people like Senator Strom Thurmond, one of Judge Thomas' staunchest supporters, into community heroes, and on no evidence, it turns people like Ms. Washington and me into traitors. This is a product of racism that shows how deeply perverse gender bias is as well.

If Thomas had been successful in painting such a picture, his analogy to lynching might have made sense. Yet he named no groups or individuals who were responsible for the accusations. There were none to be named because none existed. He contrived the evidence to support his claim or acted on no evidence at all, the very thing we fear from a judge. He angrily denounced the process which called him to answer the charges, while all the time his chief supporter, John Danforth, was manipulating it behind the scenes to assist him, but declared that he would sooner die than give up his opportunity to serve on the Supreme Court. In the end when Thomas was confirmed by the narrowest of votes, he, according to the account by his friend John Danforth, felt that "God's Will ha[d] been done."

The irony is that Thomas' philosophy of rejecting the use of racism as an excuse was turned on its head as he used racism to escape responsibility for his own behavior. Clearly, both Thomas and Chavis have political enemies. Anyone who chooses to pursue the kinds of careers chosen by the two will undoubtedly make political enemies in the process. Clearly, both Thomas' and Chavis' enemies objected to positions each had taken. Some had done so on the record, others off the record. Nevertheless, these enemies should not be used as the scapegoats for gender subordination and illegal behavior engaged in by individuals.

In my effort to reconnect with the African American community I sought a different community than the one that rejected the significance of the experience of half its population. I wanted a community that would look at gender oppression as seriously as it looked for the political enemies behind a conspiracy to bring down a good man. I was not prepared to accept the fact that I could not have such a community. Within the African American community the discussion about gender-based exclusion and subordination is long overdue. Reactions to charges of sexual impropriety such as those of Thomas and Chavis threaten to postpone discussions of the subject indefinitely. Professor Emma Coleman Jordan recognizes a "maxim of African-American participation in public commentary: Never air your dirty linen in public." Its violation carries with it a heavy penalty—a community shunning.

I searched for others who sought the same. I found several outspoken women who have shared their concerns about sexism in the community. Elaine Brown came very close to violating the maxim when she discussed the misogyny and gender bias prominent in the Black Panther Party of the 1960s and 1970s. Dr. Billy Avery has long spoken against the abuse of black women in their home, starting her campaign against this abuse in the black church. Myrlie Evers, for years a member of the NAACP national board, later its president, has spoken to the issue and urged the organization to address sexism within it. I once engaged in a discussion of gender inequity with some local leadership in an African Canadian community. The discussion was enlightening, lively, and compelling but drenched in pain. Example followed example. Earnest attempts to understand followed pained recollection. The Canadians made most of the contributions; I sat listening and intrigued. At the end one woman in the group told me that this was the first time that they had an open forum to discuss their feelings with the men in their community. They announced it as if they were describing breathing air into a portion of their lungs previously unused. I can only hope that the dialogue has continued.

One discussion does not a revolution or revelation make. The powerful charges of bringing down good men and bringing shame to the community go a long way to silence those who speak out. African American women are thus forced into a position of choosing between race and gender. When forced, we are likely to identify with race. Consequently, except for individual efforts the problems get little attention and no community discussion. Once we give up for political reasons the right to claim gender bias, the male perspective, whether right or wrong, becomes the black community perspective.

Consequently, all claims of bias and oppression lose some of their validity inside and outside the community. By raising questions of racism, Thomas and his supporters capitalized on this reality, counting on the community supporting a black man over a black woman. Thomas himself had counted on it when he used the "welfare queen" image of his sister to gain political points with the conservatives back in 1981. Ten years later the Republican senators and even David Brock could count on the community identifying with Thomas, notwithstanding their own use of racially laden stereotypes of black women, to support their charges of racism.

I could not ignore these messages and the polls. I felt their sting. I read behind their open insult every plausible negative insinuation. Yet I longed for the community that was mine before partisanship and the politics of race and gender took it away from me. The author Zora Neale Hurston describes a scene in her novel *Their Eyes Were Watching God* in which a young black woman tried in a court of law is tried in the community court as well. In a poignant passage that reminded me all too much of my own situation, Hurston wrote in 1935:

> *The court set and Janie saw the judge who had put on a great robe to listen about her and Tea Cake. And twelve more white men had stopped whatever they were doing to listen and pass on what happened. That was funny too. Twelve strange men who didn't know a thing about people like . . . her were going to sit on the thing. . . .*
>
> *Then she saw all of the colored people standing up in the back of the courtroom. . . . They were all against her, she could see. So many were there against her that a light slap from each one of them would have beat her to death.*

On October 10, 1991, as I prepared for my testimony, I spoke to my lawyers about my fear of this very rejection. "Whatever happens," I told them, "I do not want to destroy my ties with the community." I warned that the claim might be used to divide the community. Nevertheless, when I needed it most, it was not there. Nothing could have prepared me for the pain of what the rejection meant. Yet I could not bring myself to abandon it. In Hurston's book, Janie is eventually reunited with her community. I could only hope for the same.

CHAPTER TWENTY-ONE

Despite the cynicism displayed during the hearing, eventually the disclosures led to an increase in formal complaints against harassers. Complaints filed with the EEOC increased by over 50 percent in the year following the hearing. In 1992 women and men filed a record-breaking number of complaints with the federal agency, some 7,407 total. Women proved the pundits wrong and understood the difference between how women felt and acted and how they are perceived. An explosion of challenges in the workplace led employers to take action. Whether they were motivated by desire to end the behavior or the fear of liability is not certain. What is certain is that workingwomen welcomed the chance to change intolerable circumstances in the workplace and to confront employers who were previously insensitive to the problem. Rather than recoil, women and many men galvanized around the issue.

This galvanization on the issue of sexual harassment led to the collective disgust the country felt when we learned of the so-called Tailhook incident. The initial incident centered around the sexual assault and molestation of over two dozen women at the Las Vegas Hilton during an annual meeting of an association of navy pilots. The subsequent cover-up told as much about the seriousness with which some viewed sexual misconduct as the incident itself.

Despite the navy's zero-tolerance antiharassment policy, and despite the numerous payments of lip service to sensitivity to the behavior following the Thomas hearing, Lieutenant Paula Coughlin, one of the first women to complain, met entrenched resistance to her charges. Instead of investigating the complaint to determine what had happened and who had participated, top officials participated in a blatant cover-up of the matter. As it turned out, this was not the first year that behavior of this nature occurred at the annual convention of the Tailhook Association. It was simply the first time that women banded together and complained. Just prior to the incident the rhetoric led to hope that if everyone understood what sexual harassment was, it could be stopped. If the military responded this way in the face of what constituted criminal molestation, what hope was there for swift effective reaction to harassment in the private workplace? The message from the navy was a discouraging one, another hurdle to overcome.

Even before I met Paula Coughlin in 1992 at the Glamour Magazine Awards Program, my heart went out to her. As the first woman to file a formal complaint over the Tailhook assaults, she was sure to experience concerted efforts to smear and disgrace her. Though she escaped the public humiliation of having the smear conducted in front of millions of television viewers, her experience may have been worse because her detractors could act without fear of public scrutiny. Since she was still in the navy, her torment was apt to be daily and routine. Later, men who once had been friends and colleagues, who were part of the cover-up following her complaint, were likely to respond to the exposure by further harassment. I knew that she was going to be blamed. I knew that as a result she would be targeted even by those who did not participate in the original act or the cover-up. I knew that this would continue as long as she remained in the military.

When I met Ms. Coughlin, I was impressed with her energy and with the indignation she expressed over the matter. All of her life, she had wanted to fly planes. Everything about her energy and personality suggests that she is the kind of person who could take on the challenge of breaking into the male-dominated field in a male-dominated institution. She is bright, spirited, clearheaded, and motivated. A woman who willingly took a risk by entering a military which gave her little promise to fulfill that dream. She is like every daughter who is told that the opportunities to achieve are there for her in far greater numbers than for her mother's generation. Her history suggests that she was willing to work twice as hard and prove herself over and again to be considered as equal to her male counterparts. I have no doubt that it was her sense of principle, that she should be treated as an equal, which led her to report the Tailhook assault. Ironically, that sense of principle and the action derived from it led to a cruel shattering of her hope that she would ever be considered as an equal to even her assailants. Her experience reminded me that those who would judge her, the officers and pilots in the navy, saw and acted toward her in terms of her body parts—not in terms of her skills as a pilot. Afterward, protecting the status quo was more important than recognizing the humanity of the individuals who sought to serve the military.

When navy officials discovered the cover-up in the investigation of the Tailhook incident, some of those directly and indirectly responsible resigned under pressure. Yet the second investigation netted few convictions for the molestations. Admiral Frank Kelso, commander in chief of naval forces during the incident, was awarded a fourth star upon his retirement. Accountability and responsibility, lessons endemic to the military, were low, given the severity of the infractions. Kelso was rewarded for his career, his responsibility for the misconduct overlooked.

The official response to this incident compares unfavorably with the response of the Canadian government to a videotaped episode of racial harassment and hazing. Recruits to the Canadian Airborne Regiment were forced to eat urine-soaked bread and fecal matter as part of the initiation rite. One black recruit was forced to walk on all fours while wearing a leash. As if that were not degrading enough, his initiators smeared the message "I Love the KKK" on his back with feces. The same division was accused of racist acts while acting on behalf of Canada as part of the United Nations peacekeeping forces in Somalia. The hazing behavior was the ultimate expression of obedience. The racist element of the division's activities reflected and reinforced to an unacceptable extreme the hierarchical ordering basic to the military system. In the same way, sexist behavior and sexual abuse represent an extreme way of promoting a hierarchy.

Over protests from various sources, Canadian Defence Minister David Collennette announced approximately one week after news media aired the videotape that the regiment would be disbanded. No videotape of the Tailhook wrongdoing exists. All that existed was the word of nearly eighty women and formal complaints from over two dozen coupled with clear evidence that those present wanted to avoid a proper investigation. But more important, the difference between the two episodes is that the Canadian episode involved leadership with a will for accountability. None was evident in the Tailhook episode. No official entertained abolishing the Tailhook Association or official recognition of it. Clearly, that is what it will take for the message of zero tolerance to be taken seriously.

Paula Coughlin sued the Tailhook Association and settled out of court. She also sued the Las Vegas Hilton for failure to provide adequate security. Evidence showed that hotel personnel had warned female hotel security guards to stay away from the Tailhook parties for their own safety, and were thus aware of the activity that the Tailhook conventioneers engaged in. In her suit against the Hilton, Coughlin testified that the harassment from navy personnel after she complained was relentless, so extreme that she considered suicide as the only way to end her misery. Her colleagues, who resented her role in the investigation and the attention brought upon the navy, treated her with contempt and shunned her, the ultimate renunciation in a climate that preaches camaraderie. Her tormentors, no doubt, thought their actions a proper response to her "treachery" in complaining. Before giving her a poor performance evaluation one of her supervisors said that her complaint had injured *his* career. One commander recommended that she return a bonus which she had received prior to the convention when her evaluations were outstanding.

In the end, Paula Coughlin left the navy, stating that the "covert attacks" on her by her colleagues left her no other choice. With little hope of advancing in the military, she left the navy at a time when the demand for commercial pilots was low. Thus, her skills as a pilot have limited utility in the civilian marketplace. In arguing against the stiff punitive damage award, one hotel representative suggested that the hotel had suffered enough in loss of business surrounding the scandal. A jury, obviously moved by the extent of Coughlin's suffering, awarded her $1.7 million in compensatory damages and assessed $5 million in damages against the hotel. The Hilton has appealed the award. The Nevada legislature quickly went to work to undo the damage award, passing a bill in one house to elevate the standard for corporate liability for failure to protect hotel guests from sexual assaults and making it retroactive to cases on appeal. Not surprisingly, the hotel lobby in the state of Nevada, home to resorts in Lake Tahoe, Reno, and Las Vegas, strongly supports the measure.

When I think of Paula Coughlin, I am frightened for her and for many other women in military and civilian service who have attempted to pursue careers and press their claims of harassment or other forms of sexual abuse. Two dozen women formally complained of being raped or sexually assaulted by fellow military personnel during the Gulf War. Such cases seem always to precede a cover-up or mismanaged investigation and result in termination of the complainant's career. What is equally devastating is that the sexual harassment not only spoils careers but shatters dreams. Women in the 1980s were told that sexism was dead—that it was safe to have dreams and best to dream big. Unredressed sexual harassment not only takes away our dignity but spoils our belief in ourselves and in the fairness of life and conveys the message that our dreams are pointless.

As had been the case with Paula Coughlin, I relived my own experience when I learned of Suzanne J. Doucette. Doucette, an FBI agent who complained about being harassed by her supervisor, represents one more story of unofficial abuse leading to official mistreatment recorded since the hearing of October 1991. A ten-year veteran of the bureau, she broke unwritten agency rules and told her story of sexual harassment. In one incident her supervisor caught her in a choke hold from behind and demanded sexual favors. She managed to break free, but afterward the same supervisor began to devalue her contribution to the agency.

Prior to the incident, Doucette received commendations and bonuses for her performance as an agent, but afterward she was told that her evaluations would improve if she learned to get along with her male colleagues better. She filed a complaint which met with classic institutional denial. Her evaluations fell to "below acceptable." Once considered a bright, up-and-coming member of the force, she was ostracized.

Doucette's testimony about the harassment before the Senate Committee on Governmental Affairs resulted in her being placed on administrative leave without pay. She later left the force and pursued her complaint in court. She, too, abandoned her dream of service and she had to sell her home to finance her lawsuit. Yet she continued to pursue the claim not simply for her sake but for her two daughters, who adore and support her. She wants to be an example for them—to make the world better for them.

Winning a suit against the FBI may be as difficult as filing a complaint with the navy. The FBI is considered worldwide to be one of the premiere law enforcement agencies. It was venerated in a television series which ran during the 1960s and 1970s. Until the death of J. Edgar Hoover, its long-reigning chief, in 1972, the bureau refused to hire women as agents. As such, the FBI represents the classic paradigm of an institution where sexual harassment is likely to occur—a hierarchical organization which is historically male-dominated. Doucette's was not the only complaint about harassment. She was one of the few to go public with her complaint. Afterward, she said, other women started telling about their experiences in the agency. Yet it took on the average over a year for the agency to investigate and process complaints about the behavior.

The FBI, under the direction of Louis Freeh, settled the Doucette suit, and it settled sexual harassment claims raised by other female agents. In the case of two agents in California, a harassing supervisor was dismissed. Suzanne Doucette's supervisor is now retired. The two California agents remained with the bureau. Suzanne Doucette resigned, under pressure, before suing the agency.

Inescapable is the irony that the agency embroiled in its own claims of harassment and retaliation was the same agency charged with investigating my statement to the Senate. Inexperience with investigations and resistance to the validity of sexual harassment charges appears to be part of the workplace culture of the FBI. Perhaps this explains in part why the agency went along with the order to attempt to contradict my testimony despite contrary practices and procedures.

Soon after the Supreme Court adjourned for its October 1991 term, it heard arguments in Christine Franklin's lawsuit against her school. Ms. Franklin was a high school student who claimed that, from the time she was in the tenth grade, one of her teachers continually harassed her. The record shows that Franklin complained that he "forcibly kissed her on the mouth in the school parking lot," "asked her about her sexual experience with her boyfriend and whether she would consider having sexual intercourse with an older man," "telephoned her at home and asked her to meet him socially," and, finally, one day "took her to a private office [at the school] where he subjected her to coercive intercourse." The school system took no action.

Later the Association of American University Women and the Center for Research on Women would inform us through studies that sexual harassment is prevalent in high schools and junior high schools. Moreover, the studies would reveal that many times, in fact more times than not, schools did nothing about the behavior.

Christine Franklin's lawsuit before the Supreme Court was about damages. The trial court concluded that she could not sue for them under Title IX (the statute which prohibits discrimination on the basis of gender in the schools). The Bush administration had filed a brief supporting the position taken by the trial court denying Ms. Franklin's suit.

The Supreme Court announced its unanimous decision in February 1992 and ruled that Christine Franklin could sue for damages. Many of the lawyers who worked on the case were surprised at the decision, which in no way restricted the amount recoverable under the Franklin suit. Clearly, the impact of the October 1991 hearing was on the minds of the commentators if not the minds of the Court. Despite the despicable facts which led to the lawsuit, the case had received relatively little attention prior to the hearing. Upon the announcement of the decision it became a cause for celebration by women who had prior to October 1991 taken the fact of sexual harassment for granted.

I was pleased with the outcome of the suit but was all the more angry with the Bush administration, an administration which claimed to be sensitive to the problem, but which was unwilling to hold a school system accountable for neglecting to protect young victims. The hypocrisy was underscored by President Bush's assurances to Paula Coughlin that he would see to it that her assailants were punished. That promise, too, proved to be empty.

Two years after the October 1991 hearing, the Supreme Court rendered the second sexual harassment decision in its history. Not since 1986, when the Court concluded that sexual harassment was a form of sex discrimination prohibited under Title VII of the Civil Rights Act, had it ruled on a workplace sex harassment claim. Teresa Harris brought the suit against her employer, Forklift Systems, Inc. She alleged that the company's president, Charles Hardy, subjected her to numerous sexual and sexist comments: "You're a woman, what do you know" and "We need a man as the rental manager." Hardy suggested that Harris and he "go to the Holiday Inn to negotiate her raise." He asked female employees to retrieve change from his front pocket and threw objects on the ground and asked them to bend over and pick them up. Hardy defended his behavior as joking. He apologized but did not stop.

Teresa Harris lost her lawsuit at trial, even though the court ruled that she was, in fact, offended by the behavior and reasonably should have been. Nevertheless, it concluded that Hardy's vulgar behavior was not illegal because Harris' job performance had not suffered as a result. Again the suit was about damages. In essence the court ruled that because Harris could take the behavior and still perform, she had to continue to take the behavior and could not be compensated.

By the time the Harris case was argued, the second female Supreme Court justice had taken her position on the Court. Ruth Bader Ginsberg heard the oral argument in the Harris case and actively participated in questioning the attorneys. She also traded comments with her colleagues, reminding Justice Antonin Scalia that a comment directed at him suggesting that he knew little because he was a man had far less impact than a comment directed at a woman suggesting lack of intelligence because of her gender. Justice Sandra Day O'Connor wrote the opinion, for, again, a unanimous court, in the Harris case. She concluded that "Title VII comes into play before the harassing conduct leads to a nervous breakdown." She added that the law provides relief for a "discriminatorily abusive work environment" even when it does not "detract from employees' job performance."

The Court's opinion decisively affirmed the ban against sexual harassment in the workplace and strengthened the definition of what was actionable under the law. I was overjoyed at the speed with which the Court rendered its decision. To me it sent a clear message to the trial courts around the country that the Supreme Court took the problem of sexual harassment seriously. Even the separate opinion by Justice Scalia recognized the fact that further understanding about the problem was necessary before the Court could draw hard definitions which effectively eliminated lawsuits.

I agreed to comment on the case on the *CBS Morning News* and NBC's *Today* show. The night before the interview, I spent hours poring over the briefs filed in the suit and the cases cited in Justice O'Connor's opinion. It was a labor of love. To me the Harris suit represented affirmation, a victory for working women. The interview with Harry Smith of CBS went smoothly. The case is a landmark case on a prominent problem affecting working women in this country. It did not represent a panacea for all the ills of sexual harassment but it was a start. It was all the more significant because it represented only the second time that the High Court had addressed sexual harassment in the workplace since the concept was introduced to the courts in the 1970s.

I was angry and disappointed when Katie Couric of NBC asked me to address David Brock's allegations about me. The question had nothing to do with the Harris case and had not been raised by the show's producers as one of the subjects they were interested in hearing about. Yet the question was revealing especially in the context of the discussion of a major legal decision. Ms. Couric's question reminded me that no matter what the breakthrough in law and in our understanding of the problem of sexual harassment, there will always be those who want to reduce us to talking about the salacious and the sordid.

Interestingly, she did not ask me to comment on the irony of the fact that Thomas, in whose confirmation hearing sexual harassment charges played prominently, was deciding cases on that issue. Nor did she comment on the potential conflict of interest that Justice Thomas might have in deciding the Harris and Franklin cases. The emotions, anger and hostility, he displayed at his hearing regarding my claim suggest that he might have been less than objective in his review of the cases and, moreover, might even compromise the entire Court by weighing in on these decisions. Since the Supreme Court is the court of final review and given the significance of the issue, these seemed to me the more critical questions. Yet again, I became the subject of the scrutiny, not Thomas or the important issue of sexual harassment. That I may always be viewed through the prism of my detractors is not surprising. In that, I am sadly not alone. For every woman I know who has complained about harassment—those who are successful in their efforts and those who are not—unfounded accusations continue as well.

The energy breathed into the issue in the wake of the hearings was reflected in the number of suits filed soon after and the innovation with which attorneys pursued them in court. That added support led to women complaining in groups rather than alone. Women miners were the first to be certified as a class in a hostile environment sexual harassment suit against their employer, Eveleth Taconite Co., a mining company. Female bottlers and machinists at Stroh Brewery Company sued the brewery for sexual harassment. Lori Peterson, the young lawyer in the case, asserted that Stroh's advertising encouraged sexual harassment. Company work sites featured promotional posters that were takeoffs from television advertisements, such as those featuring the "Swedish bikini team." The advertising suggested that men could have both the beer and the women and that both were equally valued. In another suit involving multiple complainants waitresses from the Hooters restaurant chain sued their employer. In addition to complaining that the company failed to stop customer harassment, the women complained that the company contributed to it. Revealing uniforms which the company required them to wear contributed to the sexual harassment they experienced.

These cases are important because they represent group complaints about hostile environment sexual harassment—a new wave in the area of the law. They are important as well because they prove that the issue concerns women of different occupations and income classes. The miners, machinists, waitresses, and bottlers in these lawsuits can hardly be characterized as members of a privileged class of workers, out of touch with the reality of the work world. Rightfully, the rules applied to them in the same way that they applied to women in offices and professional settings. Finally, it seemed, the rules of law were finding their connection with the people which the law was supposed to protect. The gap between the law's protections and the law's promises was being filled.

Yet for each case that is publicly and favorably resolved there are countless others less public and less favorable to women who suffer harassment, like the surgeon in Oakland who complained during her medical residency that she had been harassed by her supervising physician. The result of her complaint was that she was constructively prevented from pursuing her career as a doctor. Only ten years later, in 1992, would she begin again the residency she abandoned under duress. She will fulfill her dream but much later and after much pain. Then there is the woman who successfully sued her Washington, D.C., employer, but has yet to collect the damages awarded to her. She had to sell her home to pay for the litigation, but she and her two sons are much closer for the experience. The successful lawsuits are important for these women as well.

Through the stories of successful complaints, all who have experienced harassment have found the community they need in order to understand the importance of their complaints. Yet in each case the dream that they had was abandoned or deferred. The tragedy in the stories goes beyond the immediate pain of the experience. The tragedy in the stories involves the waste that these experiences leaves us all with—the wasted aspirations, wasted energy, and wasted talent of gifted and bright individuals.

Paula Jones' claim that Bill Clinton sexually harassed her tests our commitment to this issue over personality. My sense of fairness and understanding of the issue lead me to conclude that Paula Jones, like other women, deserves to be heard. Instinctively, I relate to the difficulty she must have experienced in trying to tell her story. And despite those who claimed that feminists responded hypocritically to Ms. Jones' complaint, much of the leadership in women's groups agreed that the issue must be heard by the courts. Some made unsuccessful attempts to meet with Ms. Jones. Yet I was torn, because Ms. Jones was aligned with people who were Bill Clinton's political enemies—some of the very people who may have dismissed my claim and, worse, accused me of a variety of wrongdoing.

Ironically, my detractors included in their charges against me a count of conspiracy with political "interest groups." If I had gone to Washington organized with people who were Clarence Thomas' sworn political enemies, everyone certainly would have cried foul. Under those circumstances, they would have been right to assert that a woman's painful experience with sexual harassment should not be manipulated to further some unrelated political agenda. And I would have agreed with them. But the fact that Ms. Jones' supporters have never indicated a sympathy to sexual harassment makes me extremely skeptical of her judgment in relying on them for advice. One woman, who identified herself as a Jones supporter, telephoned to advise me of my "hypocrisy." Jones, she was sure, was "telling the truth" while I, she was just as certain, was "lying." Nevertheless, I am willing to accept for the moment that Jones' supporters were not all of her own choosing. And even if politics motivated some in their support for this claim, this still does not mean that we can dismiss it out of hand. Otherwise the hint of political motivation would become an irrebuttable defense against any claim, and political figures would be exempt from charges of sexual harassment. Each case must be examined on its own, with motivation and credibility taken into full account.

No matter what you make of the merits of Paula Jones' claim, it has potential for impact on the issue. High-profile claims raised for whatever purposes can impact all claims. Yet the court, not the public arena, is the best place to ferret out the truthful claims from the spurious ones. Given what many commentators have described as the hostility of the press to Bill Clinton, he is better off in the courts than in the public arena. An individual claiming to represent Paula Jones wrote to ask if I would assist her. But a copy of a contract mailed to me focused more on creating an agent-client relationship—in the event Ms. Jones got magazine, book, television, or movie contracts—than it did on creating an attorney-client relationship. I was uncomfortable with an approach that focused so heavily on the media. And before I could decline the request, Ms. Jones and her representatives held a press conference in Washington, D.C. I thought it ironic that I, the person routinely described in the press as "reclusive," should be contacted as a source of media promotion. The choice to pursue the legal claim in such a manner was a bad one for Ms. Jones. As a private citizen with limited public exposure, she does not have the resources to handle the kind of media barrage that she will encounter if she attempts to settle this issue through the media. Moreover, I question the strategy of insisting that the case be tried during Bill Clinton's second term as president. I believe Ms. Jones will fare better as a plaintiff in a suit against a former president than in a suit against a sitting president. Like or dislike Bill Clinton, many prospective jurors have a respect for the office that will put her at a disadvantage in issues of credibility.

As shameful as it will be for her if Jones' claim is false, the issue will endure. The same is true if her claim is valid. The momentum built by those women who in 1991 found their voices is much stronger than any one claim—even one directed at the president of the United States. The force of the movement they started is stronger than the politics of Bill Clinton. So widespread is the experience of harassment that the issue transcends the partisanship of any particular case in which it is raised. I have encountered numerous women who are livid about the issue of sexual harassment but who cannot recall Clarence Thomas' name, much less the politics that led to his judicial appointment. Their image of the hearing goes beyond partisan politics to the callousness and hostility of the White House and the Republican senators, and the indifference of the Democrats' response to the claim. The sense of community developed from the hearing has continued long after my testimony and the Senate vote to confirm Clarence Thomas, and it will endure beyond Ms. Jones' claim against Bill Clinton, whatever the outcome.

Though I had not practiced law for many years, as a member of the bar and a law professor, the law was more to me than the rules and remedies which people sought out to solve their problems. The law was a profession and an avocation. In May 1992 I received an honorary doctor of law degree from New College in San Francisco. Its president, Peter Gabel, is an advocate of change and examination of issues of the poor and oppressed, through compassionate affirmation of our common interests and experiences. When I spoke to the students at the graduation ceremony, I tried to impress upon them the positive contributions that went along with the challenges that they would no doubt face as lawyers. The hearing and the aftermath represented both to me.

Following the hearing, the lawyers and law professors who came to my rescue had become like family. I was proud to be associated with people who would volunteer their time out of a sense of fairness and a commitment to the confirmation process. Thus, when the ABA Section on Women in the Profession announced that it would give me a special recognition, I was proud to accept. One of the organizers of the event described it as the "hottest ticket in town." Approximately three thousand members of the association and their guests attended the function. I was even more pleased to travel to San Francisco for the August 1992 meeting because Justice Thurgood Marshall would be featured and honored at a number of events.

The entire meeting had, according to one reporter's account, "an air of exhilaration and anticipation." For me it showed a promise, a promise of inclusion. I was thrilled by the whole meeting. Yet the highlight of the meeting, for me, came when I had the opportunity to meet Justice Thurgood Marshall. The occasion was an evening program in his honor sponsored by the ABA Section on Individual Rights. The event was sold out and I was fortunate to be seated at a table near the front. Professor Stephen Carter, a former Marshall clerk and a friend of mine since law school, gave one of the tributes to Mr. Marshall. Just prior to the dinner he introduced me to the former justice or, as Mr. Marshall preferred, the retired justice. I stammered something completely inarticulate about how I was honored to meet him. I was certain that he must have thought me a blathering idiot. So awestruck was I that words, meaningful words, failed me at that moment. Later I learned, to the relief of my embarrassment, that he probably had not heard my idiocy over the noise in the room. I sat with Enola Aird, Stephen's wife, and mutual friends, George Jones and Loretta Pleasant, also contemporaries from Yale Law. The entire program was inspiring. Stephen's tribute was characteristically eloquent. I was especially moved by a tribute given by Karen Hastie Williams, another of Marshall's clerks. She spoke of the great contribution which Justice Marshall had made to the lives of many in the room and around the country. In part she stated that, without Justice Marshall, there would be no Stephen Carter, no Karen Hastie Williams, nor an Anita Hill. I could not have agreed more, and certainly she said it better at that moment than I could have.

When Justice Marshall spoke, he did so with an honest graciousness that made me admire him even more. As he often did, Mr. Marshall told a story on that evening. His storytelling reflects a rich tradition in African American culture. Yet it was more than mere entertainment; more than the reflection of a skilled trial lawyer. Justice Marshall's stories and his storytelling were part of the basis for his jurisprudence. Both set a social backdrop against which the consequences of law could be measured. On that occasion he told of a young black man in an Arkansas pool hall. This man engaged the then attorney Marshall in conversation. The young man asked Mr. Marshall if he knew anything about reincarnation. After a brief discussion on the subject, the young man declared, "If you ever find out anything about it, tell 'em for me when I come back in the next world. I don't care whether it's a man or a woman, human or goat, animal or what, just don't let it be black." The story illustrates the depth of self-hatred and despair commanded by Jim Crow laws and socially imposed segregation in the South. Clearly, the law had failed. The promises of the constitutional amendments enacted after the Civil War were meaningless and hollow—even a mockery of this man's realities. The protections of the Constitution meant nothing to this man whose dream was to escape racism and prejudice in another life, in another form.

When women around the world began to tell their stories about harassment, we realized that the law prohibiting it had just as certainly failed. Every time someone told of a job she quit or was fired from because of harassment, we learned something new about the problem. When thousands of women began to tell their stories, we all declared that we had had no idea it was so widespread. When we read about girls like Christine Franklin, we admitted to our embarrassment that we had had no idea it was so vicious. When we heard about harassers who were promoted while their victims were fired, we knew that there was more to accountability than the enactment of the law. A sense of achievement is mixed with disappointment when matters are settled under the condition that the victim keep quiet about what happened. Each result reminds us that social change is necessary if the law's promises are to be fulfilled. One measure of social change is found in politics. It is thus not surprising, especially given its context, that the October 1991 hearing provoked political change of clear magnitude and that such change has sparked great resistance each step of the way.

CHAPTER TWENTY-TWO

My mother and father delighted in their children's singing in church. It was not enough that we sang with the children's choir; they wanted us to perform in smaller groups. Joyce, Carlene, John, and Ray were required to learn the gospel songs popular during the time of their upbringing. By the time JoAnn and I were old enough to remember the songs performed by the Staple Singers, we, too, were expected to sing them as a duo in church services and musicals. When my mother mercifully forgot to request our singing, her partner, Miss Mattie, took over. "I'd like to hear a song from the Hill Sisters," she would say.

Though more of a homebody than I, JoAnn disliked public performance slightly less than I did. Each time, I dreaded the long walk to the front of the church whether to deliver the requisite Mother's Day and Easter poem or to sing "If I Could Hear My Mother Pray Again" (Mama's favorite). But we never quivered, nor did our voices shake. That would have been unthinkable. When I complained that I did not like being in front of a crowd, my painfully shy mother advised me that I would "just have to grow out of that." In 1991 at age thirty-five, I finally understood just what my mother meant.

"Why did I agree to do this?" I asked myself repeatedly as I traveled to Coronado, California, for my first public presentation following the hearing. Ruth Mandel, director of the Center for Studies of Women in Politics at Rutgers University, invited me to speak to a bipartisan group of women politicians. Though she assured me that the reception from these politicians would be better than the reception I experienced in Washington, I still dreaded my appearance. Shirley Wiegand traveled with me for the conference. She had been there for the worst of the hearing. It was only fair that she should experience some positive aspect of that ordeal. I had been so busy that I had no time to finish my remarks before leaving Oklahoma. Fortunately, Mandel had indicated that my comments needed to be about fifteen minutes in length. I worked on the airplane and completed a speech about sexual harassment entitled "The Nature of the Beast."

The extraordinary mood of the crowd on the evening of November 15, 1991, in the Hotel Del Coronado can only be compared to that of an audience at a rock concert. It was electric. Moreover, it was prophetic. Like no other, that evening foretold the dynamics of the engagement of women on the issue. Four law professors, Kimberle Crenshaw, Susan Deller Ross, Deborah Rhode, and I, addressed the assembly of women politicians to cheers and shouts of appreciation. Never have law professors ever been so enthusiastically received. On that evening the normally self-possessed, even sober, political leaders were boisterously disorderly. They shouted and whistled and stood on their chairs to applaud. For punctuation they waved pink napkins in the air over their heads like they were brandishing lassos. Neither the speakers nor the audience was used to this kind of reaction. Mandel, the conference organizer and a veteran in the study of women political candidates and involvement, was ecstatic about what she witnessed. These women foretold an era of renewed involvement as they summoned into being the political "year of the woman," election year 1992.

Back in Washington the Senate was considering the Civil Rights Act of 1991. The bill had been supported by Jack Danforth before the

Thomas confirmation hearing. During the hearing he had threatened some of its supporters with withdrawal of his backing unless they voted to confirm Thomas. President Bush had threatened to veto prior proposed legislation. When the bill came up for reconsideration after the hearing, it did so in the midst of the rhetoric which declared aversion to harassment. Passage would mean restoration of civil rights protections recently stricken by the Supreme Court decisions as outside the scope of existing legislation. Importantly, under the new law victims of sexual harassment could sue for damages up to $300,000. In addition, for the first time, jury trials would be a possibility. Never before had the plaintiffs in sex discrimination cases been allowed full compensatory relief. They had been limited to back pay and promotion or reinstatement into their old job depending on the nature of their claim. The law passed with bipartisan support and absent the threat of a veto. According to Professor Susan Deller Ross, "Lawyers in the field reported that the law quickly made a difference."

Like the new support for the Civil Rights Act, the assembly of women politicians was bipartisan. Two state Democratic senators from Oklahoma were present, as were individuals who would later work for the Republican governor of New Jersey, Christine Todd Whitman. Most of the women, though in a few cases grudgingly so, caught the enthusiasm of the event. The hearing woke up many women to the failure of progress on women's issues. The political issue was not sexual harassment. Sexual harassment is a legal issue. The political issues in 1992 for newly involved women were lack of representation and insensitivity to our experiences. That is what the hearing represented to women and men who viewed it.

When I first made the decision to start public speaking, I was driven by frustration and anger at the tone the hearing took. Later I continued to speak out of fear. I feared that if I gave up my voice this time, it would be lost forever. I would never retrieve it again. My critics accused me of having a "political agenda." Pure politics, in my experience, is ephemeral at best. I had witnessed that people change their politics to suit their own personal goals. I have even been accused of doing the same. I have not been so concerned about politics as I have issues. In retrospect, I admit that that position left me with a limited vision of larger areas of concern. It allowed me to ignore some of the faults of the Reagan administration political agenda and to work for some positive changes on specific, yet relatively minor issues. That experience caused me to distrust politics altogether. Thus, I had no overt political agenda, but I now admit that politics was an inevitable by-product of what was happening with women. I am convinced that the political awakening was not one of pure politics, but of politics driven by issues of common concern to women.

Whatever the manner women and men chose to become more politically active after the hearing, many pointed to the hearing as the precipitating factor for their activity. Nineteen ninety-two gave them a slate of women candidates from which to choose. A variety of factors contributed to the increase in women's participation in the elections: the anti-incumbency mood, the problem of gridlock, the House bank scandal, and concerns about the economy and other domestic policies. Women and men had been shaking their heads and throwing up their hands in the face of these problems. Until the hearing and the reaction to it sparked involvement in the political process, many had chosen to devote their time to their families and jobs. Family issues, work issues—these were things that they understood and had to confront daily. Before the hearing, most people were unaware that there were only two women in the Senate. For the first time, due to the coverage of the hearing, many people realized that only one or two senators were members of ethnic minority groups. For the first time, after reviewing the bungled handling of the hearing, many people realized the gap between representation and our basic concerns.

Through the magnifying glass of the hearing, we saw the face and some of the heart of the senatorial representation. We did not like what we saw. As a result, many women and men vowed to change the face of government.

I was delighted with the tone of women's political activity following the hearing. Women in grassroots efforts indicated that they had something at stake. Still, the labeling of women candidates as "one issue" candidates infuriated me. I knew that what provoked most of these women was the perceived lack of representation in the federal government—not, as was suggested, the specific issue of sexual harassment alone. This bit of manipulation of political rhetoric was nothing more than an attempt to limit the relevance of the women against whom it was directed. The labeling in the campaigns recognized the threat of their broad-based support and attempted to neutralize that support by narrowing their field of focus. Once the label convinced voters of the candidate's limitation, her opponent had convinced the voter that she had little potential for effectiveness on other issues. The "single-issue candidate" label can be likened to the old saw "A woman's place is in the home." If you can convince people of that, then you can exclude women from workplaces. Similarly, if you can convince voters that a candidate is interested in only one issue, you can convince them that they would not take care of the other issues of concern to the voter.

Interestingly, I have never heard the term used to attack a man. It lends itself more readily to women candidates probably because it plays to the perception that women are not effective leaders. For example, I have never heard of a campaign against a male member of a minority group which dubbed him a one-issue candidate. I have not heard attempts to limit effectiveness of minority candidates by similar insinuations that they are only concerned about minority people. There are two reasons for that. One is that the fear of broad-based support for men of color does not exist as it did for women who ran in 1992. A second is that the gap between the social perceptions of leadership abilities of men and women is larger than that of white men and minority men. Yet the condescending attitude toward women candidates persists despite women's proven leadership, and their detractors continue to persuade voters in that manner. Finally, as a society we have become better adept at deciphering veiled racist terms than we have at deciphering veiled sexist terms.

Despite my enthusiasm for the candidates, I declined all invitations to campaign. As a practical matter, I did not have time. My full-time teaching and administrative responsibilities in the spring of 1992, coupled with speaking on sexual harassment, left no time for political campaigning. But there was another reason I avoided politics, though I liked many of the political candidates. I dislike and distrust politics. I dislike what I see as its game playing and empty rhetoric. And despite the fact that the women running and their platforms addressed the shortcomings of current representation, I knew that they were necessarily a part of a political system.

I dislike rallies and political speeches. Thus, when Ron Brown, chairman of the Democratic National Committee, asked me to speak at the Democratic National Convention, I declined. I had always been a registered Democrat and I preferred the Democratic Party over the Republican Party. Nevertheless, the party had done little to show any real concern about the issue of sexual harassment. George Mitchell, the Democratic leader of the Senate, did little to assist me before and nothing since the hearing. Moreover, there was no clear statement from leadership denouncing the alleged behavior of one of its former members, Brock Adams, who resigned his Senate seat following allegations by an aide, Kari Tupper, of sexual assault. A bold statement of zero tolerance of the kind of behavior alleged would have gone a long way to express the commitment to ending sexual abuse in the Senate. George Mitchell never issued such a statement. The silver lining behind Adams' dark cloud is that Patti Murray ran for and won that vacated seat in 1992. When approached by Brown, I was too disillusioned with politics to participate in organized political efforts. My participation in the process would only inflame the people who had attacked me during the hearing. Among their supporters, my presence would be a rallying cry. Thus, anything I might contribute to a candidate could disappear and in fact backfire against the candidate. This was particularly so for Lynn Yeakel, who was running for Arlen Specter's seat in the Senate.

Finally, I did not campaign because I knew I would be no good at it. I am not a rousing speaker. I do not respond to the thrill of the crowd by elevating my rhetoric. I am slow, methodical, and lack charisma. My message is about changing our way of thinking about women and abuses of power, a message not easily conveyed in a rally—where people are often urged to act, not think. Though I was intent on being heard, especially during the period immediately prior to the election, I could not bring myself to campaign. Only a few campaign workers took offense at my decision, but by that time I had learned to say no with far less regret. Brown himself was quite gracious when I declined his request.

I watched the Democratic National Convention on television. Alone at my home in Norman, I listened to Barbara Mikulski declare that "never again will a woman coming forward to tell her story" be treated as I was. Tears rolled down my cheeks as I faced the fact again of the involvement of elected officials in what had happened to me. I cried out of my own sadness and my own hope. In August 1992, as Senator Mikulski spoke and introduced the female candidates for the Senate, for the first time in months I believed that change was possible—that no other woman would have to face the public spectacle I underwent. Part of me wanted to be there and knew if Senator Mikulski had asked I probably would have gone.

My name was invoked several times over the course of the convention. One occasion made me swell with pride and at the same time made me laugh out loud. During the roll call, Governor Walters of Oklahoma introduced his state as the home of Will Rogers and Anita Hill. Say what you will about the state and its politics, I had always been proud of being an Oklahoman and this recognition added to that. Moreover, at the convention it served Oklahoma's delegation well, as the crowd responded loudly. Back home in Oklahoma, Walters took a good deal of heat for the declaration but did not back down from it.

Part of me, a larger part, was glad that I was not there. Part of me knows that my specter was just as effective as my physical presence would have been. I have no regrets about being a part of the energy that got people involved. I was pleased that the party no longer ran away from me as it had during the hearing, but I was aware that, for some of the partisans, the party's embrace was just as political as its earlier abandonment had been.

After the election, I admitted to myself that I would have been afraid to live in the country if George Bush had been reelected. Any vote for him indicated to me that the White House role in the hearing and the denigration of a private citizen were proper. Moreover, I did not feel safe against further efforts to come up with false information to discredit me. I feared the FBI might again be improperly enlisted in that role. In August 1992 I addressed the Canadian Bar Association at their meeting in Nova Scotia. There some individuals spoke with me about taking a possible position with a Canadian law school. I liked the community and the people and seriously considered it as an alternative, depending on the outcome of the election. I never really pursued it and am glad that I never had to make the choice to become an expatriate. I was disappointed that the majority of the electorate in Oklahoma voted for George Bush. Yet I was thrilled that my home county of Okmulgee voted Democrat. It was a small victory but affirmed my belief in the people there.

My primary concern was the involvement of women in the defeat of George Bush. Still, Bill Clinton's election was a victory in itself. I watched the election returns at the home of a Republican friend who was voting Democratic for the first time in his life. His further contribution to George Bush's defeat was to convince his mother to vote for Bill Clinton and his father to stay at home. The election of four women to the Senate and nineteen women to the House (seven of whom are women of color and one the first Puerto Rican woman elected to national representation) showed that progress had been made. Two women senators in California represented a historic event as well. But my personal pride soared at the election of Carol Moseley Braun to take the seat of an incumbent Democrat who voted to confirm Clarence Thomas. Ms. Braun, the first African American woman to be elected to the Senate, ran after being pressed by women indignant at my treatment. This was an overdue event but one that I never thought I would see. The day after the election I talked to my mother about Carol Moseley Braun's victory. "At eighty-one," she said with pride, "I never thought I would live to see the day that a black woman would be elected to the United States Senate."

Lynn Yeakel's defeat in her challenge against Arlen Specter was a personal blow that differed from the other losses. Ms. Yeakel had made it clear that she was encouraged to run because of the lack of representation apparent from the hearing. This had energized many women in her state but had been used against her. Her community experience and leadership ability were trivialized as Senator Specter painted her as a one-issue candidate. He raised twice as much money as she did and his incumbency and past pro-choice stance carried him a long way. From a philosophical standpoint, the very narrow margin by which Yeakel was defeated represented a victory, especially given the discrepancy in campaign spending. Yet the loss was for many women around the country a marked disappointment. I telephoned her to offer my support. She was gracious in her defeat—satisfied that she had made progress and won a moral victory.

Shortly after the election, Ellen Malcolm, director of Emily's List, invited me to attend a celebration for the newly elected women senators. For the first time, I met Carol Moseley Braun and Barbara Mikulski, the two women who might restore my belief in politics if I allowed it. I had not prepared but was invited to speak. As I did, I told the story about my mother's response to Carol Moseley Braun's election. When I looked at the crowd, I noticed that Senator Mikulski had tears on her cheeks. It was only fair that we trade tears. I assumed that she was crying because I had survived the hearing and in a way prevailed by having a part in the election of the women who were being celebrated. Most observers never questioned Senator Mikulski's commitment to the equality of women. Yet even her doubters would have been convinced on that day as she welcomed her new colleagues and me to Washington. I can only imagine the loneliness she experienced with no other Democratic female colleagues in the partisan and sexist world of Washington, D.C.

Though six women in the Senate far exceeded pre-1992 predictions, that figure is not high enough. Neither are one African American and one Native American enough to demonstrate the diversity of representation of ideas and experiences of the people in the country. Much more needs to be done in politics and society in general if those numbers are to be raised significantly. Yet I still view my role outside of the political fray. Though I am often asked if I will run for public office, my thinking has never wavered. The answer is always no.

Chapter Twenty-three

The three-story brick building housing the College of Law at the University of Oklahoma, constructed in 1975, is a tribute to the flow of money resulting from one of the oil boom eras. As I cross the second floor of the nameless building, I glance up at the skylight ceiling of the two-story atrium and around at its brick interior walls—it is horribly noisy and energy-inefficient. A student, Tom March, gets my attention from across the way. "Professor Hill, have you seen the *Oklahoma Daily* today?" he asks referring to the campus student paper. As he points out the coverage, I hold my breath.

My return to campus sparked a set of angry letters to the newspaper mostly at the urging of a local politician who wanted to see me fired from my university position. I breathe a sigh of relief as I read the full-page advertisement taken out by the faculty and staff at Utah State University. A lump grows in my throat, as I read the show of support from Senator Hatch's constituents. The originators of the message wanted me to "know that not everyone in Utah supported Senator Hatch's treatment" of me.

"This will go a long way in helping get through the next week," I tell March. At this point, I felt as though I was struggling through life one day at a time and each bit of encouragement helped. This was more than a day's worth of encouragement; it actually buoyed me up for nearly a month.

Since age six, except for the three years in Washington, D.C., I have been a part of an academic community. When I began teaching and interacting with faculty around the country through the Association of American Law Schools, I knew that I had found real colleagues. In particular, the minority law professors and those professors who specialized in contract and commercial law were people with whom I shared interests and experiences. Had it not been for my friends and colleagues in the various academic communities with which I have been associated, the hearing would have been more devastating.

Professor Laurence Tribe telephoned Senator Biden prior to the hearing to tell Biden that "some women law professors" thought that my complaint was not being taken seriously. Either Senator Biden was concerned that he maintain the respect of Professor Tribe or he feared "women law professors," because only then did he distribute my statement to the Democratic members of the Judiciary Committee. On October 8, 1991, nearly two hundred law professors from around the country sent this message to the Senate:

To The Members of the United States Senate:

The Supreme Court's place in American government and society depends on unqualified public respect for its members and the institution. In this light, as law professors—including many who have not taken a position on the nomination of Judge Thomas to the Court—we strongly urge the Senate to delay action on the nomination until it can make a fully informed and considered appraisal of Professor Anita Hill's allegation. To act now would be to risk grave injury to the Court, the Senate and the country.

Sincerely yours,

This response was quick. It arrived two days after the story about my statement aired on public radio.

In the meantime, resolutions and petitions supporting either the delay in the hearing or my credibility and integrity went to the Senate from various groups of individuals. My colleagues at the College of Law along with the College of Law Student Bar Association sent resolutions of support. The University of Oklahoma Faculty Senate sent a resolution which was accompanied by a resolution from the University Student Congress. By October 14, 1991, five hundred women scholars had signed a letter which Nancy Sherman, philosophy professor at Georgetown University, forwarded to Senator Biden.

Dear Senator,

The following 500 women scholars have asked me to forward this letter to you. As signatories, we are acting independently and do not represent any organized group. The signatures were collected over the 30 hour period ending 4 p.m., Sunday, October 13, 1991; the list continues to grow.

We the undersigned are women scholars who wish to express our deep concern over the possible confirmation of Clarence Thomas to the Supreme Court. The issue of sexual harassment is one with which many of us have dealt on a personal level. We have been harassed ourselves, or know of others who have been. Because of fear of reprisal and the influence of the men involved in our professional careers, it is common for victims not to report these incidents and to maintain professional contact with their harassers. Accordingly, it is imperative that Prof. Anita Hill's testimony be taken seriously. We urge you to vote against the confirmation of Clarence Thomas.

Sincerely,

Women from twenty-seven states, Alabama to Wyoming, plus the District of Columbia signed the letter. By the morning of October 15, 1991, their numbers had risen to 750.

The ad appearing around the country from "African American Women in Defense of Ourselves" was organized by and signed in part by women from academic institutions. In part it read:

> *In 1991, we cannot tolerate this type of dismissal of any one Black woman's experience or this attack upon our collective character without protest, outrage, and resistance.*
>
> *As women of African descent, we express our vehement opposition to the policies represented by the placement of Clarence Thomas on the Supreme Court. The Bush administration, having obstructed the passage of civil rights legislation, impeded the extension of unemployment compensation, cut student aid and dismantled social welfare programs, has continually demonstrated that it is not operating in our best interests. Nor is this appointee.*

Each of these appeals to the Senate and public reflected and affirmed a different period of my life in some way. The latter, in particular, was of significance because of the portrayal of the issue in the African American community. The academic community has an important role in public discourse. On this issue, it took a solid, substantive position based on experience and principle. It was gratifying. Having my Oklahoma University colleagues' and students' support was crucial. They knew me and had shared in the struggle of the media barrage with me. Yet no petition was any more moving than the letter from sixty of my law school classmates around the world.

Dear Mr. Chairman:

It has been our privilege to know Anita Hill professionally and personally since the late seventies, when we were in law school together. The Anita Hill we have known is a person of great integrity and decency. As colleagues, we wish to affirm publicly our admiration and respect for her. She is embroiled now in a most serious and difficult controversy, which we know is causing her great pain. We make no attempt to analyze the issues involved, or to prejudge the outcome. We do, however, wish to state emphatically our complete confidence in her sincerity and good faith and our absolute belief in her decency and integrity. In our eyes it is impossible to imagine any circumstances in which her character could be called into question. We are dismayed that it has been. We know that it could not be by anyone who knows her.

Anita has imperiled her career and her peace of mind to do what she felt was right. We know we are powerless to shield her from those who will seek to hurt her out of ignorance, frustration, or expediency in the days ahead. But we will have failed ourselves if we did not at least raise our voices in her behalf. She has our unhesitating and unwavering support.

The letter was dated October 10, 1991, the day before I testified. When I read it, my stomach quivers even today. It moves me so because it expresses a caring and concern of people with whom I spent three years and some of the most trying times in my life. Over ten years later they still cared. As timeless and comforting as poetry, it spoke to me as directly as it would had I read it in 1977 when we were together in school.

The entire Yale Law School community was shaken by the hearing. Professor Elias Clark, who taught me and Clarence Thomas, wept in class the Monday following my testimony. The *Yale Journal of Law and Feminism* called for Thomas to resign from the Supreme Court the day following his confirmation. A Thomas supporter in the student group the Federalist Society countered with accusations that I was "delusional or acting out of spite." Ernest Rubenstein, an alumnus in attendance at the annual reunion the weekend of the hearing, reported that no one of the faculty or former students with whom he spoke doubted my credibility.

In the spring of 1992 Dean Guido Calabresi invited me to visit and to speak at Yale Law School. Carroll Stevens, an associate dean at the law school, arranged the trip. I anxiously awaited the trip to New Haven. I would see my friends Stephen Carter and Enola Aird and meet their two children. It was the first time since I graduated from the school in 1980 that I would return. It was the first, and only, time since I started speaking publicly that I was nearly overcome with stage fright. The experience at Yale had been the pivotal point in my educational and intellectual development. I had made many lifelong friends in law school. Nevertheless, as a woman from rural Oklahoma, I never felt "at home" at Yale.

The day before my evening presentation, I met with students and faculty including a classmate, Roberta Romano. Even then we knew that Roberta was destined to teach. She was always insightful and thorough in ways that separated her from even the brightest of her very bright classmates. Of the other, older faculty who were teaching at Yale when I was a student, Burke Marshall was especially warm. Professor Marshall had been a high-ranking official in the Kennedy and Johnson administrations. His contributions to the Civil Rights Act enforcement of the 1970s was something we took for granted as students. When I went to Washington, I more fully appreciated his importance to the era. Dean Jim Thomas, one of the most outstanding individuals in law school administration and teaching, was a major influence on my decision to go to Yale. He was as hospitable in 1992 as he had been when I visited the campus in 1977. He invited me to meet the students at the college where he was a master.

During the afternoon I had a chance to walk to my old neighborhood and visit the corner grocery and pizza parlor which I regularly visited. The owner of the grocery recognized me from the hearing. Over a slice of pizza, his treat, he told me that while he and his wife watched the hearing together he remembered me from my visits to his store. I could not imagine that of all the students he must have seen over the years that he could remember me but I was glad that he felt that he had. But none of this calmed my nervousness about the speech.

That evening the dean introduced me to the crowd of about six hundred; Stephen helped me with questions; my friend Ivy McKinney had driven from her home in Stamford to be in the audience. The scene was set for my ease and comfort. As I stepped up to the podium, I looked out at the crowd in the law school auditorium. In the back of the room, I saw the faces of two of my former professors, Elias Clark and Joseph Goldstein. All at once, I was a nervous, insecure first-year law student again. I had more than the jitters. What befell me did not go away. I progressed through my prepared remarks, never so happy to finish a speech. My only consolation was that I was spared reliving that part of the law school experience where professors ask questions.

I had learned so much at Yale. The intensity of the questioning and probing was such that I learned to expand my reasoning. The experience had given me a sense of certainty about my abilities as I faced the world. It no doubt contributed to my ability to address the Senate Judiciary Committee without being in awe of their prominence. Yet, amazingly, none of that confidence applied during my first time back inside the walls of the law school itself. The experience of being a student was so potent that twelve years later I saw myself in that role. That kind of intensity will certainly take more than one visit to undermine. Perhaps the intensity of the law school experience was what brought me close to many of my classmates, creating friendships that continue today.

Some fellow Yale Law School graduates have been less than sympathetic. In an opinion piece written for the press, one graduate was downright condescending in his sympathy with my history of sexual harassment. He suggested that my history with sexual harassment would explain why I preferred that my students call me Professor Hill rather than Anita and why I objected when a new student upon meeting me for the first time put his arm around my shoulder. But he was wrong. I would have objected to such familiarity regardless of my experience with harassment. I didn't see the student's action as harassing. I saw it as disrespectful. I defy him to recall any situation where, as a student, he had occasion to drape his arm over the shoulder of a Yale Law School professor. Moreover, I doubt if he ever referred to any of them with the familiarity of a given name, at least not while in their presence.

More important, the writer clearly failed to understand the difficulties encountered by all young women professors and particularly women of color in the classroom. More than one of my female colleagues have remarked that the male students are so uncomfortable with the idea of a woman in control of their academic destiny that they rebel and resist treating them with the deference and respect they accord male faculty. My experience at both Oral Roberts and Oklahoma universities bears this out.

Some of my classmates have been more than insensitive to my situation; some have been hostile. One in particular, a man with whom I was close in law school and since, has not returned several telephone calls made since the hearing. The insensitivity represents a slight of little significance. I would not have noticed it except that the writer mentioned in the essay that he, too, was a graduate of Yale. The hostility is hurtful. I have always worked to maintain relationships with friends and family and even acquaintances. Losing one without the benefit of explanation cuts me to the very heart of who I am. This lost friendship is one of only a few which I have suffered because of the hearing. But for me a few is too many.

On college campuses around the country, in Canada, France, Italy, and Japan, I have spoken about the problem of sexual harassment to receptive audiences. On each campus I visit, I am told of a problem of the recent past or the present with sexual harassment in that academic institution. Oklahoma State University recognized me with its distinguished alumna award in 1992. Present at the ceremony were faculty members who had taught me there years prior. But as if to prove that universities are places of diverse opinions and perspectives, someone always questions why I have been invited to campus to speak and questions the amount I am being paid. Unfortunately, these questions, rather than the issues surrounding harassment, get much of the attention of the campus and local press. Campus authorities and I mutually agreed to cancel a presentation at Old Dominion University in Virginia because some protested the fee payment at a time that tuition was being raised. Even though the payment for the speech was not coming out of tuition and I suspect that the objection was as much over the anticipated content of my speech, I agreed to the cancellation. (I was happy to learn that Susan Faludi spoke on the campus the following year and was well received.) One questioner on a college campus asked the question bluntly: "What qualifies you to earn nearly $30,000 from a two-hour appearance?"

My only response is that the combination of my experience, background, and preparation qualifies me to speak about the subject. But whether I am paid or unpaid there will be those who object to what I have to say. Despite the questions raised on college campuses, as long as diverse perspectives are valued I feel more comfortable in the academic community than any other. When valid academic perspectives are stifled for political reasons, existing in the academic community can be a nearly unbearable experience. I have learned painfully that when the academic community fails to protect the rights of faculty to state unpopular perspective, the entire community is at risk.

CHAPTER TWENTY-FOUR

In the spring of 1995, on one of about ten days in the season of clear fresh air perfect for walking, I rounded the corner to Shirley's modern brick home as I'd done many times. This time I was startled, or at least taken aback. The source of my surprise was the For Sale sign on her lawn. Plastered over it like a badge of pride was the word "SOLD." I'd known that Shirley was selling her home; I'd even known that she would, no doubt, be leaving the university and moving away from Oklahoma. But the realization of those facts only hit me as I saw the sign. I could not help feeling remorse mixed with guilt that it was so. Directly and indirectly, Shirley had borne the brunt of much of the local political animosity aimed at me and had decided that she would no longer stand for it. In the fall she would return to her native Wisconsin and continue her teaching career there. As I got to her home, I realized how much I would miss her presence, though I respected and even admired her decision to leave.

The attacks started as soon as we returned to Oklahoma from Washington, D.C. The most adamant and vocal of my detractors was Leonard Sullivan, a state politician. He began his campaign in an open letter demanding that the university buy out my contract. In his letter, which ran unedited in the student paper, the *Oklahoma Daily,* he called me a "lier" *(sic)* and likened my presence on campus to the presence of the Black Panthers. Another individual who can only be described as a local character, E. Z. Million, whose now deceased father was once a colleague on the law faculty, joined Sullivan in his campaign against me. Million even called for the resignation of Dean David Swank and Associate Dean Teree Foster. Sullivan and Million expanded their attack to include Shirley Wiegand. Through the state Open Records Act, Million succeeded in getting all the correspondence of Professor Wiegand before and after the hearing. He first sought to prove that Shirley had traveled to Washington in my support at the taxpayers' expense. When this proved to be baseless, he accused her of neglecting her duties to her students in order to go to Washington. This proved untrue as well, yet Million continued to make the claim.

To my surprise and appreciation, two state legislators, Ed Crocker, a Democrat, and Bruce Niemi, a Republican, disagreed publicly with Sullivan. In a letter to the University of Oklahoma president, Richard Van Horn, the two pointed out that the state's constitution protects educators from opposition by politicians. They expressed incredulity at the claims of political extremism raised by Sullivan. The regents at the university refused to take any action and that should have been the end of it. However, a public statement by President Van Horn gave Sullivan and Million the best opening to continue their crusade. In comments issued on Wednesday, October 16, the day following the confirmation vote, the university president announced that action against faculty could only be taken on issues that "relate directly and substantially to his or her professional capabilities or performance." Sullivan appeared to take the comments as an invitation and almost immediately began to challenge my competence to teach at the university, suggesting that I was hired only because of affirmative action, even claiming that the procedure whereby I was granted tenure had been flawed.

Million's and Sullivan's efforts to drive me from the campus would continue for years following my testimony. Their tactics included a series of burdensome requests for documents and files from the law faculty that referred to me—none of which contained any reference to the hearing.

By spring of 1992 I was worn-out. According to university policy, I was eligible for a sabbatical. Though the regents granted my sabbatical request, they did so after a debate that was unprecedented and appeared to be directed at only my application. Sullivan called for the abolishment of the sabbatical leave program. The regents took it upon themselves to review the process for all faculty.

One day a secretary discovered two clean-cut middle-aged white men dressed in dark suits and ties rummaging through the recycle bin in the basement of the administration building where I was working. They left abruptly as she approached, leaving behind several of the documents they had retrieved. Each of the documents contained a reference to me or something on which I had worked. Rumors spread that federal support for the institution was in jeopardy from the Bush administration if officials supported me in any way. Whether any official had issued a threat, I don't know. I do know that the rumors about reduced private and public funding were enough to cause me worry and some of my peers on campus to turn against me. One colleague was adamant, suggesting to Shirley that everyone would be better off if I would "just leave." I was tempted to accommodate her.

Though he never complained to me, Eric was beginning to receive accusatory questions about me from his friends and coworkers. He was asked to explain a variety of matters well beyond his nineteen years of knowledge and experience: "Why did she wait until the last minute to bring it up?" "What is sexual harassment, anyway?" Moreover, the experience with the media had left him completely shaken. He described the experience in Washington as "mind-boggling" and "frustrating." Reporters cared more about getting a story than anything. It was clear that "they had no respect for us. They were knocking us all about" and did "whatever it took to get closer to you." That experience changed Eric's dream of being a journalist. "The value of the truth has been replaced by the value of sensationalism," he told me. "Maybe you could make a difference," I tried to persuade him, though unconvinced myself.

I recall how proud he was to be reading his first book at age five and the subsequent years in which he would read in bed with a flashlight after the lights were out and all of the standardized test scores which showed his language skills well above average. I understand the value of the academic setting, the role it plays in protecting young minds from experiencing the harshness of their real-world careers before they are able to understand them. Like me, Eric saw the ugly side of a professional life before he could put it into perspective. Like me, Eric changed the course of his career in response.

Sullivan's campaign escalated with the announcement of efforts to raise money for an endowed professorship in my name for the study of women in the workplace. Gloria Segal, a state representative from Minnesota, conceived of the idea of the Anita Faye Hill Professorship. We had first met on November 15, 1991, in Coronado, California, following the presentation to her and her colleagues at the Hotel Del Coronado. Segal appeared to me to be an individual deeply touched by the hearing, but I quickly got the idea that this was not the first issue involving women in which she had taken personal action. That evening, in addition to seeing the caring side of the middle-aged politician, I saw a savvy organizer who knew what it took to make such a project happen. She told me of her idea and how important she felt it would be to follow up the events of October with research about the problem of sexual harassment and other workplace issues. The professorship would be the first of its kind in the country. In essence it would act as a research supplement to a professor committed to doing research aimed at the elimination of workplace discrimination.

The research professorship at Oklahoma could accomplish this, she reasoned, but she questioned, if I were to be awarded the professorship, what might happen if I left the University of Oklahoma. The funding would remain in Oklahoma, I advised her. After discussing the matter, my only concern was that I not have to do fund-raising for the professorship. Segal assured me that she would organize and conduct the fund-raising. I left her hotel room certain of the sincerity of her intentions but less certain that anything would ever come of it. Her enthusiasm was contagious, but I was skeptical, not wanting to expect too much—to be disappointed.

Segal persisted, contacting the University of Oklahoma development office and getting approval for official recognition of the fund. All of the paperwork was in order, including Segal's express desire that I be named to the first professorship. David Swank, as dean of the College of Law, and I worked on the language for the charge of the recipient of the professorship. It included concerns about both gender and racial discrimination. President Van Horn and Development Director Bob Bennett both signed documents recognizing Segal's preference. By October 1992 Gloria Segal and Carol Faricy, who had taken over operations of the campaign, had raised over $100,000. Faricy, an outspoken woman with a quick tongue and raspy voice, was a veteran fund-raiser, having raised money for the arts and political efforts.

The response to the fund-raising was immediate, both nationally and locally. An herbalist in Choctaw, Jim Holder, pledged to send fifty dollars a month to the fund until it was completed. Harley and Marie Brown, a couple who were members of my church, wrote letters to the local newspaper urging "concerned Oklahomans" to "pitch in and help complete the fund." A group of university faculty and staff, led by a retired journalism professor, Tom Sorey, took up a collection for a donation and to buy an ad for the local paper to show their support of the professorship. The ad listed the names of over four hundred contributors. Disturbingly, some supporters stated that they feared retribution for contributing. Donations came from women and men in nearly every state in the Union, some as large as ten thousand dollars, from alums and children of alums, but many more in amounts of five to fifty dollars. I started to believe more in the idea of the fund as the ultimate goal of the professorship.

When the university announced that it had received the amount in the fund that would allow them to request state matching funds under a five-year-old program, Sullivan responded by attacking the group in

Minnesota. Segal and Faricy were well on their way to raising the $125,000 needed in order to receive state matching funds for endowment of the professorship, when tragedy struck Gloria Segal. She was diagnosed with a brain tumor which would later take her life.

The death of Gloria Segal and the attacks on her and Faricy took away much of the energy and enthusiasm I had for the fund. The fund moved forward with the help of Dean Swank, who treated it as he had other professorships he guided through during his tenure. The fund came before the regents of the university in a highly contentious atmosphere in the early summer of 1993, when they debated whether to accept the funds. This debate, too, was unprecedented in fact and in tone. Never had the university ever questioned whether it would accept $125,000 in private donations for any reason, let alone for a reason unrelated to the area of study. Moreover, the nature of the debate focused not on the nature of the research proposed under the professorship, but rather on the person after whom it would be named. This, too, was unprecedented. The university regents had approved seventy-four previous professorships without debate.

This was also the first time that the board was asked to approve a professorship named after an African American. The irony of such a debate seemed to be lost on most of the participants until Melvin Hall, one of the board's two black members and a graduate of the law school, reminded the regents of a debate that occurred in the 1940s when it decided to exclude aspiring law student Ada Lois Sipuel Fisher from admission into the university because of her race. Mrs. Fisher, a friend and supporter, sat on the Board of Regents when they debated the Hill professorship. But instead of recognizing the irony, the board allowed Million to turn the discussion into an opportunity to air complaints about me, my qualifications, my teaching, and my research. Like the letters sent to Washington in 1991, the new attacks came from individuals whom I did not know, and from Oklahoma students I had never taught. Those in support of the professorship included one current and one former provost, retired faculty, and Dean Swank. Finally, when Regent C. S. "Budge" Lewis moved to pass the item, he stated the importance of judging the professorship on "the effect it would have on education at the college."

The 5–2 vote to accept the professorship was a moral victory. But that victory was undermined by a directive issued by President Van Horn that no university personnel could be involved in any way in raising funds for the professorship. Once again the Hill Professorship was singled out. Fund-raising for professorships had been conducted by the deans of the various colleges in conjunction with the development office since their introduction into the university.

Sullivan raised two baseless claims in order to kill the professorship. First, he attacked Segal's desire to have me serve in the professorship as illegal. Second, he threatened to bring charges with the state attorney general's office against the veteran fund-raiser Faricy. To reduce the "political heat," one spokesperson for the president's office asked me to issue a public statement declaring that I would not apply for the professorship. I was angered and offended by the request and effort, once again, to treat me differently than other faculty. I declined. President Van Horn backed down from the written assurances made to Faricy and Segal by the development office.

The threat of the lawsuit and the prohibition against university officials helping in the effort effectively stalled fund-raising. In order to maintain the integrity of the promises made to Segal and to the implicit promises made to the donors by the administration, including the regents, I began the task that I had rejected early in the process. Despite Van Horn's directive, I committed myself to completing the private donations portion of the professorship. I had no fund-raising experience; I hated to ask people for money; I felt some conflict of interest in asking for support for a fund in which I might benefit. Nevertheless, the greater principle prevailed and I started an effort to raise the $125,000 needed to complete the project.

The donations for the professorship continued to come in a steady but slow stream. I had returned from my sabbatical tired but nevertheless reinvigorated. Yet the demands of fund-raising, acting as spokesperson against issues of gender and race bias, and teaching a full load began to weigh heavily. Moreover, I was still receiving calls from individuals who were victims of harassment at various stages of their claims. Many were in search of legal counsel; others were simply worn down by the process of pursuing their basic right to a work environment free of sex discrimination. I would start the day invigorated in anticipation of the Race and the Law course that I taught at 8:00, but by the end of the day after the calls and letters and requests, I was worn-out. I was without the administrative support to handle the load, even the mail and telephone calls I received. The five members of the secretarial staff at the law school were stretched to cover the thirty full-time faculty members.

Despite the fact that none of my work was political and all was related to the legal and social issues of discrimination, I became cautious about asking for help from the staff. Fearing that I would be accused of misappropriating state money by Million or Sullivan, who were monitoring my correspondence through Open Records Act requests, I hesitated to use the law school facilities for matters related to the issue of sexual harassment. Rose Martinez-Elugardo, who had been at the law school as a secretary during the time of the hearings, decided to leave the school in February 1994. We had become friends as well as colleagues. She knew the demands on my life and understood them as well as anyone. I was delighted when she agreed to assist me with my workload on a contract basis. She more than earned her pay. With her part-time assistance and through the help of others, most of whom volunteered their time, we managed to conduct the classes, speaking, referrals, and other assistance without a professional staff. Yet, without professional assistance or more of my attention, I knew that the fund-raising for the professorship was not going to be completed by the two-year period required under the rules governing state matching funds.

By the end of 1993 I began to feel decidedly overworked and under-appreciated. David Swank had been replaced as dean under circumstances which my detractors were claiming as a victory over me. When he applied for university recognition which his years of service to the institution, including one year as interim president, more than qualified him for, he was denied. The reasons most often cited were that he had been too visible in his support for me and in dismissing the football coach, Barry Switzer. The Switzer dismissal was the culmination of a year in which a player was indicted for selling drugs to undercover agents, one player was arrested for brandishing a semiautomatic rifle in the athletic dormitory, and three other players were arraigned and later convicted for raping a woman in the athletic dormitory. Though he maintained his position as a tenured member of the faculty of the College of Law, Swank suffered at the hands of his enemies, football fans and conservative politicians. They assured him that he would not receive the recognition that others with similar service and accomplishments would have been awarded.

The administration continued to suggest that I make a public announcement that I would not apply for the Hill Professorship. David Swank's replacement, Peter Goplerud, though sympathetic to the issue of harassment, seemed not to appreciate the pressures placed on me for raising funds and from outside agitators. While assuring me he would help with fund-raising but for the no doubt well-founded fear that he would lose his job if he did, he informed me that he hoped that the professorship would attract another scholar, giving the school the benefit of the expertise of two qualified professors. In the same conversation he told me that he longed for the day when, upon being introduced as the dean of the Oklahoma University College of Law, people did not inquire about Anita Hill.

Rumors that Richard Van Horn, for his failure to take action against me, was soon to be dismissed by the Board of Regents spread. In 1994 Van Horn resigned and Sullivan claimed the victory. Eventually, the regents would replace Van Horn with Senator David Boren, one of the six Democrats to vote in favor of the Thomas confirmation. Later Boren would express regrets about the vote but make clear that his regrets had nothing to do with my testimony. Boren based his contrition on positions Justice Thomas took as a member of the Court with which Boren disagreed. Boren's new position was almost as indefensible as his argument that Thomas deserved the benefit-of-innocence standard reserved for criminal trials. Information about Thomas' position on issues was available to all of the senators before their vote. Senators who reviewed the information in their role of advise and consent were aware that those positions espoused by Thomas as Supreme Court justice were the same as he espoused in various other public positions. Boren, former Rhodes scholar and viewed as one of the more intelligent members of the Senate, could claim no surprise.

News media around the country carried stories about the continued turmoil in the state caused by my presence. In a story that ran in *The New York Times* on April 19, 1993, I was described as Oklahoma's "open wound." As poignant as some of the stories were, the conflict was most often portrayed as political, failing to capture the racist and sexist elements of the continued campaign against me. I decided to write about the episode myself, knowing that I would not be satisfied with anyone else's portrayal.

In the spring of 1994 I applied for an unpaid leave of absence for the following school year. I would write my memoirs and finish another collection of essays based on the 1992 conference on race and gender issues. In addition, the leave would give me the time to finish the fundraising for the professorship. Leaves of absence without pay are routinely granted at the university if the applicant's college approves. Outside faculty are often hired to fill the vacancies left by leaves on a visiting basis, or the salary of the faculty member on leave may be used for other purposes of the college. Unpaid leaves are viewed by departments as a way of infusing new ideas into a campus without the full financial commitment of a permanent hire or to support a onetime project. The time away from teaching allows the faculty member to pursue interests at her or his own financial expense and still maintain an affiliation with the university. Where the granting college values the contribution of the faculty member on leave, he or she is welcomed back at the end of the period. Though some faculty have been granted leaves for two years running without discussion or debate by the regents, my request for a one-year leave without pay sparked contention.

Oddly enough, the very people who claimed that my presence on campus was an embarrassment sought to block my leave. The alternative, they argued to the regents, was that I be fired. The regents, once again, allowed my detractors to infuse politics into what should have been a routine academic matter. Sullivan stepped forward to demand that I be fired rather than granted a leave, and Million took the floor at the regents meeting to argue Sullivan's case. The following day the headline of the student paper read, "Hill Keeps Her Job, Gets Leave of Absence." Consistent with the stated academic policy, the regents voted to grant the leave. Nevertheless, Regent Don Halverstadt, who voted to deny it, suggested that I should "vacate the position" and called for a review of the entire university's leave policy. And again, I was castigated for exercising a right that countless others had exercised over the forty-year life of the leave policy. And once again, the regents allowed the political agenda of a few to dictate the academic policy of the entire institution.

Despite the support of many of my colleagues and students, I was beginning to wonder myself why I did not "just leave" the University of Oklahoma. Stubbornly, I was determined not to give in to the political pressures of a handful of very vocal antagonists and a few others who were simply insensitive. More important, I was determined to see the Hill Professorship through. Had I left the university, it would have died from neglect, as had been encouraged by President Van Horn's memorandum, and the research would have never been accomplished in Oklahoma. The insensitivity and the willingness to single me out for different treatment made it apparent that the University of Oklahoma badly needed the very kind of research the professorship anticipated.

Through the efforts of friends like Tania Norris who organized individual campaigns and Ellen Gilbert, a new friend, who along with Barbra Streisand agreed to host a lunch for the Professorship Fund, the donations mounted.

"Who is Junetta Davis?" Eric asked me one day in late 1991. Her letters began to appear in response to the attacks by Sullivan and Million almost immediately upon our return from Washington. It was not until November 1992 that I got to know Davis. The sixty-something retired journalism professor with the distinct Oklahoma drawl described herself as one of the few advocates for women's rights on the Oklahoma campus during her tenure. With an area of specialty in political journalism and quick mind she was perfectly suited to comment on the matters surrounding the hearing and the university's subsequent reaction. In addition to making contributions from her retirement salary, she became an advocate and spokesperson for the fund at the regents' meetings. Rather than pelt the board with sharp-tongued attacks, she forcefully drove home her point in deliberate, though piercing language, made all the more memorable by her slow delivery. For my part, I traded my public appearances for donations to the fund.

One such engagement with the Business and Professional Women's Association proved surprisingly fruitful. When Wanda Hill (no relation) of Shawnee, Oklahoma, asked me to speak to the group's annual convention, I agreed to do so in exchange for a donation to the fund. I had had a former association with the group, and despite the fact that my schedule was overdrawn, I agreed to their request. I had no idea of what the donation would be. After my speech in Reno, Nevada, to an exuberant group of two thousand women, BPW officers "passed the hat" (actually they passed red bags) for the fund. The collection netted over $11,000 for the professorship, and donations continued to come in from the organization's members over the next few months. A reception hosted by three of my former students, Teresa Bingman, Tammy Kemp, and Sherry Wilson, and supported by my closest colleagues at the law school put the fund over the $250,000 needed for state matching funds. These students had always been a source of my pride, three talented young black women who had grown and struggled as students as I had grown and struggled my first years of teaching at the University of Oklahoma. But once again the victory of completing the fund was soured by university administration.

In anticipation of the decision by the Higher Education Regents whether to match the fund pursuant to the state matching fund program, Nancy Mergler, acting provost, suggested that I change the name of the professorship to make it more politically acceptable to that body. In a supreme act of emotional and political manipulation, Mergler suggested that the professorship be named for Ada Lois Sipuel Fisher, the first black person to be admitted to the School of Law. "The donors would agree if you suggested it." "Though I have tremendous respect for Dr. Fisher, I could not suggest this to the donors," I responded, concerned that I might sound too egotistical. The dishonesty of collecting money in one name and only after the completion changing the name was lost on her. Try as I did, I could not persuade her of the lack of integrity and wisdom inherent in such a move. Interestingly, Mergler did not suggest that the university begin its own initiative to endow a professorship in Fisher's name. The administration's refrain played once again in a willingness to compromise academic matters in order to bow to political pressure.

Raising the $250,000 in private funding was a triumph of will. Yet one more hurdle had to be met. State funding for the professorship had not been granted. The Higher Education Regents had changed their policy in December 1994 in an effort which many viewed as an attempt to avoid the issue. Prior to 1994, the Higher Education Regents reviewed applications for matching funds once the funds reached $125,000. After passing over the application for matching funds for the Hill Professorship for over a year, the board changed the amount needed to seek matching to $250,000. Once we met that goal, the university had to reapply for state matching funds.

It was by now the spring of 1995, and I had to decide whether to return to the university, where, despite the fact that the regents had acted according to stated policy, it was clear that both I and the Hill Professorship were being judged by different standards and procedures. After nearly four years of trying to function in the environment, the behind-the-scenes signals from some members of the university Board of Regents and administrators, along with some of the public debate, made me apprehensive about the prospect of returning. I heard rumors that students on campus were being told by administrators that I was at fault—that by asserting my right to maintain my tenured position, I had forced the university to take a position on the political issue of the Thomas confirmation. I had the support of many colleagues and students but I was keenly aware that they did not run the institution or establish policy.

The Faculty Senate chair, Tom Boyd, requested of President David

Boren, Senator Boren in 1991, that he meet with me to discuss the future of the professorship and my concerns that it and my career and accomplishments were in jeopardy if the disparate treatment I received from the administration continued. A colleague on the law faculty requested that President Boren meet and perhaps have lunch with me. Despite his stated open-door policy, Boren refused both requests initially, citing his fear that meeting with me might attract too much attention and jeopardize the university budget process were conservative legislators to learn of it. Later, after the state legislature completed the budget process, the request went ignored.

Apparently, on the theory that I would have to leave the state if I had no job, Sullivan finally proposed legislation to abolish the law school at the University of Oklahoma altogether. During the day the proposed legislation was to be considered, Million canvassed the halls of the capitol building declaring, "This is about Anita Hill, and it won't stop until we get rid of her." Behind the scenes, Boren told individuals he welcomed my return. But his reported meeting with Sullivan "to settle differences Sullivan had" suggested otherwise to the public, and I doubted very much the sincerity of his welcome.

Coupled with his refusal to meet with me, Boren's action suggested that politics controlled his decisions—not surprising given that he had just arrived on campus from a career in politics. I used no political clout to demand such a meeting, as some suggested. It was for me an academic matter, to be settled within the boundaries of the academic community. When our paths did cross, it was completely by accident at a university function where we sat at adjacent tables with our backs to each other. Budge Lewis approached Boren and asked if he would like to meet me. "Of course," he responded. "I did not know that she was here." He turned to where I was seated no more than four feet away and greeted me with the hearty declaration that he would be "restoring tradition to the law school." Thinking back to the tradition that had brought the most attention to the school, I found the remarks particularly insensitive. Though he probably meant traditions of quality, he simply assumed that I would see tradition in the same way he did, forgetting that when he was a student, there were few women and few students of color, and no black or female faculty. Not a tradition to which I want to return.

As I pulled into Shirley's driveway and parked my car adjacent to the For Sale sign, I questioned my own decision to return to the University of Oklahoma in the fall of 1995. I was certain that my participation in the normal campus activities would never be the same. The activities in whose involvement I had been welcomed—faculty committees, faculty awards and recognition, university projects, summer research grants—may in fact be off limits, judged by a standard and procedure limited to me, as had been my application for leave and sabbatical. A group of female students from the class before had met with me for lunch and encouraged me to return. Several colleagues had visited with me to do the same. I had even heeded the accusation of one friend who suggested that to leave would show my accusers that I lacked toughness and another who said that my requests for assurances from the university that I not be singled out for different treatment were just efforts to receive "special treatment." In the end I chalked up much of these latter comments to the perspective of those making them.

It seemed incredibly macho to me to remain in a situation of discrimination simply to prove to those who vilified me that I could "tough it out." In addition, I was aware that calls for equal treatment are often seen as calls for "special treatment" in situations where discrimination has become the norm. My chief concern at the moment was that I not become complicitous in my own denigration—that by staying I not implicitly show my approval of the institution's choice to let politics prevail over academic principles and interests. Nevertheless, I decided to return. In many ways it was a default decision but I was driven by the fact that the professorship had not been filled and might still be in jeopardy of neglect from an unsupportive administration. Despite the peace of mind that removing myself from the university promised, I was not prepared to suffer another year without a salaried position. For one more year I would make it work for me, I thought to myself.

Almost immediately I realized that very little had changed since I arrived in 1986. Ten years later I was still trying to overcome the resistance to me. When my tenure was granted, after four years of teaching at the University of Oklahoma, I thought the matter of my full membership in the academic community was settled, only to have it raised again in 1991. How tenuous my claims to the certainty of academic freedom and tenure are when politics is interjected. Even the full funding by the State Regents of Higher Education in December 1995 could not erase the acts of unfairness that others dealt to me and others like me. I could keep quiet about it—but had decided against that once and for all.

The ultimate message of how Boren felt about my presence at the university came in the law school itself. In an open forum, a first-year law student stood and asked how he, Boren, planned to address the negative publicity surrounding Professor Hill. Boren responded with a ten-minute monologue on the parking problem on main campus but never mentioned my name—as though they were words he could not bear to let pass over his lips in public.

By the spring of 1996 I was certain that the institution would never view me as a full member as long as I was an embarrassment to its leadership. And so, despite the warm welcome of support and the sincere respect of many in the student body, I knew that the fall of 1996 was my last semester as a faculty member of the University of Oklahoma. As I participated in the hooding of the law school graduating class, a variety of questions and thoughts filled my head. Since the age of six, other than the three years in Washington, I had been a member of an academic community. How was I to function outside of one? But, having escaped the political assaults and threats, seen one more class receive their degrees, and paved the way for research on issues which were crucial to me, it was now time to move on, as my grandparents did, in search of a better place.

E PILOGUE

W hat happened in October 1991 should not have happened to me or anyone else. Nevertheless, it did, and is now such an integral part of who I am that I cannot imagine how my life would be today if it hadn't. My life has been forever changed. I will never again feel as safe and secure as I did before I received the first threats on my life. One day recently in a supermarket in Norman, a friend came up behind me, without identifying himself, and put his hands over my eyes. I panicked and for hours afterward was shaken at the act and the fear it brought to the surface. I reacted in the same way when, two years after the hearing, an NBC news crew rushed toward me in my driveway seeking a comment on the endowed professorship. I had declined the network's requests for an interview. As they hurriedly approached me, I had no idea who they were or that what they might have wanted was an ambush interview. I only saw three men rushing toward me, and given my experience and the threats, I assumed their intent was bad. My first reaction was fear, but afterward, when the realization that they were simply overzealous journalists sank in, I wondered if I would ever be free to say no with confidence that the choice would be respected. Despite the fact that, as an NBC executive explained to me, the network policy was to use ambush interviews in only the most extreme circumstances, NBC chose to run the footage of me attempting to leave my home on the nightly news.

I am now more apt to speak my mind and show less patience in the face of what I think are injustices large and small. Of course, personal slights today have far less impact when weighed against the insults I suffered at the hands of certain senators and members of the public and press. More significant than the changes is the reflection that the hearing prompted. When my world appeared to collapse in very significant ways, I was forced to consider what was important to me. In an effort to rebuild what was disrupted and destroyed, I contemplated my life as I had never before done. In addition to reconstructing my relationship with various communities of which I had been a part because of my race, gender, and profession, I gained a greater appreciation for my family and friends and my spirituality. "Would you do it again?" I am often asked, and my answer is the same. I would again answer truthfully when asked. I would pursue the matter once I filed my statement. I would testify as frankly and clearly as possible when questioned. I would do it again, but I could only do it because of the great tangible and intangible support I had throughout.

One of my mother's most impressive domestic skills is her quilting. I marvel at how she takes the scraps of materials left over from sewing or worn-out clothing, cuts them into odd geometric shapes, and pieces them together in a collage of color and patterns. Then in and out her needle goes thousands of times as the top, lining, and backing come together for the completed quilt. A quilt is often my mother's winter project—her way of passing the time on the long nights she dreads. She is careful never to mix gingham with denim or organdy with wool. The browns are joined with the yellows and greens while blues, pinks, and reds are separately joined. Yet nothing goes to waste. Everything is used—bound for a life destined to continue long after each individual skirt, blouse, pants, or shirt has outworn its own usefulness.

I never learned to quilt. But as I began to patch together my life after the hearing, to pull together all of my experiences and include the one that had most recently imperiled my existence, I thought often of my mother and her quilting. And as my physical mending concluded, I was left with the task of reconciling my place in various communities of which I was a member because of physical traits or experiences—the African American community, the community of women, and the academic community. In some instances the relationships had expanded. In others they had been badly damaged—all but severed. All of the fragments and pieces had to be put together again to make up my life. In the spring of 1992 I began in earnest to learn to quilt. I decided that I would discard none of my old life—that I was better off embracing it and the changes of my life. As the autumn turned to winter, I hoped, somehow, that I had learned something from observing her.

OPEN LETTER TO THE 1991
SENATE JUDICIARY COMMITTEE

Since 1991, responsive public reaction to the problem of sexual harassment has far exceeded what the Senate Judiciary Committee displayed at the Thomas confirmation hearing. As awareness of the prevalence and severity of the problem has increased, so has intolerance of
harassing behavior. How might the Senate Judiciary Committee have
responded to my complaint in a way that would have contributed to their
own awareness of the problem as well as public awareness is a lingering
question. To say that "they just didn't get it" is not enough, for it fails to
address how they might have behaved had they understood the complex-
ity of the issue. Nor is it enough that they should simply have believed
me rather than Thomas, because this fails to establish a process for fairly
hearing information about the character and fitness of a nominee. How
could the committee (or future such committees) confronted with the
issue have been responsive to both the issue of sexual harassment and the
nomination process? What the hearing lacked and what I and others
found missing was balance in terms of credibility—mine certainly
equaled Thomas' in the matter—and balance in terms of process—the
weight of the Senate and the Executive should not have been used against
an individual citizen called upon to participate in a public process. Neither the issue of harassment nor the nomination was served by a presumption of my untruthfulness or a process skewed in favor of whoever
was able and willing to engage in the dirtiest political "gamesmanship."

Anything less than a balanced approach condemns women to second-class status and the Court to members who abuse power and authority granted to them in a public trust. Such a person can in no case be the "best man (or woman) for the job."

Because sexual harassment claims involve issues of substantive law, the nomination process should never be turned into a forum for resolution of such claims. The Senate Judiciary Committee lacks the process, the authority, and the legal competence to hear such. The charge of the committee is to advise on the nominee's qualifications. Nevertheless, since sexual harassment was central to the nominee's qualifications, the members of the committee should have educated themselves on the issue before them. Evidence that you failed to do so lies in your use of social myths to explain my testimony, your refusal to utilize information provided by experts on sexual harassment, and your deviation from your own procedural rules in hearing the testimony as presented.

Myths that support harassment and deny legitimacy of such claims abound. Society points to women's ambition and ingratitude in the face of harassment claims to show that they are insincere or unworthy of public concern. Often, those charged with evaluating a claim explained it away as a response to social or professional rejection despite the lack of factual support for such explanations. Women are accused of using harassment as a scapegoat for a variety of other alleged problems ranging from incompetence to social deficiencies described as sexually aggressive, prudish, man-hating, and erotomaniacal. Often these characteristics are attributed to the same person despite the apparent contradictions. Underlying all is the grand myth that women control male sexuality— whether at home, on the streets, or at work, regardless of the relative physical strength or social power of the participants. Consequently, the presumption is that all sexual behavior is "welcomed" because a woman either invited it or did not prevent it. At some point in the hearing and aftermath, your members employed all of these myths. Along with the public, I watched the hearing as members of your committee attributed to me motives, traits, and characteristics that were designed to further obscure the matter before you rather than shed light on how Clarence

Thomas conducted himself in public office. Your members advanced your theories despite their logical inconsistencies and lack of factual support. In doing so you pandered to myths and misconceptions about women in general and sexual harassment in particular or simply failed to distinguish myth from reality and created a world where sexual harassment is a figment of an accuser's imagination.

The reality of sexual harassment is that most women do say no to harassment but too often are stuck with the interpretation of her harasser that her no meant yes or, at least, "maybe." The idea that even forcefully saying no stops the behavior misperceives the basis for harassment and the dynamics of such interaction. Targets of harassment are all too often not in control of the harasser's behavior or the general environment in which the harassment takes place. Harassment is abuse of power manifested in the form of sexual coercion. In the same way that saying no to the use of the club rarely stops its use or the threat of it, saying no to harassment does not end it absent some greater power to back up the refusal.

Women targeted for sexual harassment are rarely the sexual prudes or aggressors described by their harassers or their harassers' apologists. Nor is every harasser an "animal" with obvious social deviancies. The prevalence of the problem supported by social research indicates that harassment victims come from all walks of life and are of all different personalities. Similarly, women rarely use harassment claims to escape responsibility for other problems in their lives: only 3 percent of the harassment claims filed are baseless while 97 percent of the cases go unreported. However, when, without fully investigating it, you presumed that my claim was a frivolous or spite claim, you advocated action based on the exception rather than the rule.

When certain members of the Senate Judiciary Committee received my statement, they acted on the myths of sexual harassment and proceeded to perpetuate those myths. In labeling me a manipulative aggressor and a political conspirator, you ignored the reality of the workplace, and moreover, that I came before the committee after your staff contacted me. As Judge Hoerchner stated in her testimony, I "did not choose the issue of sexual harassment, rather the issue chose" me, nor did

I choose to testify publicly or to make this an issue of public concern. Other than my personal experience, neither I nor you knew much about sexual harassment prior to the hearing and neither did the public. Your lack of knowledge of the problem is understandable. Some members had practiced law before election to the Senate but none had specialized in employment discrimination law specifically. Given the sharp progression in employment discrimination law since 1964 when the Civil Rights Act was passed and in sexual harassment law since 1986 when the first Supreme Court decision was rendered on the topic, it is unlikely that even the attorneys on the committee had kept up with the case-law development in the area of sexual harassment. Consequently, your failure to avail yourselves of available sexual harassment experts is inexcusable. It can only be explained as arrogance or willful ignorance. Your statements during the hearing suggest that both may have been at work.

In addition to educating themselves on the issue of sexual harassment, the committee should have adhered to established procedure and standards in evaluating the fitness of the nominee. One of the greatest disservices that the Judiciary Committee did was to unnecessarily blur the lines between a nominee's public and private behavior. The issue is one which the public and various congressional advisory committees have grappled with and which promises to become more prominent as the press becomes more and more aware of the details of nominees' and candidates' lives. But in many ways it is a false dichotomy—one set up only as a way of avoiding discussing matters which the committee is afraid to consider.

Other nominations have been called into question or failed because of behavior that, if proved, would constitute poor judgment as well as illegal activity—either a criminal or a civil violation. For example, Harvard law professor Douglas Ginsberg allegedly smoked marijuana at a law school function where both students and other faculty were present. President Bush withdrew his nomination to the Supreme Court in the face of this disclosure. Zoe Baird, a corporate attorney, was the first woman ever nominated to head the Justice Department. Baird admitted to hiring illegal aliens for child care at a time when it was illegal to do so. Her nomination ultimately failed when, after discussion, the Judiciary Committee declined to send her name forward to the full Senate. Interestingly, before the revelation about her illegal activity, Ms. Baird's nomination received bipartisan support. Each of these matters might have been considered private behavior and thus inappropriate for consideration by the committees involved in the process. Nevertheless, they became a part of the public consideration once Presidents Bush and Clinton made the nominations to high office.

Clearly, illegal behavior and evidence of illegal behavior should not be excluded from the scrutiny of an advisory committee when a nomination or candidacy for high office is at stake. Although the reviewing committee is not a court of law competent to adjudicate a claim or mete out a sanction, it must not exclude the information as private or personal. It is relevant to the question of the nominee's qualifications and character. Moreover, the committee should not distinguish between types of illegal behavior by suggesting that certain illegal behavior is private rather than public behavior when deciding whether to consider the information. The committee must be willing to explore evidence that supports the allegation that the behavior is illegal. For example, where an allegation of racial discrimination is made involving a refusal to hire a person because of race, information about racial animus that shows a propensity to discriminate must be considered. An advisory body should consider the evidence, though it may not show that the particular decision resulted from racial bias. It is relevant to support the claim of the particular incident alleged. More important, it is relevant to the character and competency of the nominee.

Evidence which has not been ruled to be a violation of the law by a court (such as the evidence presented in Ms. Baird's nomination hearing) but which raises a colorable question of a violation or suggests a disregard for the law also must be considered. This is especially so when a committee is passing on a person seeking a law enforcement position, such as a position on the Supreme Court or in the Justice Department. Often, absent a court ruling, a person offering evidence of illegal activity cannot establish with certainty that the information that they are seeking to present represents a violation of the law. Placing the burden of obtaining a court ruling or otherwise establishing a violation with absolute certainty does not serve the public interest in making a thorough determination about the nominee. Moreover, a requirement that someone coming forward establish a violation of the law in many circumstances is unreasonable. As one letter writer asserted in responding to the hearing, Thomas' behavior "indicated an attitude toward women which is not only offensive but which I fear will be harmful to all of us as we seek equality." Another declared that Thomas' confirmation "sent a clear message to those in our society who are prone to abuse the human dignity of others that it is indeed permissible to do" so. Thus, the information about his behavior was relevant regardless of whether it fit within the definitions of behavior which was outlawed. In addition, violations of public trust and evidence of such should not be excluded as relevant to the nomination of an individual to high office. Likewise, such violations are not personal information because they reflect on how an individual comports oneself in a position of authority and guardianship. As such, evidence of the behavior of Professor Ginsberg, Ms. Baird, and Judge Thomas was not private.

Consequently, certain behavior by its nature is public, not private, when a person is being considered for a high office. Illegal behavior and evidence of it must be considered regardless of whether the source of the law which makes the behavior illegal is civil or criminal in nature. Colorable claims of illegal behavior must also be considered, as should violations of public trust or evidence thereof, because the latter relates to the handling of a position of civic responsibility. These activities by their nature are public, not private. Actions which by their nature are private but which the nominee has introduced into the public arena such as the workplace or in congressional gatherings are subject to review in considering a nominee as well.

Again we must not overlook the context from which these reviews arise. A federal judicial appointment is a life-term placement subject only to removal by impeachment. Judicial appointments, which occur at the conclusion of nomination proceedings, are independent of the democratic process and should be, if they are to serve and to protect the rights of the majority as well as the minority. Such a nomination or an appointment is a prize, not an entitlement. Even presidential selection for a position does not give one the right to be confirmed to such a post. Two key factors argue in favor of heightened scrutiny of the nominee's background and qualifications—the standard often applied in the past. First, appointment to high office is a plum whose award is nearly impossible to retract. Second, the public has a profound interest in the integrity of the courts aside from the politics of any nomination. Absent a clear invasion of private matters which do not relate to the law or the ability of a person to carry out his or her role as arbiter of disputes and protector of rights, much latitude has to be given to review information about the nominee.

Presidential nominations to other than lifetime posts must to a lesser extent be subject to scrutiny as well. These nominations and subsequent appointments are subject to the will of the president, who in turn every four years is subject to the will of a popular vote. Nevertheless, the fact that they are prizes and not entitlement dictates that they, too, must be scrutinized. Actions of public officials, even seemingly private ones, may have public consequences, and a nominee who violates the law can blame only him- or herself.

During the hearing, Senator Paul Simon asked that I or someone at my academic institution provide the Senate with some guidance on how to "deal with a charge that someone makes, that is a substantial charge, but that person says, . . . 'I don't want the charge made publicly.'" Two things are of utmost importance: a thorough and fair investigation and application of the proper standard of evaluation.

Even before an investigation takes place a person seeking to provide information to the Senate should be advised of the process by a competent staff person. Secrecy about the process resulted in my own insecurities and perhaps delays in the investigation. Nevertheless I proceeded. However, others may be discouraged altogether from engaging in a procedure about which they are told they are entitled to no information. If the committee expects a citizen to participate in the process with this kind of information or information of any kind, the committee must extend the citizen the courtesy and benefit of knowing what the process is.

The investigation should be handled by a nonpartisan body or individual in the role of a neutral fact finder, experienced in investigating sexual harassment matters. In investigating sensitive issues follow-up interviews should be the norm, not the exception.

As the circumstances surrounding the hearing proved, the investigator's neutrality is crucial. The FBI proved not to be a neutral fact finder in investigating my complaint. As part of the executive branch there is, at the very least, an appearance of alliance to the president whose nominee is being investigated. The danger in this alliance was realized later as the FBI was ordered to review my testimony for the purpose of spotting additional information or inconsistencies. The bureau received no such orders with regard to Thomas' testimony. The conflict of interest is apparent: not only were the agents trying to defend their investigation but they were acting at the direction of a party whose interest was in seeing that the nomination went forward. Even though the use of the FBI in this manner was unusual, its occurrence illustrates the problem of relying on an investigator who may not be neutral or who can be utilized to serve an interest other than the fair resolution of the complaint. Secondly, the FBI has little formal experience in the handling of sexual harassment claims and no apparent knowledge of the law of employment discrimination. The agency's expertise lies in criminal investigations and background checks. Sexual harassment is a social and a legal problem—a civil rights violation. The FBI agents may be aware of the legal definitions involved but may not be aware of how to elicit adequate information about a claim.

The standard for sexual harassment information should be no different than for other information about the nominee. Thus, the claim need not present a violation of the law to be considered relevant to the nomination process. The committee should consider competent information which negatively reflects on the competency and fitness of the nominee and the ability of the nominee to fulfill his obligations to the Court. This requirement and standard of review give credibility to the process and help prevent concerns about political manipulation of such issues.

A written report with a recommendation on whether the committee should pursue the information should result from an investigation. The committee should then determine whether the information should be kept private or made public. The entire handling of my statement in this manner could have been concluded in a week to ten days. Under this time frame, had I been advised of the procedure on September 9, when I confirmed the rumors about harassment to Ricki Seidman, Senator Kennedy's investigator, or on September 12, when I contacted Harriet Grant of Senator Biden's nomination staff, the matter might have been concluded by September 23, which was the date on which I sent a statement to the committee. More important, had the matter been handled promptly and in the manner I describe, you might have avoided the leak of the information to the press. Fewer people would have known about the information and there would likely have been greater satisfaction with the process internally among the staffers.

I make these suggestions for the sake of the process and others who may have information relevant to a future nomination. I have made peace with the action I took in my own claim and have only one thing to ask of the committee. Many of you have extended to women your regrets for your insensitivity in handling my claim. Others have apologized to the American public for your poor showing in the hearing. On a personal note, I would like to remind you that none of you have apologized to my parents. At the time of the hearing they were nearly eighty years old. They have worked hard all their lives and attempted to raise their children to fear God, seek the truth, and to respect the authority of the government. Six of their seven sons served in the armed forces over the course of nearly twenty years. Putting aside my bias, I know and their community knows that they are individuals of the highest character. Your malicious indictment of me was an indictment of them and all that they have taught me. At a time in their lives when they should be enjoying carefree days of leisure activities, they still fear for my safety and well-being. At the very least, they deserve a public apology from each of you.

In keeping with your responsibility to represent *all* of your constituency in the best interest of the country, you owe to each of us the assurance that you did indeed learn from the experience of 1991 and the promise that you will fulfill your future obligations in a more sensitive and enlightened manner.

Yours very truly,
ANITA F. HILL

ACKNOWLEDGMENTS

I t is impossible to acknowledge all of the people who contributed to this book and the variety of ways that each did so. But I will begin where the book begins by thanking my family. My parents, to whom this book is dedicated, and my Uncle George Elliott were sources of inspiration and invaluable information for this book. As they have throughout my life, my sisters and brothers, Elreatha, Albert, Alfred, Winston, Bill, Doris, Allen, Joyce, Carlene, John, Ray, and JoAnn gave immeasurable support during the time I was writing this book. In addition, their telling of family stories contributed to making this book not just my story but ours. My cousins Willie Faye Parker, Berniece O'Guinn, and Eddie and Lois Hill were great sources of love and support. And Eric Hill, whose misfortune it was to live the hearing and three years following along with me, gave me amazing perspective on it all that not only enriched the book but also enriched my life.

In addition to being about family, this book is about integrity and friendship. The greatest lessons came from those people who participated with me during the hearing, making sure that my story was heard not only because of their commitment to me but also because of their commitment to the integrity of the confirmation process. Susan Hoerchner, Ellen Wells, John Carr, and Joel Paul, the four corroborating witnesses, come to mind first and foremost. I thank them for their honesty and willingness to take tremendous risks for what they believed in. Behind the scenes others worked toward the goals of exposing the truth and honoring the spirit of the process. I owe an immense debt to Shirley Wiegand, David Swank, Randy Coyne, Leisha Self, Sue Ross, Emma Jordan, Charles Ogletree, Sonia Jarvis, Kim Thompson, John Frank, Jerry Parkinson, Ray and Leslie McFarland, Janet Napolitano, Kimberle Crenshaw, Judith Resnick, Warner Gardner, Michelle Roberts, Joy West, Angela Davis, Ann Majorca, Don Green, Teree Foster, Rick Tepker, Mike Scaperlanda, Ron Allen, Gary Phillips, Keith Henderson, and Andy Coats. As well, I thank Susan, Ellen, John, Joel, Shirley, and David each for broadening my comprehension of what it meant to live the experience and thus strengthening the book.

Finally, this book is about courage—not as a single act but as a way of life. Since the hearing, the lessons I learned about bravery, endurance, and dignity in my youth have been reinforced by friends, supporters, and professional colleagues. I want to thank Ann Swank, Fred Bray, Lyn Entzeroth, Wayne Wiegand, Leon and Evelyn Higginbotham, Marie and Wayne Alley, Karolyne Murdock, Bob and Pat Richardson, Teresa and Lloyd Bingman, Tammy Kemp, Pat Kern, Mark and Libby Gillett, Bill and Terry McNichols, Frank and Edna Elkouri, Peter Kutner, Mac Reynolds, Beth Wilson, Keith and Diane Bystrom, Judith Maute, Tom Hill, Dan and Carol Gibbens, Tania and Floyd Norris, Carole Faricy, Gloria Segal, Ann Moore, Lillian Lewis, Ovetta Vermillion, Stephen Carter, Enola Aird, Drew and Kathy Kershen, Sandy Ingraham, Nina Roland, Alice Bruce, John and Wilma McFarland, John and Junetta Davis, Susan Faludi, Russ Rymer, Callie Khouri, Dewey and Katherine Selmon, Deb Parkinson, Marsha and Rod Uphoff, Andy Hall, Wandra Mitchell, Ivy McKinney, Gene and Rose Kuntz, Jim and Rita Holder, and Anne and Michael England.

In the production of this book, technical support has never been simply technical. It has included believing in the book and my right to tell my story. John Breglio, my attorney, gave excellent legal advice leading to the contract for this book and helped present to the publisher an idea for a book of which we could all be proud. Joy Johannessen read the first words of the very rough manuscript and not only gave superb editorial advice but taught me about voice and helped me to believe in my own. I would not have had the confidence to begin this memoir without her. Rose Elugardo, my personal assistant, was a partner in the production of this book as she has been in most of my professional accomplishments since the hearing. She not only typed and printed the manuscript but she also read and questioned the content and coddled and cajoled me as needed. Rob McQuilkin's red pencil and keen awareness of the work as a whole helped turn the manuscript into a book. Finally, Martha Levin's editorial observations were always excellent and well stated. Moreover, she prodded me when I needed it and allowed me to find my own space and time to write the book when that was required. I could say many more positive things about Martha but will conclude by saying that without her I never could have completed this book.

INDEX

In this index AH refers to Anita Hill and CT refers to Clarence Thomas.